I0083072

CABIN NOTES

Adventures and Misadventures
On Land and Sea

BOOKS by J. PRIVETTE

NON-FICTION
Slickrock: Notes from the Blizzard of 1993
Mole Ranch: Life in Our Log Cabin in the Mountains of North Carolina
Cabin Notes: Life on the Water 2011
Cabin Notes: Life on the Water 2012

FICTION
Bear Island Treasure (Youth Novel)

POETRY
Wake

PHOTOGRAPHY
Blackwater and Blue

CABIN NOTES

Adventures and Misadventures
On Land and Sea

J. PRIVETTE

TWO PADDLES PRESS
Oriental, North Carolina

Copyright © 2020 by J. Privette.
All rights reserved.
ISBN: 9780578768403

Part of "Slickrock" was previously published in different form, hors commerce, in a chapbook, *Slickrock: Notes from the Blizzard of 1993*. Portions of "Hurricanes" were previously published in different form on the author's blog.

With the exception of family members, names have been changed to protect the privacy of others. The stories I have written here are based solely on my journal notes or recollections of the events and may not reflect the recollections of others who also experienced the events about which I have written. Any misstatement of fact is unintentional (except as it relates to the identity of those involved).

Cover photographs © by the author.

For Beth, Taylor, and Cameron,

With love.

AUTHOR'S NOTE

This book contains both serious and lighthearted as well as, hopefully, amusing tales of danger and risk commingled with fun. At no time have I intentionally put myself or my family or friends in harm's way, yet conditions can change, and we do not control more factors than we do. Small injuries or a little pain along with anxiety and brief moments of fear enrich our experience of life and define adventure. Without the potential for consequences such as an injury, no activity is an adventure. On the other hand, the pursuit of adventure can lead us deeper into the heart of darkness than we intend and result in serious harm or worse. If that does not appeal to you, that is your choice, but I recommend that you stick to theme parks.

On one of my early rafting trips down the Nantahala River in western North Carolina, a lively stretch of mild rapids with a minor Class III at the beginning and one at the end (Nantahala Falls sounds ominous but drops only three or four feet), our guide told us about guests who peer over the side of the raft and ask where the rails are. The Nantahala is dam-controlled, but otherwise flows naturally; it is NOT a theme park. You can drown, as you can in any water, but it is unlikely. Running the Nantahala is great fun but not an adventure.

The motto of the Boy Scouts is "Be Prepared", good advice for all activities, not just scouting. I have run a couple of rivers on the heels of tropical storms with the rivers flooding and rapids double or triple in size and risk (and some of the rapids washed out due to the volume of water). These have nearly exceeded my desired balance of risk and enjoyment.

However, our guides advised us, and we kept our wits and managed the dangers reasonably. Had we ignored the risks and the appropriate preparation, we likely would have yielded our ability to influence fate. In all my outdoor pursuits, I try to be thoughtful, and I strive to be prepared. Still, excitement is good.

For me, first blood came when I was eight on a rough day in the ocean when my family was staying at the Blockade Runner on Wrightsville Beach while my father attended a business meeting. Riding a canvas inflatable raft with rubberized ends, I caught waves purely on the physics of sea water pushing a float. I was not surfing. Being wet and banged around by the waves was lively entertainment until one wave flipped the raft and slammed my face into the hard sandy bottom at the edge of the shore. My upper lip became trapped in my braces resulting in an angry, piratical sneer. I stumbled out of the ocean and up the beach. My father released the lip, pronounced the bloody tear on the inside of my lip de minimus (meaning nothing to cry about) and suggested I return to the ocean and my raft. I decided to sit out for a while, gingerly exploring the fat swelling of my lip and the painful tear on the underside. For a few minutes, I wondered how it had happened.

Soon, the clouds thickened, and raindrops began to plop and splatter the sand, so we grabbed our towels and retreated to our room on the tenth floor of the hotel. From there, we opened the balcony door for a bird's eye view of the squall sweeping across the leaden gray sea, tearing the surface into white caps and tossing umbrella tables beside the pool. Without warning, one then another waterspout dropped from the clouds to connect the ocean with the sky. I watched, fascinated, my bloody fat lip forgotten.

None of these essays is intended to be a complete or comprehensive history of the events described. My impressions are based on memory. Aside from brief notes in my journals, none of this was recorded for accuracy. In my experience, people involved in the same event often remember the details differently. Partly this may result from the passage of time; partly it may result from what we as individuals selected as important in the moment. I learned how basic those differences can be when two of my closest friends and I each remembered different numbers of helicopters we spotted during one event. The number of choppers had no bearing on the truth of the event, nor did the number change the story in any substantive way, and none of us gained anything by being "right", but each was totally convinced his memory was the best. For one of us, that was true, and it was not me.

Cheers.

J. Privette
Minnesott Beach
August 2020

CONTENTS

———————

LAND

SEA

LAND

NOT QUITE LEGAL: Hiking Core Banks

I woke at 0515, swallowed a bowl of cereal and hit the foggy road before six. The mist lifted slowly as the sun rose. Past Havelock and Cherry Point MCAS, I drove through Harlowe on a stretch of highway shooting straight into the rising sun. Then I crossed tidal waters and turned onto the road to Harkers Island.

At Harkers Island Fishing Center, several Easter weekend fishermen gathered their Kmart gear in the parking lot, piling their twelve coolers, tackle boxes, and a bird's nest of rods and reels beside the National Park ferry concession dock. Then I found Susan. I had met her by phone when I called a couple weeks earlier looking for a ride out to Cape Lookout where I had planned a hike with my two black Labradors, Ranger and Sika.

Dogs are permitted in the park, but dogs are not permitted on the ferries that deliver people to the park. In addition, only the boats that have the park ferry concession can cart paying passengers to the island. Conundrum. I had to have my own boat if I wanted to take my dogs with me. Or, maybe I could find a local fisherman willing to violate the park rules and haul me and the dogs out to the cape. Susan suggested Barnie and gave me his phone number. Barnie had no problem helping me out. "Friends" can shuttle friends out to the island without violating the rules. We settled on a schedule and price.

Susan welcomed me to the island and pointed out Barnie's house. "But I think he's on his boat because I just sold him some B.C.s." I thanked her for the introduction and pledged absolute silence regarding my source, then walked around to the water side of Guthrie's fish house where a tall, thin, weathered old salt stood beside a small white wooden fishing boat with rusty upright exhaust pipes and a wide open stern for working crab traps and gill nets. The gunwales were rubbed to the wood.

"Barnie?"

"Yep." He swallowed his reply before he had fully expressed it as downeasters do. In addition to his hoi toider ("high tider" for you landlubbers) accent, Barnie was a man of few words, taciturn, and focused on the job at hand.

"My name's Jim. You want me to pay now?"

"Nah. Let's get clear of the ferry dock. Don' wan' n'body askin' any questions."

"That's fine. We're friends, and you're just givin' a friend a ride, right?"

"Yep."

I threw my backpack aboard as the dogs leaped from the dock to the deck. It was a few minutes before eight, so we would reach the dock on Cape Lookout before the ferry departed at nine. We cast off the lines, and the diesels chugged a rocky rhythm. A light breeze ruffled the water as we passed two ospreys nesting on top of a channel marker.

As we stood in the small wheelhouse, Barnie chain-smoked his non-filter Camels. I felt like I was sailing on the *African Queen* with Bogart. *Past Time* was a smaller boat than the *Queen*, no cabin, just a wheelhouse where two could escape the rain and the wicked winds of storms and winter. Slickers were tossed under the bow, and a CB radio hung from the ceiling. Barnie steered with an old bronze spoke wheel with wooden handles. A rugged classic working boat with no pretense of a modern yacht heavy with brightwork and polished brass. The wheel controlled a rudder through a nylon line that wrapped the wheel mount and ran through pulleys on both sides of the wheelhouse walls. The throttles hung behind Barnie's left shoulder within easy reach from outside when he worked the deck.

Speed was not the purpose of *Past Time*, as the name suggested. Barnie had built her with qualities that he may or may not have possessed. I did not know Barnie, but I could see that *Past Time* was reliable, steady and strong, a well-found boat meant for long days on the water hauling loads of seafood.

Cape Lookout lighthouse rises just over three miles from the eastern end of Harkers. We eased alongside the "No Public Docking" ferry pier, and Barnie placed a hand on a piling to hold his boat in place without bothering to secure dock lines. I heaved my backpack onto the dock and helped the dogs scramble up as well. With no witnesses, I paid Barnie his full fee. I wanted him committed to picking me up without questioning whether I had the balance of his money, or the weather persuading him to stay warm at home when the time came for him to return to the cape to pick me up.

"Monday at 2." I confirmed.

"OK."

He puttered away from the dock back across the sound. Ranger, Sika, and I hiked the shoreline toward the lighthouse until I found a trail that crossed the island to the ocean beach.

The most difficult part of this hike would be carrying on my back all the water that two dogs and one adult would need for three days. There were no sources of water on Core Banks. Three gallons (one gallon per day, a frugal supply) meant over twenty pounds of water before I counted the usual supplies and gear such as tent, sleeping pad, sleeping bag, clothes including foul weather gear plus a stove, cooking pots and food for me and the dogs. The pack contained much more weight than I usually hiked with. And I would be hiking on sand, hopefully firm at least some of the time, but likely soft. My knees began to ache before I had walked a mile down the beach.

The sun climbed slowly above the horizon, and the wind swept away all sensation of heat. I felt warmth from exertion but not from the beach air. Clouds hovered motionless over the ocean. Conch after unbroken conch slipped past my feet: gray, blonde, white, blue. I would not collect any until I was returning and had consumed much of my pack weight.

We hiked and hiked, the pace much steadier than in the mountains where the trails rose and fell between summits and gaps, stealing your breath on the way up and replacing it on the way down. Despite occasional soft areas of sand, we pressed on, enjoying the open space and the refreshing sea breeze.

I had intended for this weekend hike to give me time to think my own thoughts, to pause from the pressures of a new job in a new city, to restore some equilibrium lost in the stress of having been unemployed, and the anticipation of finding employment. I brought the dogs because they were ideal companions. They would listen to me without comment, indulge my complaints without denial, and they were always happy, game for whatever I might decide to do or whatever path I chose to follow. Although their qualities may not have encouraged me to grow as a person, they were perfect for the time. I did not travel halfway across the state to an island on the sea to be joined by a noisy group of friends who would have their own baggage and agendas, tolerances, and expectations. I wanted to be alone. To walk an empty beach along an open ocean with long views. I wanted simplicity and quiet. A place I could hike, sleep and eat with time to read and write. The dogs also distracted me and prevented my thoughts from being completely self-absorbed.

Lunch was a leisurely break. Stretched out on the sand, my back propped against my pack, the beach cushioned my body so that I could relax, close my eyes, and nap. When I woke, a light sprinkle gently drifted until a drizzle picked up the tempo. A heavy drizzle followed and developed into full bore rain with curtains obscuring the softened waves quietly pushing ashore. Rain splattering onto sand makes little sound. Other than the muffled whoosh of waves sweeping up the beach, silence enveloped our world. Showers had been pulsing through all week, so I expected the rain to cease soon. Pulling on my rain shell, I sat on a dune to savor the experience and wait for the rain band to pass. Heavier raindrops began pounding the beach, popping on my jacket and pack.

I surrendered to the weather and decided I might as well keep moving north. Without any landmarks other than a continuous view of the green ocean and a string of endless sand dunes, I could not calculate how far I had hiked. I hoped to make Drum Inlet, a twenty-mile day. However, by three in the afternoon, I accepted that the rain had settled over the island, and no wind was driving it off. Pitching the tent in the rain, raindrops soaked the fly and sand attached to every surface. One wet me and two wet dogs crawled into the tent. I unrolled the sleeping pad and sleeping bag. Both dogs, and especially, Sika, the older of the two, were chilled and shivering. The heavy rain had penetrated their protective layer of fur. They curled up on the sleeping pad, insulated from the cool sand. A soft breeze fluttered the tent fly while rain fell uninterrupted.

Periodically, the rain faded to a drizzle, and I would hope for an end. But it kept returning. I settled back onto my sleeping bag and read "Big Two-Hearted River" by Hemingway. Nick Adams would have loved this hike.

Eventually, the weather spirits favored us. Just before sunset, a nice dry nor'easter blew the rain out to sea and dried the tent and dogs. Sand remained scattered into every nook, every crack, every corner. Low heavy angry clouds scudded across the sky. The ocean turned battleship gray, empty and lifeless on the surface, a scene of endless solitude.

I thought the rain had passed, and I was wrong. Twice before dawn I woke to rain dancing on the tent. When the dogs and I left the tent at 0630 to relieve ourselves, clouds still raced overhead. Convinced that more rain would fall, all three of us crawled back into bed for another hour.

After a quick breakfast, I packed a daypack with trail mix, water, rain shell, camera, etc., and we headed north for Drum Inlet. Drum Inlet illustrates the dynamic and ongoing changes in the outer islands. It moves and relocates regularly, just as other inlets appear and disappear over time. The location can vary by miles. Additionally, another inlet, Ophelia, opens and closes in the same area, usually as a function of hurricanes and the release of storm surge from the Neuse River and Pamlico Sound. At the time of my hike, Core Banks extended northeast, unbroken from Drum Inlet to Portsmouth Island. Due to a recent hurricane, the banks are now interrupted by New Drum Inlet, and Ophelia Inlet has vanished. For now.

The night before I had encountered a fisherman and asked how far the inlet was. He said about five miles, so I hoped to make the trip in about two hours. The north wind held so it was pleasantly cool. Even slogging across the sand, I was so chilled that I wore my rain shell and wished I had my fleece with me.

I passed a variety of fishing shacks (no amenities) accessible by a small ferry from the Core Sound village of Atlantic. Several wrecks hid among the dunes, each tagged by the NC Department of Archives and History. Then I approached a large well-kept building surrounded by martin houses and a satellite dish. Core Banks Club, a hunting and fishing retreat. Less than a quarter mile past the club, I discovered a World War Two era double-ended steel lifeboat riddled with seemingly original bullet holes. Unfortunately, I do not know its story. I only know that my father was once a guest at the club to surf fish, and he told me about seeing the old lifeboat and other wrecks. Just like the Outer Banks, the Graveyard of the Atlantic, Core Banks hosts many wrecks. In fact, somewhere along my route were the sites of two Spanish treasure ships that sank during a hurricane in 1750, possibly forever lost due to shifting sands.

As the day warmed, I shed my rain shell, and the air was perfect for hiking in a t-shirt. While I had trudged for two hours through soft deep sand and the angled shingle of beach when it was solid, I had yet to reach the inlet. A half our later, an old rusty Chevy Blazer, outfitted for serious surf fishing with its rods and coolers mounted on the front bumper and a camper on the back, passed me heading toward the inlet. I stopped and watched. I never lost sight of the Blazer. Either it crossed the inlet on top of the water (doubtful even when the inlet shoals) or the inlet was much farther than the fisherman had estimated the day before. I mounted a nearby hummock. Due west I could see the village of Sea Level, and northwest the village of Atlantic. Or maybe I saw the villages of Stacy and Davis. With no reliable landmarks and no GPS (the service was not yet available to the public), I could not identify anything with certainty. Ships still relied on LORAN. What I knew for sure was that I could not see the inlet I presumed I was so near.

Reluctantly, I turned back. We had a two and a half hour slog back to the tent, and then I hoped to cover at least half the distance to the lighthouse since I needed to be at the lighthouse dock for Barnie to pick us up the following day. The walk back was hard and hot. We were walking with the wind, so there was no breeze to cool us. The dogs, ever enthusiastic, sometimes walked alongside me, sometimes dashed off to smell something invisible to me. Despite having a light day pack, the difficulty of walking through sand for so many miles day before and that morning hurt my shoulders, feet, calves, and thighs. But we marched on and reached our camp soon after noon.

I struck camp after a short lunch break. The sun, higher in the sky, penetrated the clouds so that, even sitting at rest in the sand with the soft breeze tumbling over the beach, we were feeling the heat. No doubt the sun on the dogs' black fur heated them more than me. All three of us were thirsty. I gave them as much water as prudent. We still had twenty-four hours before Barnie returned with his boat, several more miles to hike, and no water other than what I carried.

The afternoon was tough. The pack was lighter because of the water we had drunk, but it was the second day of plodding through sand with a load. Anything less than firm sand reactivated my pain centers: knees, back, feet, and neck. We trudged on, and what passed for landmarks from the previous day, such as the shape of certain dunes, odd tufts of sea oats, flotsam and some shells, appeared more quickly than I expected. So we pushed on though at a steadily declining pace due to fatigue.

I began to notice that my head was drooping, my eyes seeing only the feet below me trading sides one after the other. I was scarcely aware of the ocean opening to the horizon beside me. Then I spotted a sea horse with its tail curled by my foot. Long dead and desiccated by the heat, it lifted my spirits nonetheless. I have found a handful or so in my time on beaches, and they are always special because finding them is so rare. Wrapping it in a bandana, I placed it in my pack and began to focus on selecting a few good conch shells. They would add weight, but I knew I would regret passing over the most exceptional ones. As many as I had collected in my life, Core Banks offered the most prolific selection of large and colorful conchs I had ever seen. Part of me wanted to gather them all, but that thought was merely a measure of their beauty.

Standing at the edge of the ocean, relaxing a few moments and watching the waves break, I noticed far to the north a darkening sky. It could have been more clouds or more rain or a storm. Looking about, I considered options for shelter, and there were none. No matter what might approach, I had only my rain shell to help keep me dry. The dogs had their fur with its water resistant outer coat and downy undercoat. I could see the lighthouse and the tops of the trees adjacent to it, but we still had more than a mile to go.

I tried to accelerate my pace so that I might make camp before the weather caught us, an illusory hope more than an action plan. The sky became angrier and darker, clouds over the mainland a wicked black. But then the sky started to brighten, clouds over the sound parting, and columns of sunlight moving across the water. Sun lit buildings on Harkers, so I thought the threat had faded.

But the storm had merely slipped behind me to the east and formed over the ocean. Rain fell, first as a drizzle that swiftly became a deluge. Rain poured over my rain shell and down my legs into my boots. My feet were soon swimming in wet wool and rain water. The lighthouse disappeared, completely obscured by the torrent. Searching for a sign of relief, I turned around and saw the sun lighting the beach and the clouds opening to blue sky.

When the squall moved down the islands, the wind surged, and the sun released a shock of warmth emerging from the clouds. I watched the squall sweep over Shackleford Banks to the west toward Morehead City and Atlantic Beach while Harkers Island glowed with the golden afternoon sun tinted with the pale green of what I call "storm light".

Another half hour of walking brought us to within half a mile of the lighthouse and its restricted dock, so we made camp. I wanted to be sure Barnie did not have to wait for me, and I hoped I would not find myself waiting futilely for him. I believed he would return for me, but I know how islanders of all sorts can be. They can change their minds without notice, change their schedules without alert. They act in their own time, more mañana than urgency. Plus, weather is always a factor, mainly due to boat safety.

The last thing I wanted to do was have to ask the Park Service for assistance. I had violated the rules, so I should have, by rights, been on my own to find a solution if Barnie failed to show. Although entirely acceptable to me, Barnie failing to pick me up would be a problem. I knew no one nearby with a boat. It would not be like having a flat tire and calling a friend with a car or even flagging down a passing motorist for help. My dogs and I were on an island during an off-season holiday. The weather had been rotten enough that most people would have avoided coming out to the cape. No water, as I have noted, but also, no phone or other way to call for aid. I was depending on Barnie, my newest "friend".

Nothing to do about it, so I pitched the tent, tossed my pack inside, watered and fed the dogs, then ate some dehydrated rice and beans. The skies remained unsettled, but I convinced myself the bad weather had moved away. Again, I was wrong. Before the sun had fully set and night accented the periodic flash of the lighthouse beacon, rain returned. More wind and more dismal weather descended. One bright spot because of the lousy weather, no biting bugs. There are thousands of acres of marsh near the ocean and the banks, fertile ground, literally, for things that bite, sting, and draw blood from humans. I will always take the rain over the mosquitoes, sand fleas, horseflies, green-head flies and any other voracious insects.

I slept well due to extreme fatigue, mild pain, and the soft rhythm of rain on the tent all night. Dawn brought cool air and a light fog. I took my time eating breakfast, drinking tea and striking camp. I had several hours before Barnie was due and only a half mile to trek. I wanted to be waiting when he reached the dock so that we could evacuate immediately without explaining ourselves to the rangers. Before he arrived, I strolled along the beach looking for stray doubloons or reales and fine shells. Plenty of shells were scattered along the shore.

When I reached the dock early afternoon, I was careful to drop my gear off to the side on the soundside beach. I tried to look casual, a camper waiting for a friend. One ranger approached and asked if I needed help. "No, I am waiting for a friend who is picking me up in his boat." The ranger's smile belied his skepticism. But he left me alone. Just before Barnie arrived, the park ferry docked to pick up the few visitors who had spent the day on the cape. I could see Barnie's boat heading for the dock, so I shouldered my pack, called the dogs and prepared for a quick trot onto the dock and a jump onto *Past Time*. Again, Barnie did not bother with dock lines, and I ignored the rangers standing above him. Then the interrogation began.

Addressing Barnie, "You know you can't carry paying passengers."

"I'm not paying. We're friends." I replied.

Addressing Barnie again, "So tell me this guy's name."

I interjected, "He knows my name is Jim." I was not chancing that Barnie might have forgotten or never bothered to remember in the first place.

"Only the boat with the ferry concession can bring paying passengers out here." He glared at me.

"I know. And I know that the ferry cannot carry dogs even though dogs are legal in the park. So I asked my friend Barnie to give me a ride." The ranger frowned and scowled at us both, convinced Barnie and I were not entirely forthright about our arrangement.

Barnie ignored him completely. With me and the dogs aboard *Past Time*, Barnie quietly put the boat in reverse, eased past the ferry, and pulled away from the dock while the ranger continued to lecture in a louder voice and accuse us of a violation he could not prove. Throttling up once he cleared the dock, Barnie scooted across the sound, getting gone while the getting was good.

BUSH AX in MY HEAD

After high school, I postponed college and moved to the rolling hills south of Morganton where I lived in an old farmhouse off the main roads and a half mile down a dirt farm path. The closest "town" was an intersection named Casar, ten minutes by motorcycle. The property belonged to a couple from my hometown. It was the mid-seventies, but the sixties had not passed for everyone, including these two. Both had government jobs and hoped to move out to the property and homestead when they had saved enough money to update the house with plumbing and electricity.

The house had two doors off the front porch into two rooms, each of which had one set of windows with glass, the other set without. The rest of the house was without doors or windows. But summer lingered in the foothills, so the openness was comfortable.

Another friend of mine, Carl, was also staying at the house. In fact, he had been living there alone for a couple of months and was eager to visit his home, so he left the day I arrived after showing me how to start his dirt bike, where the spring was (down the hill under a large beech tree), and pointing out the trail that led down to the river. My first task was to build myself a bed. I had brought a small mattress with me, and there was a motley stack of lumber in an old barn near the house.

Carl had made himself a rope bed. The rope supporting his mattress was not sufficiently taut to let me "sleep tight", so I opted for wooden cross pieces. Nailing two by six lumber to four round legs (the diameter of small telephone poles) formed the frame of the bed. More two by six slats gave the bed its cross-support and a solid platform for my mattress.

The first night alone at the house was, frankly, creepy. I barely knew where I was geographically, had no telephone (cell phones did not yet exist except for celebrities and limousines), and knew no one within shouting distance (one house). Carl said the neighbors were friendly and did not mind if used their phone as long as I paid for any long distance calls (any call I would make would have been long distance). When the sun disappeared below tree line and then yielded fully to the dark, there was not a speck of light anywhere except for the stars. I lit a couple of candles and tried to read.

Pressing on me was the kind of silence and darkness when only night creatures move. Raccoons, possums, snakes. Bears were unlikely but possible. Mostly, my anxiety sprouted from being a stranger in a strange land. I knew nothing about the woods surrounding the house, and I had never ridden a motorcycle, my only means of escape faster than my feet. I stretched out in my bed and looked at the gaping hole where window panes should have formed a geometric pattern of rectangles stacked neatly atop one another, a gaping hole through which anything might crawl, climb, or jump through the window sill, low to the ground. A box against the wall in the corner near the head of my bed made a convenient table, a place for my candles, book, journal, flashlight, and knife.

After trying to read for a while, I blew out the candles and found myself in a black void. Neither walls nor doors nor windows were visible. The room was a soundless vacuum, sensory deprived. I tried not to breathe, to be quieter than the soundless space. Listening, I could hear nothing. So I listened harder. Still nothing. I began to talk to myself in an imagined whisper. "Nothing to fear, nothing to fear. Carl has done this so can you." Tautly paralyzed, fear prevented any movement. That scared me more. Why can't I move? Has some invisible force seized my will? Crazy and uncontrolled thoughts kept spiraling through my anxiety.

I have no recollection of falling asleep, like a haunted house guest in a horror film who has unknowingly swallowed the host's drug-laced nightcap. But I had been asleep because I woke from a nightmare knowing that someone or something had entered the room through the glassless window. I peered into the darkness and could see nothing. Carefully, I reached for my flashlight, eager for illumination but not really wanting to see what was near me. Click. The room was empty. Under the bed? I jumped to the floor and stood far enough away to shine the light into the shadow. Nothing. But what about the other rooms that were also open to entry? I eased through the door and flashed the light into all the dark corners. Breathing returned. And I needed to pee.

I tested the knob on the front door without making a sound. Then I turned it slowly, careful to prevent the anticipated click. Pulling it into the room, I shined the flashlight onto the porch and slashed the beam along the tree line looking for the reflection of eyes looking back at me. Nothing. I cradled the light in my armpit while I peed off the porch. I would go no farther. The night was pleasantly cool, the night sky dusty with stars. Despite my fear, the night was peaceful. Whew. Maybe I could handle this solitude after all.

Back inside I checked each room once again and crawled back into my bed. I tried to read myself to sleep, and my eyes soon blurred, then closed. The next time I turned over, dawn had dampened the room with a chill morning mist so I snuggled deeper into the warmth of my blankets and fell back to sleep. Sun shining through the windows surprised me. I had slept well.

With a cup of instant coffee in my mug, I stepped onto the front porch to a world that had metamorphosed overnight. Rays of sun lit the lingering mist like smoke drifting among the trees, and the woods appeared open and inviting. Comfortable with my isolation in the bright light of day, I savored the coffee as I strolled around the house and wandered into the adjoining pasture. Cool. I needed to write in my journal and play some guitar. Despite being horrible at both, the idea gave me purpose, a plan, actions on which to focus. I walked down to the spring and made a mess of the silt at the base of the spring where it collected in a shallow pool. After letting the pool settle, I tried again and scooped mostly clear water, cool and sweet.

I stuck close to the house and avoided thoughts of night and loneliness. Carl had said he would be gone "about a week". Although I tried not to, I fixated on the amount of time I would be alone. Would it be a week? More? Maybe less. Yes, that would be ideal. Carl said "about" and that could mean less. As the afternoon sun warmed the house, my confidence surged. I had just needed to get a first night in a new place behind me to know that there was nothing to fear, nothing to worry about.

As the sun drifted below the horizon and the light in the house dimmed, I fixed some dinner and considered whether I had adequate provisions. Carl had told me that Casar was just east down the main road several miles. There was a small country store with the basics. Canned goods, bread, soft drinks and such. Of course, to get there, I would have to ride the motorcycle. Carl had quickly told me how to start it and how to shift gears. Could I remember the instructions? As soon as I wondered whether I could, I couldn't. If I could not start the motorcycle, I could not replenish my provisions. I was stuck. Damn it. Alone, trapped, confined. I began to convince myself that I would exhaust the provisions before Carl returned. The neighbor's phone was an option but I did not have the phone number for our friends who owned the house. They lived twenty miles away and only visited the property occasionally on weekends. Calling someone hundreds of miles away in my hometown seemed utterly foolish and futile. No one there could help. My options evaporated as my anxiety swelled. What could I do?

I lit a couple of candles and hopped onto my bed with my attention locked on the gaping black hole where a window with glass should have been. Another night exposed and vulnerable in a room that could not be locked or secured against anything or anyone. I tried to read but constantly found myself checking the empty window for anyone looking back at me. The sill was just the right height for someone to stand outside and peer into the room less than five feet from the foot of my bed. How stupid. I had spent nights alone in the woods before. Not many, but some. This was better. Solid walls surrounded me, except for the vacant windows. My anxiety simmered and flared in a terrifying cycle. Irrational thoughts controlled. My heart pounded. Why had I not waited until Carl returned to move in?

I deferred sleep as long as I could but eventually, long after midnight, slipped into unconscious slumber. I woke midmorning, relieved that I had rested so completely, but uncomfortable that so deep a sleep left me defenseless and susceptible to whatever goes bump in the night. In any case, I had completed another day, crossed off another night alone in the interminable wait for Carl's return. My apparent dependence on his presence irritated me, but there it was, real and true. I should not have needed him and promised myself that I would not. I just needed to get past a few anxieties like dwindling provisions.

I remained uneasy. I sat outside on the porch and wrote a letter to a mutual friend, our former high school guidance counselor, Roger. In frank terms, I told Roger about the dearth of provisions, my lack of experience with the motorcycle, and my hope that Carl would return within a week as he had said. I withheld any revelation of serious concerns, much less fear, and felt content just communicating to a friend. I walked out the dirt road and posted the letter in the neighbor's mailbox. I had thought I might bump into them and introduce myself, but no one was home.

Night brought back most of the disquietude I had come to expect. In ways that did not matter much, I accepted the unprotected house and the unguarded room while remaining nervously vigilant. Staying up late worked its magic once again, and I was surprised to wake long after the sun had risen. In a strange way, I began to reconcile my discomfort knowing the days were clocking past, and sooner than when I began, Carl should return. My dependence annoyed me which offset some of my anxiety.

Borderline depressed, I accomplished nothing, and that too pissed me off. I should have been chopping wood for autumn, fixing doors, patching leaks. Our friends had offered the house rent free in exchange for our help with repairing the old long-unoccupied place. I needed to get to work, but I was not sure where to start. How useless could I be?

Every day was long and slow, but each day seemed a bit shorter than the day before as I ticked through the calendar. The weekend after I sent my letter to Roger, I heard a vehicle coming down the dirt road. It could not be anyone I knew. If I had had a gun, I would have grabbed it. A car parked in front of the house, and Roger got out.

"Hey man, what the hell you doing here?" I was pleased to see him.

"I got your letter. You seemed pretty desperate."

"Really? No, I'm fine."

"Sure didn't sound that way. I knew Carl was not returning when he expected, so I thought I should drive up and see if I could help."

"Shoot, I'm glad to see you but sorry you thought I was sending an alert."

"No problem. I wanted to see this place anyway. Carl's told me a bit about it, but I couldn't picture it."

In a single unanticipated moment, my anxieties vanished. A friend arrived, and my loneliness drifted into the ether. No more nights alone with my imaginary fears. An easy ride to the store to grab some victuals. Someone to talk to. I assured Roger that I was enjoying my time alone and my letter had been reportage, not a cry for help. He let it go as a good friend would. We drank some beer and chatted by the fireplace. What had haunted me the preceding days and nights no longer existed.

Carl eventually came back, and work proceeded. He had a clear idea of what needed to be done, what the priorities were. We processed fallen timber for firewood, our only heat as the autumn chill arrived and winter hovered a month out. We installed windows and doors to protect us from rain and cold winds. And we cleared overgrown myrtle hedges alongside the house.

The hedges stood nearly twelve feet high, the trunks thick with untended age, the limbs woven with old vines. We chopped the tangled limbs with a bush ax, a curved two-sided blade suitable for slinging into thickets. The leverage of dropping the bush ax blade quickly through the myrtle sliced a lot of limbs and vines with each stroke. The work was steady without much exertion. I just worked my way down the length of the hedge making good progress with only a mild sweat, wearing gloves and no shirt in the Indian summer air. Then, one swing caught a stout vine and bounced back, the outside corner of the bush ax blade recoiling into my head.

It hurt, but I felt the top of my head with my hand, and it seemed fine. My hand was gloved, so I looked into the palm of the glove and saw blood, more blood than a scratch.

I called Carl. "Hey, I just hit my head with this damn bush ax. I don't think it's bad, but I need for you to take a look since I cannot see the top of my skull."

Carl sat me down on the porch and pulled my hair aside. "Doesn't look good, but let me get some gauze. Maybe we can patch it up." He brought out our first aid kit, handed me a stack of gauze and told me to hold it in place applying pressure.

"How do you feel?" Carl had pulled out our first aid manual and looked up concussion.

"I'm doing okay I think." Then I wavered. "Maybe a bit woozy." Blood trickled down my scalp and behind my ear. "I guess it's bleeding worse than I thought."

"Yep. I think we need to call the rescue squad."

"Really? No, not really. Is it that bad?"

"Well, the bleeding is not stopping, and you probably need stitches." I acquiesced, and soon we heard a siren echoing over the hills.

Two pickup trucks arrived first, each equipped with the flashing red lights of volunteer EMTs and firemen. "Where's the guy?"

With my hand still pressing the top of my head, I replied, "Right here."

"You got hit with a bush hog?"

"No, a bush ax."

"Geez, we thought we were coming to pick up someone decapitated by a bush hog."

"Sorry to disappoint you. Head is split but still attached."

They laughed. I chuckled nervously at their enthusiasm for seeing a decapitation. An ambulance soon followed and rushed me over hill and dale on winding country roads to the nearest town with a hospital, Rutherfordton. The ER nurse quickly shaved my hair around the wound, and the doctor stitched me up. "You'll be fine. We thought you had been decapitated. Heard it on the radio."

" Nope, just a bush ax."

Exhausted from the attention and adrenalin, I slept the sleep of the dead, but alive. And the local good old boys had a tale to tell though not as good as the one they heard on the radio.

Mac and Trish, our friends who owned the property, introduced us to a couple of their co-workers, Kathy and Catter, who lived in a big old Victorian house in Morganton with five dogs. Kathy and Catter were "hippy chicks", a bit of a Mutt and Jeff couple, Kathy tall, lanky, and assertive while Catter was short and mousy. They showed up at the property one day to go for a walk with the dogs. Before they left, they told us that their landlord had given them notice that they would have to get rid of the dogs, or he would evict them. They asked if we would keep them.

They were a medley of mixed breeds and sizes, the smallest an almost toothless old terrier and the largest a combination of German Shepherd and Great Bernard plus all types in between. Short hair and long, tall and short, hyper and chill.

Autumn had settled into the foothills, frost on the pumpkins as it were. With all the dogs running around and cool days for working, a new energy permeated our efforts. Bathing in the river became much more bracing, something we saved for the clearest days when the sun warmed the rocks in and along the river.

Carl and I moved our beds into the other front room where there was a small brick fireplace. We kept a fire at night before we went to sleep and then lit one again in the morning. The days shortened, and we spent the dark hours beside the fireplace talking philosophy, playing guitar, and dreaming about our futures. The dogs each found their own space scattered around the room, those with thin fur closest to the fire until we crawled into our beds. Then the dogs jumped onto the beds with us. We laughed about three dog nights or five.

By the time Carl left the property for another visit back home, I had learned my way around and welcomed the solitude. I knew the trails along the river, trails through the woods. I enjoyed hiking the autumn woods with the undergrowth receding and the views opening up. On one trip with the dogs, I found the skeleton of what must have been a dog, possibly a deer dog that got lost and starved. I knew that sometimes happened. I collected the teeth, and we continued down to the river, well upstream from where we usually bathed. As we strolled along the narrow trail, I heard a faint buzzing sound. I scanned the area but saw nothing. Then one of the dogs yelped, and another. Two suddenly ran off down the trail whining. The old terrier stood still whimpering, quivering, frozen in place. Then I saw the hornet's nest, a hole below the roots of a dogwood tree. Three or more stung my arms and neck. I grabbed the terrier and jumped into the river. Several hornets were trapped in the curls of the terrier's fur, lifting their stingers and stinging the poor dog repeatedly.

I picked the hornets out of his fur or smashed them if they were too tangled. He must have had a dozen or more. Only the biggest dog had stayed with me. He had jumped into the river before I did, and none of the hornets had followed him. I hoped the others had run back to the house. The terrier trembled as I carried him, and we hiked cautiously down the trail, alert for more nests. I had never encountered ground hornets before, but the sound of their muted buzz became permanently etched in my memory. With future encounters, as soon as I thought I heard a buzzing, I stopped, identified the pathways of the hornets to and from the nest, gave a wide berth and ran past the threat. In the present, I hoped that the toxins from the multiple stings would not sicken the aged terrier. His eyes swelled almost shut, but otherwise he seemed okay once he had a nap and a long overnight rest.

Although not all the dogs were waiting at the house, all arrived before nightfall. A couple had swollen eyes, but I could see no other injuries from the hornets.

While Carl was away, I finally took the motorcycle to Casar. We had run out of dog food and some basic food supplies. Once I turned onto the main road, I loved the power of the motorcycle rushing up and down the hills, wind in my face. The old country store was a classic, dimly lit, carrying a modicum of much and a lot of little. This was a place to visit every few days, not a source for monthly supplies. I loaded a 25 pound bag of dog food into my backpack, mounted the motorcycle with confidence and roared back west toward the house. As I approached the dirt farm road, I slowed, downshifted, turned off the asphalt and crashed. In a flash, the front wheel slid through the dirt and I tumbled off, my head hitting the ground with enough force that I thought I had busted the helmet. But I had not. Nor had I expected that a dirt bike would be so tender in the dirt. Oh well.

Autumn eased into winter, the days and nights colder and colder, the pile of blankets on our beds deeper. Carl and I decided that trying to live in the open house during the winter would not be practical, so we planned to leave after the Thanksgiving feast that Mac and Trish hosted with lots of their friends. A vegetarian affair with the centerpiece a pumpkin stuffed with grains and vegetables. A macrobiotic menu about which I had been learning. But including wine. At the end of the meal, Carl drove me to Mac and Trish's real house with its view of Table Rock perched over Linville Gorge. The next morning, Carl dropped me off beside the interstate so I could hitchhike back east to my grandparent's farm. My grandfather had agreed to let me borrow his truck so Carl and I could move our belongings from the foothills house to our homes.

I did not expect an easy hitch as my route incorporated an interstate, a major highway through the Research Triangle Park (before the interstate that cuts through today) into Raleigh followed by another major highway heading toward the coast, then a backroads highway to my grandparent's farm. Maybe the hitchhiking gods were watching over me. I made the trip almost as fast as I would have if driving myself. My last ride was with a spicy character in a red Corvette. He even knew the small town near where my grandparents lived.

I asked him what he did for a living.

"I'm married to Madame Bogart." He smiled proudly. "You heard of her?"

Oh yes. Madame Bogart read palms and healed the sick. She operated her business in an old house on US 301, the predecessor to Interstate 95 that carried all the traffic from New York to Florida. She also ran seemingly endless ads on AM radio, so everyone in the eastern part of the state had at least heard her name. I could not stop grinning though I did not want her husband to think I was laughing at him for declaring his occupation as being married to her. But he clearly liked his Corvette. Conversation made the time pass easily, and soon we pulled into my grandparent's driveway.

As always, my grandmother had a feast laid out for me, this time mostly Thanksgiving leftovers with turkey, ham, fried chicken, and pork loin, all the meat I missed at our mountain Thanksgiving. Mashed potatoes, creamed corn, collards and green beans seasoned with fatback, beets (I passed on the purple slices), cucumbers and onions in vinegar. Homemade rolls. Except for the beets, I tried to eat it all. I had left the macrobiotic vegetarian diet in the foothills.

The journey home should have been uneventful. The pickup truck held all our goods comfortably. But rain threatened, so we covered the back with a heavy canvas. We stopped in Chapel Hill at Carl's sister's house. The rain fell steadily. Carl worried that everything in the back of the truck would be drenched overnight. I assured him it would be fine, but he wanted to pull back the canvas and see how wet it already was. I promised him everything was dry, but pulling back the tarp would break the surface tension and allow the rain to penetrate.

"That makes no sense," he declared.

"But it's true," I replied. We argued a couple of minutes before he pulled the canvas back to expose our gear.

I knew what I knew about canvas from sleeping in canvas Baker tents and Wall tents in Boy Scouts. And I knew how my grandfather treated his tarps to keep his valuable cured tobacco dry on the way to market. In short, I knew what I knew. What was under the tarp was dry, but now the tarp would leak at least where he had folded it back. He was angry as was I. It was a sour end to our venture, and I was ready to put it all behind me and get home. The drive home the next day was quiet and bitter. I dropped him off at his house and helped him unload. Much of our gear had been soaked by the rain under where he had folded back the tarp. Unsurprisingly, he admitted no error, and I said nothing more.

Only with the passing of time have my memories of living in the foothills found a place of contentment in my mind. I had learned a lot that would prepare me for adventures in the mountains I had yet to imagine, whether camping, backpacking, or living through winter. Several years later I bumped into Carl in the grocery store of the small town where I was a young lawyer and he was temporarily assigned as a young medical resident. We embraced and said we were glad to see each other, and I was. But a bruise lingered between us, and we have not seen or spoken to each other since. Growing up can be that way.

J. Privette

LINVILLE GORGE

First Attempt

For a couple of years while I while I was in college, Curt was my hiking partner. Curt was already out of college though I do not know if he graduated. We tried to grab a few days on the Appalachian Trail every other month or so. It was a long drive from Chapel Hill, so we typically arrived at the trailhead late afternoon with only enough daylight to hike in a mile or so before making camp. Because we knew we would not hike far the first night, we indulged our menu, ignoring the weight of our first night's meal, taking a whole hen or big rib eye steaks, potatoes for baking, salad fixings, a couple of beers and a bottle of wine. Curt always took a flask of whiskey. We rarely turned in before midnight the first night out as we chatted beside the campfire.

Curt claimed to have been a US Army Ranger, trained in the skills of hand to hand combat. I never really believed him but went along with the tale since it seemed so important to him. He told good stories sitting beside a campfire. His father, Big C (as in C note), owned a print shop and, reportedly, spent some time in prison for counterfeiting our nation's currency. I believed Big C had been a counterfeiter even though I had never met the man. I don't know why, but Curt as a Ranger seemed less plausible than Big C as a felon.

Curt's girlfriend was friends with my girlfriend, so the four of us had beers together every couple of weeks. That is how Curt and I met and began talking about going hiking. Curt wanted someone to hike with and, I guess, so did I. I liked for Curt to backpack with me because he carried a .45 caliber pistol, the same one the Army gave him when he was a Ranger. I didn't care where the gun came from, just that he carried it, and we had protection from any obnoxious, loudmouthed hillbillies we might meet. We never met any on the trail. Murphy's Law. Whatever you are prepared for never happens.

After a few autumn hikes, Curt and I thought we should try some winter camping. In winter, night comes early, so we decided we would camp at Linville Gorge which was a few hours closer to us than the Appalachian Trail in the Blue Ridge mountains. The gorge is extremely steep beginning where the river is a quiet pool at the top of a two drop twisting waterfall that slices through the vertical canyon wall at the top of the gorge.

Neither of us had ever hiked in the gorge, a designated wilderness area, but rumors were that the place was crazy with copperheads in the summer. So winter seemed the ideal season for camping there.

We plotted our gear meticulously. Gloves, wool caps, wool shirts and pants (Curt's were GI, of course), heavy socks, down coats and down sleeping bags. We did not intend to hike anywhere the first night as we assumed it would be nighttime when we arrived. Plus, we carried a whopping load of gear including at least twice the amount of food we needed. Just to be safe.

Curt met me at my garage apartment, and we tossed his pack in the back of my Land Cruiser. He helped me gather my pack and the rest of my kit, hopped into the Land Cruiser, and we started the slow grind west to Linville. A few hours later, we turned onto the snow-covered dirt road that ran along the western ridge above the gorge. The snow was several inches deep, but the four-wheel drive pulled us forward easily.

Darkness squeezed in. Stars scattered across the black winter sky cast the only light. Even so, the snow glowed dimly, accenting the blackness of the woods around us. Crunching through the fresh snow, we turned into what appeared to be a parking lot; it was wider than the road had been. We were several miles from pavement and, aside from our tire tracks, there were no hints of life. No people. Just the cold, muffled stillness of a wilderness winter night.

We stepped out of the warmth of the Land Cruiser into sharp, piercingly cold air, our fingers aching as we opened the back door and pulled out the tent bag. In minutes, my body chilled, and I zipped on a down vest and coat. My toes were feeling the cold before we finished pitching the tent beside the Land Cruiser. Our hands hurt from pushing the tent stakes through the snow and into the frozen ground below. Although it was clear and had been sunny just before sunset, the temperature plunged as quickly as the sun had disappeared. It was below freezing with a forecast low of fifteen degrees before sunrise.

Curt was tossing our gear into the tent while I set up the camp stove in the back of the Land Cruiser. No reason to set it in the snow where we would have to squat to cook over it. Unscrew fill cap, fill with fuel, close fill cap, pump the primer, light and then fiddle with the control until the flame stabilized a steady thin blue. Curt unrolled our sleeping pads in the tent, then unstuffed his bag so it would loft up while we were cooking (pouring boiling water into pouches of visually unrecognizable but salty freeze-dried entrees) and eating dinner. Yummm. At least it was hot. He asked if I wanted him to unstuff my sleeping bag while I messed with dinner. I thanked him and said yes.

"So, where is your bag?" Curt asked.

"In my pack."

"I don't see it in there."

"Maybe it fell out in the back here." I shuffled around some loose gear, but did not uncover it. "I'm sure it's here somewhere," I declared with something less than total confidence. It is like the moment when you first think you might be lost or caught doing something you should not be doing. Bravado evaporates into a spike of raw, dry-mouth fear as you try to maintain control over your emotions, your story, your excuse.

With flashlight in hand, I dug desperately through my backpack, searched the tent and removed every loose item from the Land Cruiser. Nothing.

We debated the possibility (and folly) of me essentially bivouacking in my down outerwear. At freezing, it might have been possible, even though it would still have been uncomfortable. I doubted that I would sleep much as my body chilled. I could imagine the full body violent shivers that would rack me head to numb toes if I attempted an overnight without a good winter bag. There was no way it would be smart to stay overnight without a sleeping bag with temperatures in the teens.

We reached my apartment at three in the morning. When I switched on the light, I spied a neat black stuff sack sitting on my chair. Curt drove home alone.

Second Attempt

A month or so later, we decided to return for the hike we had failed to make. I remembered my sleeping bag. Once again, we arrived in the dark, and the parking area was covered with several inches of snow. Repeating our efforts from the prior trip, we set up the tent and loaded our gear inside. I fired up the stove, we boiled water and ate a delicious dehydrated dinner followed by hot tea and a wee dram. After the long day and long drive, we crawled into our down bags and soon slept the sleep of the truly weary.

Morning was dull and overcast with light flurries and a temperature near thirty degrees, much warmer than the original trip. We loaded our gear into packs and found the nearby trailhead. The trail was clearly cut along the contour of the upper gorge. Nevertheless, frozen snow is slippery and, at certain twists in the trail, it would have been easy to be distracted by the steep drop into the gorge, the river flowing below, and fail to pay attention to our footing. A simple slip could have sent us tumbling down the mountainside toward the river.

We reached the river after an hour. The brilliance of the snow along the river bank contrasted with the blackness of the deep pools and current rushing between the rocks. In the larger eddies, small ice flows that looked like lotus pads the size of dinner plates spun lazily. Though the sun had risen, the day remained dull, gray, and cold. Snow flurries floated in the soft breeze, but we were warmly dressed with lots of wool and heated by hiking. The trail continued alongside the river...until it did not. The trail simply vanished.

We pressed on, searching for where the trail might begin again. We stared into the forest and tried to conjure a hint of pathway obscured by the snow. We pushed aside tree branches in case a fallen limb or sapling was hiding the trail. Nothing, nothing and more nothing. The trail had to continue. Our map clearly indicated a trail following the river, but we could find no evidence of it. Because Linville Gorge is a wilderness area, trails are not marked or blazed as, for instance, the Appalachian Trial is. We reviewed the map again, checked the compass (for what that was worth since we could clearly see the river beside us).

"What d'you think?"

"Well, I don't want to camp right here. But, if we can't find the trail, we can't continue to the next intersecting trail that leads us out of the gorge."

"So we have two choices. Backtrack or bushwhack."

I looked up the slope of the gorge above where we stood. If we climbed out, the good news was that we would have to intersect the road along the ridge. The bad news was that we would not know whether last night's camp (and therefore the Land Cruiser) would be north or south from where we emerged from the gorge.

"The safest decision would be to backtrack. We know the trail is clear, and we have an idea how long it took to hike down here. On the other hand, we also know how steep it will be hiking back up. From here, the slope up the gorge if we bushwhack looks pretty good, a steep hike through the woods. Plenty of altitude gain, but not too steep. Then again, we can't see the entire route and can't know what we will run into as we climb. But it sure seems like it would be shorter than backtracking."

Curt and I tossed pros and cons back and forth for several more minutes before he suggested we "go for it". Climb straight up the side of the gorge. We finished an energy bar each and stepped into the woods, meandering among the trees in an effort to take the least steep route.

As we climbed, the side of the gorge became a bit steeper, but we could still hike upright even though we found ourselves relying more and more on trees for handholds. Short breaks to catch our breath increased. The ground was covered with snow, but under the snow was decayed leaf litter, an often slippery underlayer that prevented us depending on traction from the snow. The hike became a slog. Still, we were happy to be making an adventure out of our thwarted hiking plan. Who would have thought anyone would be crazy enough to climb out of the gorge off-trail? Yeah, look at these two fearless fools wandering in the woods during winter where no one could find them if anything went wrong.

Suddenly we found ourselves standing at the base of a nearly vertical rock wall twenty feet or so high. The options for skirting the rock on one side or the other were covered in snow dusted leaf litter and offered no secure footing nor a gentler slope. Much of the rock was exposed, so we thought we could actually climb it, hands and feet. No, we had no rope. And when I turned around to look down what we had already climbed, I realized that one slip and only the closest tree or a long fall would follow. Like the proverbial boiling frog (scientifically false by the way), we had climbed a steepening incline without noticing how much our exposure had increased.

"This wall looks nasty."

"I know, but I don't see any other way to continue."

"I'd suggest that we retreat and take the backtrack route, but I'm not sure we can descend safely from here. If we begin sliding, we might hit the bottom of the gorge before we stop or break a bone on our way down an uncontrollable slippery slide."

"Well, I have my hiking stick, so let me see how high I can get."

Curt began a cautious climb and used his hiking stick to brace himself when he had to stretch for a hand or foot hold. In effect, I tried to spot him in case he slipped. Without being anchored, I likely would not have been able to stop him. I might have blunted his fall, but I suspected that his fall would cause both of us to tumble. Tense and sweating, Curt eventually reached the top of the wall. I started my climb. The first ten feet were not bad, but then I felt gripped by my exposure. I could not find anything or any way to secure my position. Curt grabbed a small tree with one hand and extended his hiking stick down to me with the other. I was scared to trust that he could hold me, or that I could hold the hiking stick if I slipped. But it was the only way up. And it worked. The stick gave me just enough stability to trust the rock, and I quickly topped the wall, sweating as if I had stepped out of a sauna.

We stood still for a few minutes scanning the surrounding woods and reexamining the wall we had just climbed.

"I can't believe we tried to climb that. It may be the dumbest thing I have ever done when hiking."

"Yeah, but we made it, and the slope eases from here toward the top of the gorge."

"Thank goodness. We really should have backtracked."

"But this was exciting. A good story, huh?"

We munched energy bars and drank water once more as we tried to stop sweating. Wool saved us from hypothermia. Then we began a slow pace through the forest toward the road we knew waited for us somewhere up above. As we had noted, the grade of the gorge slope eased near the top, and we had an easier walk out once we left the rock wall below us.

We popped out of the woods onto the snow-covered road and guessed that the Land Cruiser was somewhere to the north. Thankfully, we were right and soon reached the end of our unplanned hike, relieved to drop heavy packs, heated some tea, and ate a hot meal.

As we packed the Land Cruiser and rode the three hours back home, we reviewed our trip, our decisions, our adventure. We both concluded that we had been dumb and very lucky. Without the proper gear, we never should have attempted climbing out of the gorge. Even in an emergency, it would have been foolish because of the number of unknown conditions that we encountered. But we had done it, and it is a good story if only because no one else would be that stupid and get away with it. For my part, the lessons learned would return to me several years later when some friends and I took a winter hike in Slickrock Wilderness as a blizzard later termed "The Storm of the Century" approached. That is another story.

PADDLE OR DIE:
RAFTING the LOWER GAULEY

The Gauley River is a dammed river in West Virginia. Each autumn, the Army Corps of Engineers opens the Summersville Dam to release massive volumes of water from the dark, cold bottom of Summersville Lake, creating the finest whitewater in the eastern states and some of the most exciting whitewater anywhere in the country. There are dozens of rapids rated from Class III to Class V, raft-eating hydraulics and more undercut rocks than anyone can count. The Upper Gauley is non-stop exhilaration. The Lower Gauley offers some respite between most rapids; promotional info describes it as a roller coaster. As a novice to both the Gauley as well as whitewater rafting in general, I was only allowed to run the Lower (minimum age 14).

I was a young banker living in Charlotte when a co-worker and friend, Mark, asked if I would like to run the Gauley. He had run it a couple of times and thought I might enjoy it. Not knowing what questions I should ask, I asked none and agreed to join him and some of his friends on an October raft down the Lower river.

I had never paddled whitewater, just canoed lakes and creeks and, a couple of times, paddled through the salt marsh to Bear Island on the North Carolina coast. As far as I knew, whitewater was just a river running over rocks. I had surfed in the ocean and knew that there was also a surfing terminology applied to whitewater, so I guessed I was sufficiently prepared to drive up to West Virginia for the experience.

The departure date approached, and I stumbled providentially (prophetically?) onto a couple of articles a week apart regarding people drowning while rafting or kayaking in whitewater. I started asking more questions. Is this safe? Do we have a guide? (I did not know how to steer a raft and did not think Mark did.) How hard is it, really? Mark laid out an overview. Guides. Self-bailing rafts so that we would not stall at the foot of a rapid only to lose control and swamp-and-swim in the subsequent rapids. PFDs. Wetsuits. (Yes, he said, the water is that cold. So I knew I could add hypothermia to the list of deaths I could suffer.) Helmets. (I *need* a helmet? Yep, lots of rocks, and if you flip or swim, the river will be pushing you exactly where you do not want to be. It was beginning to sound like a motorcycle wreck.) What is "entrapment"?

The trip would include a big lunch at midday on the rocks beside the river complete with plenty of juice and hot cocoa. (I welcomed some part of the day that would be familiar and enjoyable.) Take a waterproof disposable camera. (About which I thought, I will be holding a paddle for dear life and not sure when I could use the camera.) Mark, ever sure of himself, convinced me that I would be a wimp to back out. Even his girlfriend was going. (Yes, I know how sexist that sounds, but I was beginning to picture whitewater aficionados as weight-lifting masochists with a penchant for death by concussive drowning.)

I resigned myself to a low probability of survival and researched self-rescue techniques for hydraulics, learning that the ability to swim was mostly irrelevant. After all, better to flame out than fade away, right? I tried not to analyze any more.

The morning of our run, we gathered at the outfitter's camp far from the put-in. It was dark, the low clouds dour and menacing. There was nothing auspicious about the day. The skies literally cried as we rode the tired old, whining school bus up the crooked mountain roads with nothing between us and the invisible bottom of the gorge except some second growth forest clinging desperately to the steep mountainside. It seemed a good day to die.

I could not relax. What an idiotic idea to go whitewater rafting in the remote backcountry where rescue was impossible. More than once, the driver navigated tight switchbacks that required backing up to make the turn, the rear of the bus hanging over empty space as he burned the clutch to hold his place on the hill. Tension gripped my chest, starving my lungs, my heart hammering an increasingly loud, staccato beat. Shit! I was scared.

After what seemed at least an entire day, our driver pulled off the road into a gravel parking lot in the trees, a typical trailhead. There was no river in sight. Where was the river? We shouldered the eight-person raft for the half mile hike down to the river along an old jeep trail. Thankful that fear had not paralyzed me, I was relieved to be doing something, anything, happy even to be sweating inside my wetsuit (when I really needed to pee), despite the black neoprene squeezing my chest, constricting my breath, its claustrophobic embrace smothering me. Damn this was a dumb idea.

We arrived at the river. It did not look too frightening. It was the middle of nowhere, and the climb out of the gorge was virtually impossible up vertical rock walls, but the deep black water swirling past us looked only cold and deep. Still, fear lingered at the edge of the woods from which we had emerged, its shadow looming just behind me inside the impenetrable forest, a fiend biding its time. You had to think of James Dickey's novel and movie, *Deliverance*.

Suddenly, everyone was hurrying to pile into the rafts, grab a seat and jam a foot underneath a tube for bracing. There is no such thing as "holding on" in a whitewater raft; there is only staying in. With a wink and a chuckle, Mark pushed me to the bow of the raft asserting it was the safest place to be. He sat behind me.

I reflected on the morning safety talk that the outfitters gave hours earlier. "Rule number one: Stay in the boat." (Another movie came to mind. In *Apocalypse Now*, when Chef gets off the river boat to scout the jungle for mangoes, he instead runs into a tiger. After fleeing wildly through the forest, he leaps back onto the river boat and keeps yelling, "Never get out of the boat. Never get out of the boat.") Once out of the raft, options for rescue diminished by the second as the current seizes the person, pulling them under or away from the raft and hurtling them toward the next rapid and other life-threatening hazards such as undercut rocks, strainers or eternally recirculating hydraulics where a body can rise and sink below the surface until not even bones remain.

Before I could ask myself once more (already too late), why am I doing this, our guide, a petite young woman (so much for my image of the masochistic weight-lifters) pushed us into the current. She walked us through some perfunctory commands like "Left forward" and "Right back". The raft swung lazily as we dipped our paddles more or less in unison to spin or ease forward in the flat water of a quiet pool. Then she called "All forward", and the raft lurched with the combined effort of eight paddles. The surge reassured me and felt like control. Ahead I could see a small wave rising from the surface, and we plunged into a standing wave that swallowed me whole, the cold water slapping me awake and bringing me back into the moment. The river had doused my nerves. "Wow! That was wild!" My friends laughed as I turned and smiled. No one behind me had even gotten wet.

Our raft paddled well. Our guide complimented our strength and ability to coordinate, counseling that her steerage was entirely dependent upon us pushing the raft faster than the river current. Otherwise, we were helpless as any stick or leaf floating and twisting with the river's whims.

As we approached each rapid, our guide would name it and tell us what class it was rated. Most of the rapids were Class III and Class IV (Class VI being theoretically unrunnable). She would brief us on the best set up and line of attack, control of which was entirely in her hands as we only provided the locomotion she commanded. When we slid onto the upstream tongue of a rapid, she would exhort us to "paddle, paddle, paddle" until we were clear. A few times, while waiting our turn to enter a rapid, we held back, idly holding our position with faint strokes of a few paddles and watched as paddlers ahead of us were tossed from their raft or simply fell into the river as the waves bucked them off the raft. All morning, we never lost anyone from our raft.

We stopped for lunch on a large rock beside the river. The guides laid out gobs of deli meats and cheeses, tomato slices, mustard, mayonnaise, a variety of breads, peanut butter and jelly for the vegetarians among us, and a selection of chips along with gallons of koolaid and water. Despite the wet suits we wore, the water came from the bottom of a mountain lake at fiftyish degrees, so hot chocolate was welcome. Naturally, there were cookies with Oreos a favorite.

We relaxed on the sloping boulder and relived a few of the bigger rapids. As a neophyte, I had been unaware of the practice of naming each rapid. Of course, we began with an easy Class III, Fuzzy Box of Kittens with other downstream rapids named Chainsaw, Back Ender and Junkyard, where the guide warned us not to swim and to avoid touching the river bottom because of the risk of trapping a foot (the feared "entrapment") in one of the old cars that had been pushed off the canyon lip in years past. Our raft crew chatted eagerly about our prowess; everyone had stayed in the raft. Although none of us believed that we exhibited any special skill, our success pumped us for the remainder of the river.

Some of the upcoming rapids had names that did not reveal their severity. Upper Mash was rated Class IV followed by Lower Mash, a Class V.

Nearing the end of the day and the end of our run, our guide invited us to tackle the next rapid straight through, saying "we usually run the right side or the left side of this bowl because it is a hydraulic. You have all been paddling strongly, so would you like to run it down the middle?"

"What's it called?"

"Heaven Help You."

"Hell yes! Down the middle."

She should have clarified that *she* had never run it down the middle. We were quite full of ourselves. We had almost survived the Lower Gauley and believed we could handle anything. No one distinguished the difference between hubris and luck. Because we were not yet off the river alive, humility would have been more appropriate.

Our guide admonished that all must listen for her commands, paddle as hard as we could, and keep paddling until she commanded "Rest!"

We lined up and began an easy, steady communal stroke. Ahead, the bottom fell out of the river in the shape of a huge bowl broad enough to swallow that old school bus that had delivered us into the gorge. We could not even see the bottom of the bowl until we reached the lip. Down we slid, accelerating with the current, paddles dipping and pulling, dipping and pulling, all quiet except for the sound of the river roaring around us. The raft bottomed out, and we started to rise up the far side of the bowl, still dipping and pulling in unison as a crew.

We stalled. Just when we felt we would crest the downstream edge, we hung motionless for long enough to sense the lack of movement, and then felt the raft being sucked inexorably backwards. A sense of nausea shot through me. Hydraulic! The rapid seized the stern tube of the raft and pulled it under. The side tubes folded just forward of the stern. Our guide leaped to her feet as the tubes sank beneath the water filling the back of the raft and leaving her standing knee deep on the stern tube with one hand gripping the PFD of the paddler in front of her.

Her high pitched scream indicated true terror, "Paddle, paddle! Harder, harder!" With all the fear of being swallowed whole and being trapped in the endless cycle of a bottomless hydraulic, we poured all of our energy and strength into faster, harder, deeper strokes. Her emotional cry ended only when we sneaked over the back of the rapid. Slowly, as if in a time warp of slow motion, the river had gently yielded; she let us go.

Our guide heaved with relief as she confessed she had never tried to run the center and never would again. We cheered ourselves nervously, raising our paddles in the traditional celebration of triumph, like knights raising their swords, shocked by the danger and humbled by forces we could not control.

Our guide assured us that the rest of the river was reasonably calm Class III rapids. "Oh, but there is one exception. The final rapid is a Class V called Pure Screaming Hell."

With those few words, our guide cancelled the relief we were feeling. There would be no safety until we passed Pure Screaming Hell, and there were seven rapids leading up to it, one named Rattlesnake. I could not see any good coming from a rapid named Rattlesnake even though it was only a Class III.

That night, after warm showers and dry clothes, we sucked down plastic glasses of cheap red wine over steak dinner at the outfitter's camp. Sitting outside at long picnic tables in the dim light of sunset beside the deep forest, everyone shared tales of near death experiences on rapids east and west. One story was current, the story of a raft on the Upper Gauley that same day. In the middle of a Class V hydraulic, a raft speeding downstream in the current peered into the water and saw what appeared to be a white disk just under the surface. Puzzled, they looked up at the shore and saw the crew of an eight-person, self-bailing raft, theoretically unsinkable just like ours. The white disk was the bailing bucket of the fully inflated raft trapped on the bottom of the river, sucked under and held there by the hydraulic. I drank another glass of wine, relieved to be alive.

DON'T DROWN the CHILDREN

Paddling Carter's Lake

My wife, Beth, and I love both our children dearly, and we raised them dayhiking, paddling, flyfishing, and camping. We are protective parents who preach caution and preparation when outdoors: proper gear coupled with a good plan (that someone else knows), maps, water, extra energy bars, appropriate gear and clothing (wool/synthetics, not cotton), and emergency blankets to stave off hypothermia. Without scaring them when they were young, we weaved into our conversations on the way to camp and while sitting around campfires stories of people who made poor decisions that exposed them to avoidable risk. We also taught the two of them that risk is not always avoidable. Serendipity, chaos theory, and accidents all can contribute to outdoor ventures going wrong. So you need to know how to start a fire, make a shelter, attract searchers, and maintain your logic while suppressing emotions, especially fear.

Nevertheless, the best laid plans can jump the track so you must be prepared for the unpredictable, the difficulties that cannot be anticipated.

When we lived in Atlanta, we sometimes drove north to Carter's Lake, one of several manmade hydropower lakes in the Georgia mountains. Creation of the lake required the tallest earthen dam east of the Mississippi and filled the gorge of the Coosawattee River, a river formerly wild with rapids running through a deep gorge. Sadly, the rapids have been drowned 450 feet below the lake surface. The novel *Deliverance* by James Dickey is based on the damming of the Coosawattee even though the fictional river in his book is named the Cahulawassee, and the movie was filmed on the Chattooga River where it forms the boundary between Georgia and South Carolina.

On our first trip to canoe the lake, my wife and I loaded the canoe with three black Labradors, two folding chairs, a cooler filled with drinks and lunch, and our two-year old daughter bundled, as always when we were around water, into a pfd, a lifejacket. We paddled a couple of miles up the lake to a muddy, red clay and quartz rock beach. The water was conveniently shallow near the shore, so we could laze in the lake, the dogs could chase sticks thrown into deeper water, and our daughter could play along the water's edge (still wearing her pfd) without us worrying that she would drown.

It was a hot summer day, the sun searing as we swam and sank into cooler water. By the time we decided to head back to the boat ramp, everyone, including the dogs, was exhausted. My wife and I were in no hurry and took our time stroking the canoe across the flat calm lake. The dogs immediately curled up and closed their eyes. Our daughter, seated in the bottom of the canoe at my feet, leaned on the gunwale and trailed her hand in the water. Tired and relaxed, she seemed to enjoy the feel of the refreshing lake water. There were few boats of any sort on the lake, so we could watch the shoreline for potential beaches for future paddles. The sun burned our shoulders and heads, amplifying the fatigue we felt.

Paddling can be mesmerizing and soporific: the steady rhythm of dipping the blade, pulling the stroke, lifting the blade, repeating the stroke, watching the water drip like a line of crystal beads while you recover the paddle and repeat the stroke. Dip, pull, lift. Dip, pull, lift. Dip, pull, lift. Again and again and again. With neither wind nor current to resist, we coasted easily through the water. Even our daughter began to nod as she rocked with the pace of the paddles, her hand tracing a lazy pattern through the lake.

Then she was gone. In a moment that did not even imprint an image on my brain, our daughter rolled over the gunwale of the canoe and sank into the lake. 450 feet. The only thought that flashed through my mind was 450 feet of lake beneath us. Deep dark water. She had barely made a splash. I pushed the paddle into my offside hand and reached over the side just behind the stern as we continued to slide through the water past where she fell. I did not have time to tell my wife to stop paddling. I could not even take a breath as my hand clutched our daughter's ankle, and I lifted her from the lake. As I embraced her upright on my lap, she woke, surprised and confused while my wife suddenly registered the small sound of a splash that had marked the instant our daughter slipped into the water. Before she could fully form the fear of asking "what happened?", I had our daughter safely back in the canoe.

"She fell asleep and tumbled out of the canoe." Beth did not need to hear more.

We have no idea how long the whole event took, but I would guess less than three seconds. Had our daughter breathed, she would have drowned even though we should have been able to resuscitate her. The pfd kept her afloat, or she would have plunged like a stone into the depths of the lake where I doubt I could have found her. By the time I would have jumped from the canoe, I would not have known exactly where she had entered the lake. The longer I searched, the deeper she would have sunk. The deeper she sank, the darker the water, and the less visibility. In Carter's Lake, visibility might have vanished completely within ten feet or so. And, of course, there is a limit to how deep I could have free-dived even with her life at stake.

In the end, the experience may have been more traumatic for me and Beth than for Taylor. She does not remember anything about the incident except what we have reminded her over the years. Back then, I never wore my own pfd, keeping it loose in the canoe. If I had applied the same practice to our daughter, she would still be on the bottom of Carter's Lake, unreachable, lying in the lightless, frigid depths of an ancient gorge under 450 feet of water.

Flyfishing on the Jackson River

For several years, we shared with a few friends a rustic fishing cabin on the Jackson River in Virginia. The Jackson is an excellent trout stream that received little fishing pressure because it is private under an old King's (or Crown) Grant that conveyed not only the land on the banks of the river but also the fish, the fowl and all other creatures within the property. It is a cold, tailwater fishery with water released from the bottom of Gathright Dam on Lake Moomaw less than a mile upstream of the cabin.

The river provides varied depths, speed, and bottom types. Swift shallow rapids occasionally break the steady pace of the current. Wading where the current is swiftest is fine so long as the fisherman is careful with his or her footing and pays attention to the bottom and water depth. For convenience and fireside conversation, we divided the river near the cabin into different section names: Above the Falls, Below the Falls, Cabin Pool Rapid, the Cabin Pool, Middle Pool, the Ledge, etc. Below the Falls, the bottom mounds toward the center of the river with gravel, the easiest of footing. Above the Falls is angled slab rock that can twist an ankle or pitch a fisherman off balance. In the Middle Pool, small to medium round boulders covered with moss are scattered; if the shape of the boulders does not trip you, the slippery moss might. Still, except for the couple of deep pools like the Cabin Pool, in normal conditions the water is never over your head. Although this sounds reassuring, we mostly fished in waders to stay warm. If water fills the waders, as when a person might fall into the river, a huge bubble of air can be trapped at the boots and float a fisherman's legs above the head, in effect pushing the head below the water. With no assistance or leverage to regain your footing to stand, drowning is a real possibility.

Beth and our two children learned to flyfish (always catch and release) at the cabin, and they learned the risks. Naturally, they also learned what types of bottom were where, how deep the various fishing spots were and how to carefully and safely navigate the moving river. Still, my wife and I made sure we could see the children when they were fishing. The Cabin Pool formed a ninety degree angle in the river. The Cabin Pool was too deep to wade, but someone floating in the pool had a view both up and down the river which was purely hypothetical. Anywhere else on the river, our views were limited by bends and banks. So we usually fished within fifty yards of each other at least in pairs.

One afternoon, Taylor and I hiked downstream to fish the Middle Pool while my wife and son headed upstream to Below the Falls where the water is less than knee deep and the bottom is reliable gravel for good traction and footing even when moving through the current. The Middle Pool is not quite knee deep at the bank then drops to almost waist deep near the center of the river. The main current and channel rushes along the far bank, and big trout often hover there. My daughter cast into the current along the far bank where it enters the top of a shallow rapid. I cast upstream into another small rapid and drifted my fly in the channel against the far bank.

The action was modest and the fish average for the Jackson, 8-10 inch rainbows. But I had caught a few big browns in the same pool on previous trips, so I fished it hard and switched flies regularly. We had fished nearly an hour when my daughter climbed out onto a comfortable grassy flat between the river and the woods. She took a break while watching the water for feeding fish. I tied on another fly, still hoping for a big brown. As can happen when you fish, I had eased closer and closer to the current along the far bank where I expected the big browns to be feeding. I went from not quite waist deep to waist deep in the river. I was paying attention because I did not need to cross any farther, and I did not want to wade any deeper.

The river water flowing from upstream began to cloud and become muddy, and I also noticed a few sticks, small at first, then larger. My brain took a minute to comprehend what was happening. The Corps had opened the dam. Because it is a flood control dam, they only open it to relieve the flood waters filling the lake, but there had been no rain. As I started to realize that I was standing in deeper water than just minutes before, my daughter called to me from the shore. "It looks like the river is rising." And she was right. I shuffled against the increasing force of the current to return to the shore.

"Your mother may not notice what is happening. We need to hurry upstream to see if they need help. And keep a sharp eye on the river in case your brother has been swept away in the current."

Waders are not made for running, but neither of us had time to stop and sit to peel them off. We ran as best we could, cutting through the woods while keeping a watch on the passing river. More and more debris cluttered the dirty current and collected along the banks. If my wife or son were in the deeper part of the pool Below the Falls, they had likely already been knocked from their feet, or they could be trapped on a rock or shoal in the middle of the river with no safe way to wade ashore.

I later learned that the river rose so quickly that Cameron, 5 years old, found himself deep enough that the current was beginning to slosh over the top of his waders. Beth was too far downstream to help him until she could fight her way against the current with a stout stick that luckily floated within her reach. He had made it to the gravel bar, so his footing was secure and, with his mother's support, the two of them crossed the slab between them and the shore. By the time Taylor and I arrived, they were climbing out of the river, frazzled but safe.

Cameron had kept his wits as had Beth. They worked together without letting fear paralyze their actions. Even though neither they nor I had ever considered the situation of a dam release and suddenly rising river level (all of us knew there should have been a warning horn), everyone analyzed their options and made decisions without delay. What could have been a tragedy of the worst sort instead became a learning experience and a good tale for chilly nights by the campfire.

Rafting the New River

A couple of years later, we joined another family for an overnight rafting trip on the Upper New River in West Virginia. It was the second trip for our group so, when the outfitter offered paddling our own duckies instead of riding a raft with a guide, my daughter and I said Yes. (A ducky is simply an inflatable kayak with no deck and loads of fun.) Taylor and I had run the Nantahala River in western North Carolina in one a few years earlier. Like a raft, you cannot sink a ducky. They float high and are forgiving for amateur paddlers running rapids. They keep you wet but safe.

For the first day, the rapids were mild, and we mostly rode the river current using the paddles to steer but not to propel us forward. Nearing our campsite for the night, one guide suggested Cameron might like some time in the ducky too. He agreed and climbed in front of me, his hands free so he could hold the lines along the tubes. We approached a railroad bridge, and the guide alerted us to a series of rooster tails below it. Whoop dee doos. The rooster tails always look intimidating because they are formed by a wave train in which each wave rises steeply and drops the same so that they appear impassable. The river picked up speed as we neared the first wave. "Hang on," I advised my son. Then Bam! We punched the ducky into and through the first wave, and each one that followed doused us thoroughly. Taylor and I laughed the whole way through. Cameron turned and glared at me.

"I want to get back on the raft."

"But wasn't that fun?"

"No."

As we slowed in the flat water beyond the small rapid, I signaled my wife's raft, and we dropped off my son. He was fine, but he had not enjoyed feeling out of control. I understood.

Late afternoon, we camped on a wide sandy beach beside the river and across from a railroad pinned to the mountainside. Our guides instructed us on river etiquette, emphasizing the "boom box" where we would perform our scatological functions. "You can urinate anywhere, but we have to pack out the solid waste." They placed the "boom box", an old ammo box, back in the woods about fifty yards. "Follow the trail, and you will find a Tupperware container with toilet paper inside. If the container is not there, it means that someone is ahead of you using the boom box. Wait your turn."

"Why is it called a boom box?"

"Good question. Avoid urinating in the boom box. If you do, and if you close the box, gas can build up with the excrement, and the pressure may release with some force. Boom!"

Everyone laughed, but everyone knew how embarrassing it would be to be the person who caused a boom in the boom box.

The family friends who had invited us to join the trip did not have a lot of outdoor experience and knew that our family camped regularly. They wanted at least one family along who they were comfortable asking questions that might seem obvious to others. Plus, their children would have our children for companionship. The father, Jack, was a successful real estate developer who kept himself in top physical condition. Tall and muscular, he could intimidate strangers unintentionally, but he was a good and gentle soul. A couple of hours after the guide's instructions concerning use of the boom box, after most of the rest of the group had made their visits to the woods, Jack approached my wife to clarify the boom box logistics. What he pictured was bending his six foot six frame over a small square of Tupperware and attempting to direct his waste into the tiny target; in addition, he could not stomach the thought of removing the toilet paper from the already-soiled Tupperware and then replacing it afterwards. When my wife explained that the Tupperware only held the toilet paper, and the boom box only captured the solid waste, Jack's relief was loud and palpable. He scurried off into the woods, returning later with a broad smile of satisfaction.

Our camp beach was ideal except for the teeming population of granddaddy longlegs. In certain places, the thin vegetation on the ground appeared to move. Although they are certainly in the arachnid family, I have a hard time thinking of them the same way I think of spiders because they are slight of frame and can easily be removed by pinching a thin leg and tossing the critter away onto the forest duff. Still, a big number of any insect, venomous or not, can be obnoxious when living outdoors as on a camping trip. Stupidly on my part, when we set up our tent, I left the door open to let the evening air cool the inside before we went to sleep. We later noticed a congregation of granddaddy longlegs and swept out as many as we could and zipped the flap closed.

Our guides prepared a hearty and tasty meal over the fire, then everyone sat around the coals talking and telling stories until the day's fatigue led us to bed. Beth, Taylor, Cameron, and I stretched out our sleeping pads and sleeping bags and lay down. With soft, cool sand below the tent, everyone but me quickly fell asleep. I read with my headlamp for a short while then clicked it off. The tent was instantly black. Outside were muffled sounds from the guides packing away our food and the whisper of the river flowing past. It seemed I was only one wink into slumber when a scream filled the night. Grabbing my light as fast as I could, I pointed it at my son.

"What is it?"

"A granddaddy longlegs just landed on my face." Think about the movie *Alien*. Our son was trembling as my wife comforted him. We learned the next morning that Jack was relieved that it had been our son and not himself who had freaked out over a granddaddy longlegs.

We scoured for other critters to excommunicate from the tent, and then all of us returned to sleep once more. A couple of hours later, a blaring train horn shattered the peace and quiet of the still night, waking me from a restful dream. Because I knew the sound came from a train, and knew that the train tracks hung from the mountain on the opposite side of the river, I did not intend to fully awake. I turned over. But the ground shook and rumbled, the horn grew louder, and the huge light leading the engine turned our night camp into daylight aiming for our tent. My somnolent brain leaped into emergency mode. The train was coming through the camp, tons of steel, engines and cars, charging from the canyon wall, somehow crossing the river and plowing through our campsite. All of us would die. I had to see it and unzipped the flap of the tent just as the engine's light rounded a curve on the mountain and continued rolling down the tracks. Safe.

The sun rose above the mist upriver, and the guides cooked another satisfying meal, a breakfast to fuel another day of paddling the river and rapids. Guides often talk about the dangers of the trip, building anticipation and suspense among the paddlers to enhance the glory of success, and they particularly emphasize the rapids with the biggest myths or legends. For the section of the New River that we were rafting, the BIG rapid was named Surprise, the only Class III we would run. The guides had mentioned it in the pre-launch briefing, and spoke more about it before and after dinner the night before. Now they reminded us, in most serious tones, that Surprise would mark the end of our day, the end of our trip on the river. We needed to prepare ourselves mentally because the rapid had a tricky route that kayakers (and duckies) often failed to survive. With a series of huge waves, a wickedly fast current and massive boulders beneath the river, we would have to be sharp to make it. I am sure the tension and heart rates rose measurably among the group paddling.

We struck camp, laughed about the midnight scream from the granddaddy longlegs landing on Cameron's face like the larval, face-sucking, chest-bursting xenomorph in the movie *Alien*. None of us were laughing *at* my son; we were chuckling nervously about how we would have reacted the same way had it happened to us. Maybe it helped tenderize the tension of the rapids that awaited us downstream. Gear loaded on the guide raft, my daughter and I strapped on our pfds and settled into a spare rhythm with just enough effort to steer the ducky. The sun hung bright in a clear blue sky, mountain forests framed the river, and the water cooled us when it splashed into the ducky. We floated as a group, occasionally jumping into the river to float with the current and cool off. Eventually, the guides announced that Surprise was just beyond the next bend in the river.

Our lead guide advised me how to approach the rapid. "There are three big waves in quick succession. Take the first two head on, but...this is important...you need to twist the bow of the ducky to the right before you hit the third wave. It is more powerful than it looks, and it comes at you from an angle. The third wave is the Surprise. Miss your twist to the right, and it will flip you."

I worried about my daughter's safety. "You said the boulders under the rapids are big. How deep is the rapid? Do I need to worry that we could get trapped underwater if we flip? Or will we be slammed against the rocks?" Helmets and pfds are essential whitewater gear, but they cannot protect a paddler from all risks and hazards.

"She'll be fine even if you flip." I had to accept his confidence as we accelerated toward the rapid.

The rafts ran it first, each disappearing in the waves once they dropped over the entry ledge. And then we were hurtling over the same ledge and headed for the wave train rising three or four feet above the river. Both of us hooted as we plowed face first into the first wave and then the second. For one brief moment, I could see how the third wave would throw a right cross current at us, and I dug the blade of the paddle into the water, back paddling with as strong a stroke as I could muster to force the bow to face the final wave. As soon as I thought I had made the move successfully, the wave slammed the bow back into the current, and my daughter was tossed from the ducky and vanished into the rapid. The ducky was flying down the river as I scanned the tumultuous whitewater looking for any sign of her. She popped up right beside me close enough for me to grab and hold her arm as the rapid spit us out into the current below. I feared the trauma of falling from the ducky and swimming a Class III rapid might cause her never to paddle whitewater again. But I looked into her eyes, and she was smiling. No fear, just the excitement of adventure.

NOT for SALE: 1978 Toyota Land Cruiser FJ40.
One owner.

A year after high school, I decided to go to college and managed to get accepted very late in the admissions process. Needing transportation to and from home without expecting my parents to chauffeur me, I bought a used Toyota Corolla five speed, white with yellow racing stripes, cheap but sort of sporty.

Instead of attending the cavernous lecture hall with stadium seating for Chemistry 101, I regularly read Thoreau at the Carolina Coffee Shop on Franklin Street. I ate enough omelettes to have them make mine with mozzarella, which was not offered on the menu, instead of the standard cheddar. My tactics did not help my GPA but spawned an epiphany of sorts. Despite majoring in Marine Biology, I had never in my life had a creative thought about science of any sort. I can picture vividly the moment of my revelation, standing at the urinal in my dorm suite surrounded by cold cloudy tiles. On the other hand, reading Robert Penn Warren, Charles Olson, and Ezra Pound in the library between classes, coupled with my informal study of Thoreau, enlightened me to a different path. I would become a poet, a notion that to that date had never breached my thoughts.

I changed schools at the second semester, matriculating at St Andrews Presbyterian College, a small liberal arts college in the Sand Hills of North Carolina. Never had I been surrounded by so many creative and energetic people. Potters and painters, photographers, poets and short story writers. Isolated as we were outside a small town with virtually no current culture of its own (except Mrs. Ford's, aka Norma's, diner: meat and two for 75 cents), the students made their entertainment on campus with music and readings seasoned with alcohol and recreational drugs. Several jazz greats were born in or associated with the area: Dizzy Gillespie, John Coltrane, Rufus Harley (a black bagpiper who played jazz), Billy Taylor, and Thelonious Monk, to name a few who garnered their fame outside of North Carolina. Due in large part to St. Andrews' writer-in-residence,

Ron Bayes, the college attracted a roster of accomplished if lesser known artists, especially poets, to introduce us to the real world of creativity.

Seeking a break from the insular campus, I made my first journey to the Outer Banks to surf with a classmate, Mark, from Florida who was a more experienced and capable surfer. Though he grew up in Florida, he had surfed Cape Hatteras several times. I grew up in North Carolina an hour from Emerald Isle but had never visited, much less surfed, Cape Hatteras. Mark convinced me I had missed most of what life had to offer, and we mounted a minor surfing expedition in late fall anticipating glassy waves and cold water. I mounted my surf racks and surfboard on the Toyota Corolla, and we headed north toward Roanoke Island, then crossed east to Nags Head and Whalebone Junction where we turned south on Highway 12 for the 60 mile stretch of sandy highway down the narrow island that leads to the cape. Frequently we could see simultaneously both ocean and sound from the highway. The strip of asphalt was that narrow.

On our eight hour trip to the Banks, Mark told me endless stories of surfing up and down the east coast. I had only surfed the Crystal Coast, an unnamed island that extends east-west from Fort Macon at Beaufort Inlet through Atlantic Beach to Pine Knoll Shores, Salter Path, and Indian Beach to Emerald Isle and Bogue Inlet, the ocean closest to my home but more than a hundred miles due south of the wild beaches of the Outer Banks. Cape Hatteras is the point farthest east in North Carolina where the northbound warm river of the Gulf Stream closes into the shore and sometimes collides with the icy southbound Labrador Current. Wild sea life abounds. In addition to fish, whales, eagle rays, and large sharks migrate in sight of the shore. There is no land between Greenland and Cape Hatteras, so ocean storms have unlimited room to build. The Graveyard of the Atlantic earned its name with both sea and shore littered with vessels caught off the Banks when a storm coalesced in the North Atlantic.

The first day, in moderate waves, I almost drowned. Mark had warned me how the waves off Hatteras appear as gentle swells but peak with a flick of the wave lip that is strong enough to fling a surfer backwards off the wave. I listened and dismissed his description as hyperbole, the experienced surfer trying to psych out the younger grom. Mark caught waves immediately. I struggled to find a good position in the lineup and could not paddle quite fast enough to match the wave speed. Hoping to see how Mark was making his waves, I looked down the line as he paddled out and watched as he crested a wave only to be tossed suddenly backwards through the air as if pitched by the hand of Posiedon. I was laughing when he surfaced.

He was laughing too. "Told you so." He stroked up the face of another wave and ducked under the lip before it could pitch.

With arrogant ignorance, I knew it would not happen to me because it never had. Of course, I had never surfed Hatteras either. I attempted once again to get into position. A fine wave began to rise in front of me. This one I could catch. I paddled toward the wave, slowing just before I reached the face so I could spin and pull down the face. But before I could turn, the wave leaped skyward, and the lip lifted me free of the water, heaving me shoreward through the air. The wave pushed me to the bottom where the turbulence of the broken sea rolled me around on the sand and held me down. I tried to claw for the surface, and my face barely emerged when the following wave rolled me again. When I tried to reach air this time, I did not make it before the next wave took me back to the sand, flipping me around like a rag doll and wrapping my ankle leash around my neck while I tried to push toward the shore. At the edge of the beach, another wave knocked me back, buckling my knees in the receding wash. When I finally crawled onto the beach, I could barely catch my breath. Never had I faced waves of such intensity.

Trembling with relief, feeling that I had almost drowned, I collapsed on the beach. I looked out at the breaking waves and saw Mark catch a fine ride, streaking across the face of a green wave as it peeled parallel along the shore. I raised my hand so he would know I had gotten out of the water. Reflecting on the thrashing the ocean gave me, I was confounded that the conditions at Hatteras could be so different from what I was used to surfing. Intellectually I understood the exposure of the Outer Banks and the power of an uninterrupted sea, but this was the same Atlantic that I surfed farther south. Could it truly push so much more energy? Yes it could, but I remained in denial since I had been skunked. I had not caught a single wave. Mark caught several more waves before he returned to the beach.

We camped at the cape for a couple more days, but the wind picked up and the surf was mostly too blown out to ride. It did not matter to me. I had tasted Hatteras and wanted more.

The following year, Mark went to Italy to study art. I convinced the college to let me do an independent study and spent the spring semester traveling west through the North Carolina mountains and into Tennessee. When summer started, I was in the Tirol of Italy for a summer session studying literature at Schloss Brunnenburg, a castle owned by Mary de Rachewiltz, the daughter of Ezra Pound. Mark had returned to North Carolina from Italy and landed a job with the National Park Service in Manteo with lodging near Coquina Beach south of Nags Head. While I was trekking around the Italian Alps, Mark had all the surf he wanted on the Outer Banks.

When I returned from Italy late summer, I immediately headed out to the Banks where I tracked down Mark on the beach with the expectation that he would have a place I could crash. On my most memorable day of the long visit, we rode perfect six foot swells all morning. The sun was hot, the ocean a deep clear green unwrinkled by a single ripple of wind. When we finally stopped for a late lunch, Mark introduced me to carbonara, a heavy egg and bacon (prosciutto if we could have gotten any) pasta dish he had learned in Rome. We prepared a dozen eggs, a pound of bacon, and a cup or two of parmesan mixed into a couple pounds of linguine. We devoured it all then returned to the ocean for an afternoon of surfing.

Even as I departed the Banks, I knew I had to return. I was supposed to spend the academic year at SUNY Buffalo studying with the poet Robert Creeley, one of the Black Mountain poets. However, by the time I received my acceptance letter, college had started, so I decided to head back to the Outer Banks. Mark had moved north to Duck while still working for the National Park Service, but he and his roommates had an extra bedroom in a cottage a couple blocks off the ocean. Perfect. I landed a job at the Aquarium on Roanoke Island and commuted almost thirty miles down the Banks each day. Autumn had arrived, the blues were running, and the ocean was cold.

The timing chain on my Toyota Celica (I had totaled the Corolla in a one car brain fart accident) broke, so I took it to a local mechanic. I did not consider the mechanic's location across from Jockey's Ridge, the tallest sand dune on the east coast, a place high enough to launch hang gliders. After all, fixing the timing chain should have been a matter of ordering the part and installing it. Since I am a mechanical idiot, the repair seemed simple to me. Weeks passed, and I watched the car sit idle on the lot as I rode to work each day with Mark. I called periodically, and the mechanic blamed the delay on the parts supplier. Driving past one day, I stopped and checked on the car. The hood was cracked open, and the head had been removed from the engine block. My dim bulb of a mechanical brain flashed true for a moment. Jockey's Ridge was across the highway. The prevailing winds, and especially storm winds, most often blew out of the west, covering the highway with sand from the Ridge, covering my car with sand, blowing sand under the hood and into the engine block. Shit!

I politely chastised the mechanic, and he assured me the part was arriving the next week. It did, and I retrieved my car after paying an obscenely large repair bill. I could not imagine how much damage the sand must have done inside the engine and soon saw the effects. The car consumed a quart of oil every time I filled it with gas plus a quart about every half tank of driving. I kept a case of oil behind the driver's seat.

With the arrival of winter, the ocean was frequently too rough to surf. I shot photos of Mark trying to get out in ten foot plus waves during a nor'easter that had blown a calm sea to a rage of whitewater chaos breaking along the bottom of the piers. Luck was with him. He never made it past the first line of breakers while the cross current carried him a half mile south in about five minutes.

Back then, the area around Nags Head mostly closed for the winter after Thanksgiving. I quit my aquarium job and returned home, immediately placing an ad for a used Toyota Celica 5-speed, fast and sporty. I had pledged to myself that I would not lie about the condition of the car and answered every question truthfully. The buyer asked about gas mileage but never asked how much oil it burned. I would have told him, I swear. It sold quickly to an enthusiastic teenager (funded by his father) who was hot for a fast car, and I was again in the market for a vehicle.

Unlike a lot of guys I have known, I have never had a fascination with cars. I would never have bought the second one if I had not wrecked the first one. I did not enjoy the process of buying a car, hated the negotiations and games. This time, I decided to buy a vehicle that I would want to own the rest of my life to avoid more acquisition pains. When in Italy, I had driven an old British Leyland Land Rover owned by Mary's son, Sizzo. He had asked me to drive down to the river and collect small boulders for landscaping around the castle. The Land Rover had a drumming diesel and right hand drive. I loved it. Unfortunately, in the aftermath of the mid-seventies Arab oil embargo and the need for improved gas mileage and reduced emissions, you could not buy new

Land Rovers in the US, and used ones were hard to find. Thumbing through action shots in four wheel drive and off-road magazines reminded me of the Japanese version of the British Land Rover, a Toyota Land Cruiser FJ40. It sounded like a beast.

When looking at used FJs, the three speed shift on the steering column had not appealed to me. Even the three speed shifter on the floor did not suit me because I knew I would be driving highway speeds periodically. But 1978 was the first year Toyota added four on the floor. That would work.

The FJ did not offer any standard amenities. No power steering, no air conditioning, and only the most basic AM/FM radio. Perfect. A purely functional vehicle with none of the fancy accoutrements found in contemporary Jeeps or even pickup trucks. Fewer systems to maintain or to fail. I liked everything I read. Dreams of crossing rivers in Alaska, climbing mountain trails, driving remote beaches to the best surf breaks. I called a buddy who worked as a salesman at the local dealer. They had none in stock, but he said he would find one for me.

He located one in fire engine red and had it delivered. I added locking hubs and a cheap radio with a cassette tape player. Yes, I could imagine keeping it for a lifetime. And for forty-two years I have.

Once again deferring college, I worked construction four days per week leaving me time to drive to the mountains or the beach for a long weekend every week. Money for gas and enough time to enjoy my days off. I drove the back roads and avoided the interstate once I learned how little the FJ liked highway speeds. Fifty miles per hour was as fast as she wanted to go. With her short, narrow wheelbase and rigid suspension, highway speeds created a fair amount of shake, rattle, and roll. Fine. I took my time. Patience soothed my soul at the end of the workweek.

In the mountains, on and off the Blue Ridge Parkway, I drove calmly. The dirt forest service roads that spiraled down into the dark, heavily wooded coves required the lazy crawl of four wheel drive. The roads led to places so dark and remote that I always carried my shotgun without ever knowing whether I might need it for a two- or four-legged animal. With a USGS topo map in hand, I explored any hashed jeep trail, path, or forest service road that was wide enough for me to pass. I might have gotten stuck, but low four gave me a final solution any time I needed it. Ironically, the low gearing meant that only occasionally did I *need* four wheel drive. Mostly, it was a convenience that gave me the confidence to go places I should not have ventured.

Deep in the woods, I could hike off trail, follow creeks, and scramble up boulders. I looked for intriguing names on the topo map. Lost Cove, Lost Cove Cliffs, old quarries and mines, abandoned homesteads. Cemeteries appeared everywhere. As did forgotten places like Edgemont and Mortimer. I searched for places where the topo lines nearly merged solid to indicate cliffs. And I was always alert for a paired hashing that showed a jeep trail.

Looking for the interesting place names, I catalogued lots of prosaic names: Long Ridge, Sassafras Ridge, Persimmon Ridge (not to be confused with Simmons Ridge to the west), Timber Ridge. Cold Mountain, duplicative of at least one other in the state. Some names warned me off, like Breakneck Ridge, Big Rough Knob, and Rattlesnake Cliffs. Other names piqued my curiosity. What is an Apple Hole Knob? How did Schoolhouse Ridge come by its name (most communities lay along the creek valleys)? Who was Billy's Knob named for? Or Ned Mountain or Marks Mountain? What happened to earn a mountaintop the name Polecat Knob? There is no shortage of skunks in the state, so what made this one special enough for a name?

When I was not in the mountains, I regularly headed to Emerald Isle, a short one hour country road drive from my home through forests and farmland, a place wild enough to be home to alligators, one of which some fools decided to gawk at roadside as I passed, ignoring the animal's land speed. The winter beach was barren, rarely even a walker as far as you could see. The sea was usually glassy with gentle offshore breezes, deep blue reflecting the cloudless sky, and I had the island to myself. With bright clear days, the sun warmed the sand dunes, and I would tuck up between them, sheltered from the northerly breeze, for a nap between surf sessions. Once my arms were exhausted to the point of barely being able to peel off my wetsuit —noodles - I would soak up one more bit of sun to dry off then drive to a small seafood restaurant beside the tidal marsh off the causeway to Swansboro. Fresh fried shrimp, oysters, scallops and flounder piled high with a bottomless glass of sweetened iced tea. In a booth by a window with a view across the marsh and White Oak River, I gobbled seafood, exhausted and aching from a day chasing waves.

Snow is rare in temperate eastern North Carolina, so the FJ rarely experienced winter action. But once, in 1982, a beautiful early spring blizzard dropped over two feet of snow on the coast. I was taking spring break from school at my parents' cottage on Emerald Isle when the weather service warned of blizzard conditions. My parents decided to return home. The one hour trip took them almost three hours as conditions deteriorated. Even though I had the FJ and could easily have gone with them, I stayed for the storm. Winds rocked the cottage with sixty mile per hour gusts. Snow quickly drifted into the low spots between rolling sand dunes. As the sun set, the snow blended into the bright sand of the dunes, the two seeming one.

After dark, I scanned up and down the island looking for lights in other cottages. Only street lights shined through the blizzard. The cottage continued to rumble and jump in the gusts, and the snow spun violently. The lights flickered a couple of times before I heard the pop of a transformer. I peered out a window. The island was dark with not a light in sight. I had known I would likely lose power, but ever hopeful, I wanted to keep it for the heat. No such luck.

At dawn, the sun rose in a clear sky, the land covered in snow down to the high tide line of the ocean. Snow on the beach created an incongruous scene. Dark blue water accented by the blinding white of snow blanketing the dunes. After exploring the beach, I scouted the landward side of the cottage where I found the snow had drifted three feet in the valley formed by the roadway. I grabbed a short board without a fin and surfed down the driveway. Although far from perfect, it was fun and completely out of place. I had used the board on sand but never on snow.

The FJ has always attracted attention. Once, when I worked in Atlanta, a traveling Swede saw it parked across the street from my office and inquired about buying it. "Sorry, not for sale." People told me regularly they wanted to buy it if ever I did sell it. A good friend reminded me often that I should leave it to him in my will. Although I eventually drove it very little in Atlanta, as it was poor for commuting with the hard start and stop traffic of rush hours, I kept it in our garage and occasionally went for short drives.

When we left the city to move into a 19th century log cabin in the mountains south of Asheville, I was delighted to have held onto it. The pastures at the cabin had not been cut in years. Briars stood four feet high and thistle topped eight along with all kinds of tough, woody weeds. Thinking that no riding lawn mower could cut through the thick growth (and not wanting to invest in a tractor), I hooked a section of steel fencing to the tow ball and drove the FJ around the pasture as if mowing. The fence section successfully knocked down and, to some degree, "cut" the years of overgrown weeds so that the lawn mower had a fighting chance in spring after the winter freeze. The briars, with thorns tough as nails, punctured every single tire with uncountable tiny leaks. The FJ became a work vehicle for running to the hardware store and exploring unpaved mountain roads leading back into old hollers and homesteads, some occupied, some not. Ironically, when exploring an old jeep trail across the road from the cabin, we found ruins of an old livestock barn and the body of an old yellow FJ without an engine. I have always regretted not dragging it off (assuming I could have located the owner or proven the absence of one).

Driving the FJ always brings smile to my face. It is unlike any other land vehicle I have driven, even its ancestral cousin the Land Rover. The combination of a narrow wheelbase and loose steering allows the FJ to float from side to side in the road, much like sailing a sailboat in small waves, the rudder responding with a slight delay to the skipper's hands on the tiller or wheel. I gently weave down the roadway, on land but feel like I am at sea. Although this motion is not ideal on interstates, I avoid them almost entirely.

Without much exaggeration, there is nowhere the FJ cannot travel. Hunting at the back of a friend's forest, we reached a long stretch of muddy track that was nearly three feet deep with black mud and blacker water. I engaged four wheel low, a setting that gears the FJ like a slow tank, and it plowed steadily through the mud hole without hesitating. Slick red clay mud can be more troublesome, but ice is the worst. Anyone can drive in snow until it becomes so deep that your bumper plows more than the wheels ride over the snow. Southern snows tend to be icy without being deep, so plowing is rarely a problem. Nevertheless, ice is a true hazard.

During winter storms, friends and neighbors often comment how easy I have it with the FJ. They envision unrestricted travel regardless of conditions, just put her in gear and press the accelerator. I always assure them that, once wet snow is packed on the road, it is really ice, and a four wheel drive vehicle has the distinct disadvantage of slipping with four wheels instead of two (this without explaining that four wheel drive is really two wheel drive just as two wheel drive is really one wheel drive). And then there is the random moving obstacle course of other, unskilled or irresponsible drivers who never bother to account for the conditions. Rob, a neighbor and close friend, sent his son to work knowing that a snow storm was likely to strike before his son's shift was over.

"You don't mind picking him up, do you?"

"Actually, I do. You should not have let him go to work. No one should be out in this weather."

"Yeah, but you have four wheel drive."

"True, but I am not worried about me. It's the other morons on the road who endanger those of us who know how to handle the snow." Rob looked puzzled. "Yes, Rob, I will pick up your son, but you have to ride with me."

"Why?"

"So you can understand why I do not recommend anyone go out in this shit."

On the way to the store where his son worked, the traffic was slow, the roads mostly still just wet not frozen. Traffic proceeded lazily but with a noticeable sense of haste, an urgency among drivers to be back in the safety of their own driveways and garages, to escape the hazards of rush hour combined with tricky driving conditions. Approaching stoplights, too many cars were trying to be the last car to slip past the yellow light before the red light froze them in their vulnerable spot on the roadway. Pulling away from stoplights, cars jumped forward at the instant the light turned green without waiting for the car ahead of them to begin rolling forward or the cross traffic to clear the intersection. I patiently gave cars in front of me a generous margin in case I slid at a stop light or stop sign on ice that could be difficult to spot in the falling snow. When we headed back toward home, the temperature had dropped enough to freeze parts of the roadway. At one stoplight, cars had to stop on an incline. I held back a few car lengths. When the light turned green, wheels were spinning and whining all around while cars fishtailed trying to gain traction and climb the gentle rise. Cars slipped to the curb, and I would lightly accelerate past them before the driver could turn his wheel back into traffic. I kept my distance and glanced over at Rob. He was whiteknuckle tense.

"Don't worry. I can get through this. It just takes intense focus to anticipate what other idiots will do." I paused so as not to seem angry with Rob, then asked him "Do you understand now why I thought your son should not go to work? Climbing the mountain is often the easier part than getting down." Rob nodded stiffly, not looking my way, eyes fused to the road, still anxious.

On the highway, some cars crept while others sped as if on dry asphalt. The fast ones slid briefly when they crossed a bridge, and a couple floated off the road into the snow-covered grass median.

"Should we stop?" Rob was kind-hearted and caring and wanted to help those who ran off the highway.

"Hell no. It's an interstate. The highway patrol will see them, and I have no intention of becoming the target for the next moron who fails to drive safely for the conditions. We're going home while we can."

Once we crested Mine Hole Gap, our route followed a gentle decline the couple of miles to the turnoff to our neighborhood. I pulled up Rob's driveway and let him and his son out.

"Rob, let's not do that again."

"No, I agree."

A couple days later, we reviewed our experience over a glass of cabernet from Rob's illustrious cellar. Rob had decided that he would not be sending his son to work in similar conditions in the future, a future that was sooner than we expected.

The mountains of North Carolina get relatively little snow except above 3000 feet. We lived in a log cabin for several years in a cove at 2400 feet elevation and laughed at the cars coming down the mountain with several inches of snow on the hood while we had only flurries. However, the last year we lived in the mountains, a series of snow events rolled through. From early December through the middle of March, there was never a time that the ground was entirely free of snow. One of the first big storms came the night of our annual Christmas party. Fifteen inches of dry powder. Only people who lived in the neighborhood could hike to our house. Most wore snow boots and brought a pair of slippers for inside. Some people are ninnies about tracking snow into their homes, but we never were.

Our friend, Rob, was feeling poorly, but his wife hiked down the hill to join us. When she decided to head back home, so much more snow had accumulated that I offered to drive her. It was an uphill trudge through deep powder with snow continuing to fall heavily. I drove her up the hill in the FJ and pulled up her steep driveway with ease. Unfortunately, as I rolled down the driveway, I managed to slide out of the tracks I had made going up. One rear wheel dropped off the edge of the concrete into a deep drift, and I saw that I was close to smashing their mailbox. I stopped where I was, got out, left the FJ where it was and hiked back home down the hill. I could have moved the FJ, but I would have had collateral damage with the mailbox. Sometimes, just because you can does not mean you should.

With the snow lit by holiday lights, the scene was magical. Standing in front of our house, I reflected on the serenity of having a warm home, bright with holiday cheer and friends. But I also knew we were moving soon. The 2009 Recession had ended my business, and we needed to reduce our overhead to make it through what we expected would be a long economic recovery. We had decided to sell most all of what we owned and move onto a sailboat. Pending the survey and sea trial, I would pick up the boat in Annapolis in a couple months. Our daughter chose to stay in the Asheville area to work and continue college. We gave her our Subaru, and I decided to sell the FJ.

My last long trip in the FJ stretched from the mountains to the coast. Our black labrador, Scout, rode shotgun as we slowly rolled eastward at no more than 55 miles per hour, sluggish in the impatient speeding interstate traffic. Once beyond Raleigh, traffic diminished, and fewer vehicles objected to my presence. When we arrived at the marina where our boat waited, we unloaded the FJ, and I posted a sign in the side window offering it for sale.

A day or so later, a young man pulled up in his Range Rover when I was standing beside the FJ. "Cool jeep."

"It's a Land Cruiser."

"Yeah. How much you want for it?"

"I'm asking $4500."

"Oh! I was thinking maybe $500."

"Oh well." I thought to myself, you don't even know what an FJ is, so you do not know its value, and you are not worthy of owning one. Pride seasoned with a touch of snobbery is common among FJ owners. Comments about my nice "jeep" became common. Anyone who called the FJ a "jeep" revealed their ignorance, and I instantly knew they were not potential buyers. No one who does not know the difference between a jeep and an FJ should own an FJ. In the end, only one gentleman knew what he was looking at. His son had owned an FJ some years earlier, and he thought he might want one again. But the timing was not right for him.

We cast off a week later than planned. We were taking the sailboat to Charleston for a nephew's wedding. I parked the FJ at a storage facility and wrapped it in a tarp not knowing when I would see it again. We had no plans beyond Charleston.

Our voyage south was pleasant with long hot sunny days and remote anchorages. Life could not have been more peaceful. Then our lives took an abrupt turn. Beth discovered a lump in her breast. When we docked at the marina in Oriental, I realized that I would not be selling the FJ. Not only had Cameron admitted that he wanted to keep it for when he was old enough to drive, but we needed it as we moved to Greensboro for Beth's treatments. My FJ would never again be for sale.

DUCK SWAMP

Soon after I left grad school, a two-man firm hired me in a small town in eastern North Carolina where many of the residents were avid hunters, especially duck hunters. They hunted mostly mallards and wood ducks locally on the river that flowed through town and in the canals, creeks and ponds on the surrounding farms.

When I had last hunted, it had been doves over corn fields during high school afternoons, so I was keen to get back into the outdoors. Hunting nearby was so convenient that I could meet a hunting partner at 5:30 AM, drive to a wildlife landing, launch the canoe, float the river and be in my office, shaved and showered, by opening.

My parents' home was only an hour away, so in anticipation of wanting to keep myself busy during the Thanksgiving holidays, I asked my father to see if any of his hunting friends knew where I might hunt ducks. One friend suggested a small swamp off a country highway down a dirt farm road. I knew the general location and was certain I could find the swamp.

I pulled off the farm road beside the woods and peered into the ghostly darkness of flooded woods. Green duckweed floated on the surface of the stagnant water. There was no way to know how deep the swamp might be, but the friend had assured me he had hunted it without problem. He had also advised me that the action came swiftly right at dusk and ended as quick.

I tugged on waders and clipped my shoulder straps in place, grabbed my shotgun from the trunk, dropped some shells into the front pouch on my waders and carefully eased down the slope into the water. Near shore, the water was nicely shallow, the bottom soft, but not muddy. I listened to the silence and then eased through the water as stealthily as possible, both to avoid disturbing wildlife and to avoid being seen. Who knew what the shadows might conceal? About the middle of the swamp, the water had risen to my waist, so I found a big tree to lean against, breaking my shape and letting me rest while I waited for the sun to set. Swamps can be unnerving in broad daylight. This swamp was plenty eerie with the sun setting, the dim light ever darkening. I knew I would have to find my way out in the dark, so I searched the surroundings for landmarks I could identify after dusk.

Suddenly I noticed a series of ripples disrupting the smooth water to my right. What the hell? Because I was standing in a swamp, I naturally thought of snakes, venomous snakes like big fat black water moccasins that like to bite and hold as they inject their venom. But I reminded myself they should be hibernating as cold as it was.

The ripples continued, and I watched the movement of the water, listening for a clue to what was moving toward me. Then I heard a "whack" as something big slapped the water. I looked in the direction of the noise and spotted a big round furry head cruising along. And I also noticed something I should have observed earlier, a beaver lodge, a massive mound of intertwined sticks, branches and limbs that rose from the swamp less than fifty feet from where I stood. The furry head ducked under the water, the swamp regained its smooth surface, and the beaver vanished into the lodge.

Witnessing the beaver for those moments was worth more to me than all the wood ducks that soon fell from the sky. I marveled at the ducks' speed and agility as they dived into the swamp woods and dodged trees and limbs while plummeting to land on the water. There were so many ducks dropping at once that I felt like I was shooting at the trees more than the evasive ducks.

Then it was dark, nearly too dark to see, as I trudged my way back to the shore and climbed up the embankment. I knew I would return if only to watch the beaver again.

THE ALLAGASH

When I turned onto the square in Concord, Massachusetts, I had no idea where I might find a room to spend the night, but there was an inn across the town common that looked promising, so I pulled into the parking lot. Concerned that I could not afford the rates, I approached the desk clerk tentatively, almost apologetically, to inquire about renting a room. He offered me an inexpensive room in the old part of the inn with shared bath at the end of the hall. Perfect. I could afford it. Colonial Inn on Monument Square had accumulated some history since its first building was constructed in 1716 and housed munitions used in the first skirmish of the Revolutionary War in 1775. Later owned by Henry David Thoreau's uncle, John, Thoreau lived at the inn while attending Harvard.

I had started the day's journey just outside Washington, D.C. where I stayed with cousins, and had driven the interminable Jersey Turnpike, crossed the George Washington Bridge, and closed my sunroof when I found myself rolling under overpasses in The Bronx where the interstate was lined with burned and stripped vehicles. From my view of The Bronx, the borough recalled photos of cities bombed during World War Two. Once I cleared New York City and entered Connecticut, traffic clogged to a crawl. On the passenger seat, I had an old cassette player (CDs did not yet exist) and popped in a tape of James Taylor singing "Traffic Jam"; "Damn this traffic jam, how I hate to be late…." But I was not bound to a schedule; I just needed to meet friends in Bangor, Maine the next day.

Weary from sitting in the car all day, I realized that I was close to Walden Pond and pulled on my shorts and running shoes. Out the front door and across the square, I ran an easy pace the couple of miles out of town until I spotted the pond. I wandered down the shoreline where I reached the granite and chain outline of Thoreau's cabin located on a small cove off the main pond. (A replica of the cabin is located farther from the shore.) As I scanned the pond and reminisced about *Walden*, I heard the sound of a distant horn, a train riding the rails at the southern end of the pond, a train that inspired Thoreau to comment, "We do not ride on the railroad; it rides upon us." The moment connected me with Thoreau and his Walden Pond experience in a way that reading the book never had. Direct and personal, a shared experience. The shady forest surrounding the pond cooled and relaxed me while I appreciated my fortuitous discovery of the old inn. I had not planned to stop in Concord, but I should have and was delighted that I had, because my journey was ultimately to paddle the Allagash Wilderness Waterway, a place where Thoreau too had paddled. We would put in on Chamberlain Lake, his starting point, and pass his camp on Pillsbury Island in Eagle Lake.

Four friends from grad school were waiting for me in a shopping mall parking lot in Bangor, and we caravanned north to Fort Kent where we met our outfitter. Pitching tents for the first of many nights, we helped the outfitter load our canoes early the next morning and backtracked south. The drive was about three hours, half of which was on a gravel logging road where the only rule was "Logging trucks have the right of way." Loaded with cut trees and speeding along the unpaved road, the trucks trailed clouds of thick gravel dust without regard for any tourists in their path. At Chamberlain Bridge, we unloaded the canoes and packed our gear. Don, Susan, John, and Christy paired off in two of the canoes. I alone would paddle a 17 foot whitewater canoe solo, so we added two buckets of heavy supplies to provide ballast in my bow and set off. The lake was smooth as I turned back to watch the bridge disappear behind us with Mt Katahdin in the distance.

Soon, we exited the Thoroughfare, and the main lake opened ahead of us. The wind crossed our bows from the north raising white caps and pushing against the sides of the canoes. Fighting the force of the wind, I tired quickly, so we stopped for a short break on a large rock in the middle of the lake. The others were fighting the wind but not in the same way as me. The bow paddle could maintain forward motion while the stern paddle steered, as is customary in a canoe. I had to manage both without stalling my forward motion; if I let the wind seize the bow, I would immediately be blown south toward shore with no way to turn the canoe west against the wind. I found a pressure point where I could paddle only on my left side and hold the bow against the wind while moving westward. It was exhausting not to switch paddling arms, but it worked. For a while. Eventually, the wind and waves piling against the bow overpowered the fatigue in my arm, and the canoe swung south. I could not turn it, so I headed for the shore and waved to the others to continue to Donnelly Point, the nearest camp site that we had identified during our break.

When I reached the shore, I climbed out of the canoe and began to tow it alongside the beach. I had not walked far before I noticed moose prints. Yes, we had arrived in wild country no matter how many loggers there were in the great north woods. Don and Susan paddled near me to be sure I was okay. They got out of their canoe to see the moose prints and then turned for camp.

Although everyone was exhausted from having driven from North Carolina to the border with Canada and then back into the wilderness where we had a rigorous first day of paddling, all of us were also enthused to be on the Allagash, tents pitched, and cooking over an open fire. We slept deeply in the cool northern night, the wind keeping the biting bugs at bay.

Our first morning on the waterway set the routine for the rest of the voyage. We rose soon after dawn, started a fire for coffee and tea then ate breakfast. While sipping our morning drinks, we packed our personal gear and loaded the community supplies into the five gallon buckets that served as waterproof containers. We expected our passage, almost 100 miles, along the waterway to require about ten days of paddling, but we did not hurry. Surrounded by forests, wildlife, and copper-tinted clear lakes, we intended to absorb the beauty of the scenery as well as the experience. A long way from home, there was a likelihood that most of us might never paddle this wilderness again.

We crossed Chamberlain Lake and passed through Lock Dam, a very short portage, into Eagle Lake where we paddled alongside Pillsbury Island past the 1857 site of Thoreau's camp. The paddle down Eagle Lake was uneventful, and we arrived at Ziegler camp early enough to swim and bathe, replenish our water and take some photos. Diving deep in the copper-colored lake, the bottom covered with round stones from a million years of eroding granite and ice age glaciers, I never saw a fish. Good thing we had not planned to depend on fish for food. Still tired from the previous days of travel on both land and water, we enjoyed another restful camp.

At the end of Eagle Lake, we entered Round Pond, aptly named, a small circular bay surrounded by heavy forest. We also encountered our first moose. We heard the sound of a small waterfall, the moose standing in the shallows to one side of the river, urinating, before we saw its horse-sized bulk. We laughed about the name of the Canadian beer Moosehead, a new image in our minds. It watched us pass without interest, but we were thrilled to have seen our first moose. (John, the only one of us who had paddled the Allagash before, failed to see any moose the previous year and only two the year before that.) A small creek at the northern end of the pond let us into Churchill Lake, a larger lake swept by north winds that were not as intimidating as the winds on Chamberlain but resisted a straight crossing. When we reached the northern shore of Churchill, we were happy to camp at High Bank, a pleasant open shady site with a grand view south across the lake. Once again, there were no bugs, no black flies, no mosquitoes and no no-see-ums because of the wind. I will take the wind and a hard paddle over the plagues of biting insects any day.

At High Camp, I finally had settled into the rhythm of our journey. Writing in my journal while I scanned the area and enjoyed the changing light of a setting sun, I began to reflect on how special the wilderness waterway is. Sure, there were occasional sounds or sights that reminded us of the modern world, but mostly what we saw were relics of older human activity, wooden dams to float logs down the river, logging equipment like old trains that once hauled the cut trees to the dams, and some roads providing access to the trucks and loggers. We ate well and slept even better.

Fog swallowed our camp site the next morning. The shoreline, less than fifty feet away, was practically invisible. The lake was silent; there was no wind. We lit a fire and heated our water enveloped by a bubble of mist. I began to fantasize.

"You know what would be perfect this morning?"

"What?"

"A big bull moose looming out of the fog as it grazed on the lake bed. That would be so magical."

The others laughed but agreed, and we continued loading the canoes knowing the heavy fog would make visual navigation challenging. Hoping the fog would lift or thin, we took our time preparing. We launched the canoes and eased through a narrow inlet into Heron Lake. I hugged the left shoreline as the others followed.

"Look!" I hissed softly to the others and pointed to my left. Almost chest deep and barely visible was a dark mass obscured by gray mist. When the moose lifted its head, we could hear the water running off its antlers and its mouth chewing the lake bottom vegetation on which it was feeding. I let a couple of strong silent strokes of my paddle carry me close to the moose and shot a couple of photos. Behind me, John used his telephoto to shoot me in the same frame with the moose, my face locked into an irrepressible grin of satisfaction. Perfect. And a fine start to the day.

A short distance later we arrived at Churchill Dam, a mandatory portage. The park service required all paddlers to unload their canoes so their gear could be ferried downstream to Bissonette Bridge in a pickup truck. Just below the dam was Chase Rapids, Class III, and more rapids appeared farther downstream. Don, Susan, John, and Christy grabbed their paddles and hopped into their canoes and shot down Chase Rapids. Behind them, relieved of my bow ballast, I pulled into the entry channel and almost immediately capsized as the river hit me broadside at the top end of the rapids. I bounced across the rocks until I could lift my legs into the submerged canoe, then I rode the water-filled canoe past the rapids where Don waited. He had noticed my paddle precede me down the river and realized something had gone wrong. However, I was not injured, so I pulled the canoe to the bank of the river, and Don helped me empty the water. We reloaded the canoes, and the rest of the run to Umsaskis Lake was fast with easy whitewater. We camped on the northern end of Umsaskis at Sandy Point.

Umsasksis was the first location with a distinctly Native American name. We all liked scanning the map for the native names of creeks, brooks, ponds and lakes. Umbazooksus Lake, Chesuncook Lake, Caugomcomoc Lake, Musquacook Deadwater, as well as the landmark mountain visible far to our east, Katahdin (Ktaadn), northern terminus of the Appalachian Trail. Not all of the native names rolled off our tongues like Umsaskis did, but we appreciated the history despite not knowing the meanings. Naturally, there were plenty of Anglicized place names like Otter Lake, Shallow Lake, Upper and Lower Russell Ponds, Clarkson Pond, Chisholm Brook, Sweeney Brook, and Lost Popple. In a wilderness filled with innumerable water courses, ponds, and lakes, the names are almost as entertaining as the travel itself.

Another inlet named The Thoroughfare carried us from Umsaskis into Long Lake where we confronted light northern winds again then entered another river section that connected us to Harvey Pond. Harvey Pond ended at Long Lake Dam, another splash dam that the loggers built to force the river to pool behind it until they released the water with a flood, a manmade flash flood, sufficient to float the logs downstream even during low water. The remnants of the dam were clearly visible with rocks and timbers extending the entire width of the river. At low water, as when we were there, the old dam was a tricky hazard to avoid with steel rods, big timbers and rock piles protruding into the channel. With plenty of daylight left, we ran the dam and then pulled to the right shore to camp. It was a grassy open campsite that looked inviting. Unfortunately, as we prepared dinner, the no-see-ums attacked supported by a legion of mosquitoes and several dozen black flies. For all the biting buggers we had avoided until then, that evening settled the score. We piled into one tent to talk and bitch about the no-see-ums that inevitably sneaked in with us and whose bites continued to irritate us. We played cards and games behind the protective screening that held the clouds of insects at bay then dashed to our respective tents after nightfall for sleep. In the morning, we were ecstatic to step into the morning mist and find the bugs had abandoned us.

This was the longest outdoor self-powered trip I ever attempted. Lots of time for reflection and self-reflection. And a spectacular amount of time to simply live the moments, the waves of rapids over rocks, the sweep of wind over the lakes, ever-changing shoreline along the rivers and lakes, wildlife anticipated and seen or unseen, the colors of sky and water, the textures of lake bottoms, tree trunks, tree lines, and stones. Feeling your body captured by currents, washed by falling rivers, cleansed by lakes. The sensations of thirst or hunger. Fatigue and rest. Deep sleep or sounds of unknown things that went bump in the night. The insane buzzing of small insects that you cannot chase away. Concern, anxiety, and fear of what a wilderness can throw at a person, especially if they make a mistake or choose poorly. Surprises that may or may not threaten your safety. Our time in the wild is time to note what we ordinarily would pass and overlook. Time to see what we often fail to notice. Time to appreciate the unappreciated.

From Long Lake Dam, the river current carried us swiftly downstream and through a few rapids into Round Pond (if one is good, two is better?) where, once again, the north wind slowed our progress. We aimed across the pond, then hugged the shore in the bit of wind shadow that helped break the worst of the force until we could re-enter the river just above Round Pond Rapids. The current sped us onward as we paddled toward Allagash Falls. But we stopped at a nondescript campsite named Croque Brook (translated as "Crunch Creek", possibly a reference to the increasing number of rapids) up a steep bank beside a narrow section of the river with more thickets than woods. There were more river miles than we could navigate before sunset to allow us to reach Allagash Falls. More and more brooks intersected with the river and sped us downstream until we reached the longest portage of the trip – around Allagash Falls. The portage was short, flat, and easy along a well-worn trail, especially with five of us to share the burdens of canoes, packs, and gear.

We set camp below the Falls. The next day of our journey would be our last. So we refreshed ourselves by swimming where the Falls, thundering over 40 feet of rock, tumbled into a pool of deep black water that swirled with foam where the river crashed at the bottom of a double waterfall, one on each side of a rocky island. Don, John and I swam to the island, and John and I climbed to the top of the rocks to see where the river poured over. Mist formed rainbows in the sunlight, and we found a circular pool, ten feet across, at the top where the right side of the river rushed over the edge. We could see that the pool was lined with moss, and the swirling current of the plunging river created a whirlpool effect. John and I slipped into the pool cautiously because we could not see how deep it was. Waist deep, our feet reached the bottom of the pool, and we could lean against the wall as if restfully settling into a Jacuzzi. The sun was bright and warm enough to offset the chill of the cold river water. Sitting, talking, and smiling happily so near the end of our trip, John and I relaxed in the spinning current of the pool. On top of all the joy of the paddling and the wilderness, the pool was surreal, an amenity from another world.

When we decided we had soaked long enough, both of us rose and slid back onto the surface of the stone around the pool, feet dangling. John stood first and screamed. Before I could ask why, I saw his legs covered with small leeches, and he shamelessly stripped off his bathing suit. I stood, looked down at my legs and saw the same. "Shit! Leeches!" I pulled off my bathing suit as fast as John had, then we rapidly searched each other for leeches hiding in the hidden places on our bodies, places we could not see ourselves, literally the cracks and crannies we can personally never examine. The little parasites were everywhere. In an instant I realized that the moss that seemed soft and welcoming along the side of the circular rock pool had actually been a colony of thousands of leeches waiting for fools to immerse themselves in the inviting pool at the top of the Falls. It was a good title for a horror film, "The Pool at the Top of the Falls". John and I hurried as quickly as we could without slipping and busting our proverbial asses to the base of the island and dived into the deep water below the Falls, sweeping our legs and all other parts with open hands to eliminate the little suckers before they attached and began to feed on our blood. In spite of the shock and trauma, we could not stop laughing. Who would knowingly relax in a pool of leeches? Who would fail to notice that the attractive "moss" covering the side of the pool and swaying with the current was actually thousands of leeches? Who would publicly strip naked in broad daylight standing fully exposed in the middle of a river? Who would inspect a friend's most private regions in full view of spectators? We laughed all the way back to camp but slipped our bathing suits back on before exiting the river. It was a strange end to the day and the trip but memorable.

Our final day was more miles than we usually paddled, but several brooks tumbled into the river along the route, accelerating the current. Also, below the brooks were more rapids, faster water combined with mid-river obstacles. With several days of handling canoes behind us, the current and the rapids presented excitement and a swift ride to the end of our voyage. We drifted apart as the two-person canoes could paddle more quickly than I could solo. Nevertheless, I was content to be making my own pace and seeing the last of the river in my own time. Within sight of the bridge near Allagash Village, our take-out, I raced down the river full of confidence until a huge rock rose up before me. I could not dig my paddle hard, deep, or fast enough to turn the bow and slammed into the rock with the current pushing me up, twisting the canoe into a rollover capsize. Back paddling with as much force as I could, the river spirits smiled on me, and the canoe slipped off the rock and back into the current running downstream. Several minutes later, I cruised into the shore and stepped out of the canoe. Our week on the Allagash was complete.

BLUFF MOUNTAIN

Harry, my father-in-law, and I woke early and drove to Creston Volunteer Fire Station at the west end of Three Top Mountain for the annual fisherman's breakfast. It was Opening Day for trout in the mountains of North Carolina. With frost on the ground, winter more than spring, the station buzzed with fishermen (eating) and volunteers (cooking breakfast). What a spread they served. For less than four dollars each, Harry and I received a plate of scrambled eggs, sausage, biscuits and gravy, and a cup of seriously hot coffee. Neither firemen nor mountain folk mess around when it comes to fueling your body for a day outside, especially in winter. The station was warm, murmuring with friendly conversation, and we took our time savoring breakfast and sipping coffee. We talked about fishing, but food had priority.

Harry and Claire, my in-laws, lived near the crest of a ridge at about 4000 feet elevation, up a steep and winding gravel drive, directly across from Bluff Mountain. During our many visits, we saw snow, flurries and wisps of flakes when it was not winter or fall, in every month except July. Their south-facing yard dropped to an old grove of Christmas trees, and their broad deck, framed by old poplars, gave an eye-level view of the mountain with its waterfall pouring off the summit except when it froze solid during extreme cold.

When we left the station, Harry and I drove around for a while exploring the backroads that twist and turn and wind along the creeks and valleys between the ridges and mountains. Ashe County, where Harry and Claire lived, is rural and rugged, the homesteads scattered. Many of the county residents still relied on subsistence farming with a large garden and raising their own animals. They supplemented their meat with deer, an occasional bear, and of course trout. Turkey and grouse live in the woods but were challenging to hunt.

Harry suggested it was a good day for a hike, so we returned to the house and enlisted all interested for a hike to the base of the waterfall on Bluff Mountain. Only Beth, my wife, joined us. With lunch packed into daypacks and plenty of water, we drove to the gated road to the cemetery that stood on a knoll below the mountain and above a cow pasture with its crumbling barn. The cemetery held lots of Hodgsons, and several graves were marked with nameless, dateless tombstones. Two stones at the base of a double-trunked hemlock could have been 150 years old given the size of the tree. But we soon realized that the cemetery was a fruitless detour that would not lead us to the north face of the mountain.

From the cemetery, we found a faint trail to the south leading up a ridge along the eastern side of an extensive rhododendron hell ("thicket" in the vocabulary of flatlanders) that reached 12-15 feet high, the leaves dark glossy green, the branches thick, tangled, and resistant to hikers slipping through. The trail we trod seemed to be a game trail recently used by deer. We followed it alongside the rhododendron, angling up the ridge for fifteen minutes or so without finding a break that would lead us over the ridge and down to the creek that began at the base of the falls. Eventually, we bushwhacked through the hell and descended to an overgrown site of an old homestead. Beyond the homestead site, we found tire ruts that seemed to be the old track we should have been hiking. Turning south, we headed upstream into open second growth woodlands of locust and oak. Autumn leaves from the previous year thickly covered the ground. White blossoms of bloodwort peeked above the leaf litter. Nearby were patches of juniper and periwinkle, bright green and fresh like the bloodwort.

Bluff Mountain is an unusual formation with a rare fen, a wetland not commonly found on top of a mountain, the source of the waterfall. The southern slope of Bluff Mountain was just that, a long gently sloping rise to the summit. The north face, on the other hand, had a precipitous cliff as if the face of the mountain had broken off in a cataclysmic landslide long ago. The creek tumbled between two arms or spur ridges formed by the broken face of the mountain, and we continued to follow the secondary branch until it connected with the main creek where we stopped for lunch. Harry cooled his water bottle in the creek while we ate sitting on the rocks in the sun, a gentle wind in the trees and the creek gurgling along between the boulders in its rocky bed. It could have been good native brook trout water, but we did not see any fish at all.

As we continued to ascend, the arms of the mountain squeezed the cove and the ground steepened so that we were required to cross the creek a couple of times in search of a slope we could traverse. We took one last break before heading up. Beth stayed behind as Harry and I climbed the final 150 yards to the base of the falls. We quickly learned that scrambling up the rocks in the creek bed was the only way up. After thirty minutes of hand, foot, and knee climbing, we reached the base of the mountain where the falls ended and the creek began.

From the base, any route higher was both wet and vertical, so we stopped and took photos as we caught our breath before the knee- and ankle-twisting descent down the wobbly rocks we had just climbed. Although not a major feat of mountaineering, Harry and I both felt satisfied with having reached the falls and completed a hike that we first discussed a couple of years before. Never again would we stand on the deck of his and Claire's house musing about the view of the waterfall and saying to each other "Wouldn't it be neat to climb to the base of Bluff Mountain Falls?" We met up with Beth on the way down and left the creek behind as soon as the cove opened up. The retreat from the falls through the cove below Bluff Mountain was shady, quiet, and relaxing as we strolled through open forest where spring had started. A flock of turkeys, spooked by our voices, skittered past us fifty yards away. We returned home with good memories of a fine day in the woods.

J. Privette

WILD THINGS

When we had lived in our log cabin in a narrow cove south of Asheville for a few years, with the children getting older, we moved into a small neighborhood less than ten minutes from the cabin, mainly because there were lots of children in the neighborhood, and the house had more than one bathroom.

For many years, nature had called me in the middle of the night. Sometimes I could go back to sleep but often I simply stretched out on the sofa and read until my eyes closed. On the night of this event, when I slid out of bed at 4 AM, I tried to maintain an empty mind so that I would not wake myself fully. But I could hear one of our cats, Moonie, a gray and white fluff ball, banging a screen on a window onto our back deck. When inside, he wanted to be out; when out, he wanted to be in, and he expected, as cats do, that the humans of the household would open and close doors as needed no matter the time of day or night. He could be obnoxiously persistent in the wee hours before dawn. I looked out the den window and could see only night, so I could not chase him off or otherwise dissuade his banging.

As I headed back into the bedroom, the noise resumed. I realized it must be Taylor, our then-teenage daughter who had a habit of keeping late hours, and I could not imagine what she might be doing to make such a racket. Despite being somewhat irritated, I simply wanted to get back in bed and try to sleep until morning. No sooner did I crawl under the covers than my cell phone on the bedside table rang. My nocturnal wandering, now accented by the ringing phone, woke my wife, Beth. My frustration with Taylor increased.

I looked at the screen, and Caller ID revealed that it was Taylor calling. I looked at Beth and said, "It's Taylor, and I bet it's a damn butt call. She's been making a lot of noise…." My rant had not ended when Beth cut me off and calmly instructed me to answer the phone.

"Taylor might be sick or something. Just answer it."

Exasperated, I punched the button to answer the phone. "Taylor, what are you doing up there?"

She replied in a soft voice, just above a whisper, "Daddy, I think someone's trying to break into the house. It sounds like they're on the front porch. Cameron heard it from his room and came to get me."

"OK. I'll go check."

Still convinced that it was our cat or maybe a raccoon, I slid out of bed again and walked quietly into the den where there was no noise, then into the foyer from where I could see the front porch through the dining room window. I neither saw nor heard anything on the darkened porch.

Often in horror films, the character searching for the source of a disturbing sound heads for the basement and carefully descends the stairs without turning on a light. The action is completely illogical. If you go into your basement for a tennis racket, you turn on the light so you will not fall down the stairs and so you can find the racket. The movie character looks foolish, if not stupid, seeking to locate a potential threat without using the one advantage they retain over anyone or anything hiding in the dark. Illumination. If they are surprised (usually), the audience cannot help but comment on the folly or lack of thought.

When I saw nothing through the window, my brain reinforced its bias for either a cat or a raccoon being the source of the clatter. Without even considering whether to flip on the switch for the porch light mounted right beside the door knob, I unlatched the deadbolt and stepped out onto the door mat looking to my left toward the outside of the dining room window. Seeing nothing, I took another step across the porch. Only then did I notice a shadow of motion in my peripheral vision.

Time slowed to a crawl as I turned toward the front porch railing, looked down and found myself within a short reach of the brown-fringed nose of a black bear with its head above my knees. Time abruptly accelerated. Fear and panic automatically seized control of my body, and I stumbled backwards into the door frame before falling onto the door knob and into door as I scrambled to get inside before the bear caught me, mauled me, and entered the house where my family was unprotected. All I could yell was an extended "Shiiiit!" as I slammed the door closed and clicked the lock.

Neither Beth nor the children knew what was happening, but they could hear the pounding of a desperate father and the yell. For them, it was clear that I was being attacked. Beth hid under the covers because she had no way to exit our bedroom without passing the foyer. Taylor pulled Cameron into their upstairs bathroom, and she began to dial 911.

In the meantime, breathing so hard I could not speak, I managed to utter loudly, if not clearly, "Bear." Following a few more gasping breaths, I called out, "It's okay."

Beth and the children joined me in the foyer, each telling their piece of what happened and what they thought had been happening to me. Distilled, they all thought that the person or persons who were breaking into the house had overcome me, and I was badly injured or worse. The same person or persons had entered the house, and Beth along with the children were on their own to defend themselves. Scout, our wonderfully loving and loyal black Labrador, finally woke and came out of our bedroom, curious about the hubbub.

When I scratched his head, I said sarcastically, "Thanks for all the help, watchdog." It is good that he did not understand me.

It took several minutes for all of us to reduce our heart rates. Once we knew the "attacker" was not human, we needed to see what we could see outside on the porch, but this time I first turned on the light, then we looked out of both windows that opened onto the porch. Nothing visible, so I eased the front door open and stuck my head out cautiously. Empty porch. All of us searched for signs of the bear. Nothing. Scout wandered around the porch sniffing but otherwise blasé.

"Scout. Don't you smell the bear?"

Hearing the word "bear," Scout alerted, hackles raised, and declared "Ruff!" Tough guy on deck. Semper paratus. Semper fi.

As we collectively reviewed the situation, we agreed the bear was attracted to the bird seed in the feeder hanging off the corner of the porch. The bear left tooth marks but the metal feeder was mostly unharmed. Beth recalled that the bird seed she had purchased that week contained fruit in addition to sunflower seeds. Usually we fed the birds only sunflower seeds. Apparently the fruit aroma invited the bear strolling down the street to investigate our feeder.

For most of the years we lived in the mountains, we did not have any bear problems. More often than not, "wild animal problems" are "human problems" that tempt wildlife to visit feeders, trash cans, pet food on the porch, greasy grills. At our cabin, a bear once folded the pole holding the bird feeder to the ground. A stout rod of steel, the bear literally bent it to its will until the rod lay parallel to the yard, seeds freely scattered on the ground. In the same side yard, Taylor once observed a young bear jump onto the stone wall at the base of the ridge and then dash into the woods. But mostly bears avoided our homes even when the nineteen year cicadas hatched and provided the bears with so much protein that mother bears gave birth to three or four cubs rather than the customary one or two. The forests on the high ridges filled with bears that year, and several descended into the valley to explore the neighborhoods of Asheville.

Our solution, as with other "human problems" was to remove the enticement. We took down the bird feeder. No more bear visits.

A month later, we thought (as if we knew anything about bear behavior) that the bear had likely moved on and found food elsewhere. None of our neighbors had reported seeing any bears. So, we hung the feeder back on the corner of the porch near the kitchen window where the railing was twelve feet above the ground. Even squirrels were hesitant to try to steal from the feeder hanging on a slippery piece of steel with a long drop below. A few nights later, our entire family heard the banging on the porch like we had heard on the first night of the bear's visit.

This time, we were excited. We gathered in the kitchen and switched on the light. A black bear was perched on the four inch wide railing like a ballerina balancing on its paws while it pulled the feeder to its mouth to eat the seeds. We snapped a few photos then decided we should not encourage the bear to become a "human problem" by getting too familiar. When we tapped on the window less than two feet from its face, it tiptoed along the railing, gently jumped onto the porch, and casually walked down the stairs.

JIM, JIMMY, JIMBO

James Brian Samuels. Born March 10, 1897. My grandfather. Not my real biological grandfather, but the only one I ever knew. He was my father's stepfather, though my father never called him that. To my father, he was Mr. Samuels. To me, he was Granddaddy.

My father used the name "Mr. Samuels" in the most familiar of ways. Just like I said Granddaddy. I am sure he could have said "Dad", but Mr. Samuels was not his father. My father had known his father who died when my father was ten. Nevertheless, he said Mr. Samuels in the same way that he would have said Dad. It never sounded stilted or forced, never as if he owed or intended any kind of formality. I think he just could not think of the man with silver hair, the man who was old enough to be *his* grandfather, as someone named "Jim." On the other hand, I had never known my real grandfather, also a James, so to me he was Granddaddy. Of course, at that time, my father was still Jimmy. In a family with three living Jameses and one deceased, I was left with Jimbo which suited me far better than Junior. I knew grown men named "Junior" and always felt badly for them, their name suggesting they were something other than real men, full grown, no matter how tough they were.

Mr. Samuels was a hardworking gentlemanly farmer when he met my grandmother. He was in his fifties; she was several years younger. He was a widower with six grown children. The more field hands in the family, the fewer hands to hire. My grandmother had been widowed some seven years, raising a boy on her own. She was a schoolteacher when they met and married. My father was in his last year of high school.

Mr. Samuels never graduated from high school. In fact, he never made it past eighth grade. He was one of the smartest men I ever knew in the ways that matter. He knew the earth and people and the ways things work. He was grounded. He had started life poor and worked his way to prosperity. Day labor to tenant farmer to land owner.

Farming in his time, more so than these days, was more art than science. A man, a farmer, had to know the feel of rich soil under his fingernails, the smell of fecund earth in his nostrils. A man had to have a sense of what was right with his crops. And what was not. Farming was a calling, an individual and spiritual commitment, not the kind of corporate business that it has become today. The farmer held his own between his farm and his God, feeling his way through weather and seasons and cash flow. The farmer was on his own, aided mainly by family and community. The farmer knew the importance of giving back, caring for the land, rotating crops, and sowing for the future.

As a man whose day and business was, by its very essence, a solitary effort, the farmer's success was measured in large part by his integration with others. Meals for a sick neighbor, disking a field for an adjacent farmer whose machinery was down needing a part that would not arrive for a week when the rains would likely make it impossible for him to return to the fields. Farming instilled and fostered the essence of community, a shared fate. There but for the grace of God go I. Do for others as you hope they will do for you in your time of need. Treat your neighbors as you hope to be treated by them.

I know that Granddaddy was not a perfect person; I still haven't met one. But I know he was a good man, good hearted and generous. He said nothing if he could not say something good. If I saw him angry, it was not more than a couple of times, and he only simmered, never boiled over; his face may have flushed, his eyes narrowed, but he never said an angry word, never lashed out to satiate his anger verbally. And he would never raise a hand to anyone. I suppose some of that was due to my age and him wanting to set the right example for me. Still, I know that he lived as he lived, without pretense, and it was not in his nature to speak ill of or to others.

In my younger years, I spent the kind of time many kids used to spend with their grandparents. I visited their home on a farm in rural eastern North Carolina, outside a town called Fremont. Fremont was a name that always sounded like it was a place that grandparents belonged. In fact, to me at the time, it seemed like there were more grandparents in Fremont – not just mine, but other people's too – than anywhere else I had ever been. For a small town, there seemed to be a lot of old people. Everyone seemed to be my grandparents' age. Sure there were a couple of exceptions, but they were mostly the few of my parents' generation who had not left the farming town for jobs in the city.

My visits were pure escape. Whether for a day or a weekend, a holiday or a reunion, it was always a time for food and fun and usually other grandkids, nieces and nephews. It was a place without rules. Truthfully, the rules that applied at home still applied at the farm, but there was no one to enforce them. The kids ran through the woods, down the dirt road beside the house, exploring the creek through the culvert and collecting all manner of sand, mud, clay, briars, hitchhikers, crawdads, and general filth. The parents relaxed in the house, talking and drinking coffee and iced tea and asking periodically whether there was something they could do to help with dinner. "Helping" with dinner meant hurrying it along.

Dinner was the magnificent spread of food convened midday in the South. Supper was the evening meal. After smelling the baking of rolls, the roasting of pork, and the simmering of ham hock-seasoned collards for a couple of hours, a person's brain will seize control, stomach juices flood, saliva collect uncontrollably at the corners of your mouth, and your hands reach for anything edible. Sousemeat, pig's feet, a pinch of fatback, leftover sausage, maybe an extra deviled egg if no one was watching.

During these periods of waiting for the meal to be served, a passel of pickles and peanuts would be consumed. Well, not so much consumed as inhaled. Anything that seemed set to eat was tasted and re-tasted for readiness and flavor.

Granddaddy quietly held the organization together until the meal was prepared, the table set and all the participants seated. Then, he said grace. And he meant it. He knew, in a way that I could not at that time in my life, how much he had for which to be thankful. He could look around the room and count his blessings. Children, grandchildren, nieces, nephews. Blood kin and those related through marriage.

Granddaddy was a great Southern cook. His food was simple, filling and exploding with flavor. Southern cooks are not shy with salt or pepper or fat. I was schooled by pre-dawn country breakfasts of scrambled eggs, link sausage (his own hog and recipe), cornbread on an iron griddle, grits and biscuits. With grapefruit, orange juice and hot coffee. It is important to note the hot that describes the coffee because so many people today think of hot coffee as a euphemism; back then, for a farmer rising at 4:00 AM, hot was critical; sort-of-hot was a waste of time.

I loved his biscuits. This frustrated my mother no end. Of all that Granddaddy cooked that was homegrown or homemade, his biscuits were not native. The biscuits were store bought in one of those pressurized pop open containers. Pillsbury. I could eat them two at a time. My mother made her own drop biscuits from scratch. From scratch is a lot more trouble than from a can. I didn't know then how much it hurt her for me to comment that Granddaddy's biscuits were better.

Granddaddy taught me to scramble eggs. Now this may seem as easy as boiling water, but I have found that is not so. Almost everyone I have ever known scrambles their eggs by cracking them into a bowl, then whirling, whipping, and whisking them with a fork until the yolk and the clear viscous "whites" mix. Granddaddy, efficient as ever, cracked his straight into the hot iron skillet. But I have run ahead of myself.

First, he cooked his sausage slow. He raised and slaughtered the pigs himself, then took the parts he wanted ground for the sausage, instructed the processor what spices to add in what amounts. He knew what he wanted from the hogs he raised. The links blackened, shrank and splattered in the iron skillet until he had everything else ready to eat. Then he set the sausage to drain on a paper towel and broke the eggs directly into the still hot sausage grease. I love hearing the sputter of eggs hitting the grease. Breakfast is nearly ready to eat. After cracking the number he wanted to serve, he stirred the eggs calmly, pausing occasionally to finish setting the breakfast table. Butter, strawberry jam, orange marmalade. Honey. Salt and pepper. He kept the eggs cooking but not too quickly. Just before he thought they were perfect, he lifted the skillet from the range and raked the eggs into the serving bowl. He never served the eggs directly onto a plate. Then, we both sat down, he blessed the food, and we feasted.

As I grew older, grew to know him better, I began to realize how important it was for me to learn as much as I could about what he knew. I began to ask questions. I know now I never came close to asking enough questions, but I am thankful that I asked what I did.

The secret to scrambled eggs is breaking them into the hot skillet and removing them just before you think they are ready because it is the nature of eggs to hold heat and to continue cooking after being removed from the heat. Thus, cooking them until they are done will guarantee you overcooked, dry eggs every time. I still get comments about my methodology, not all of the comments being complimentary. But I know what I know, and I know that Granddaddy made the best breakfast I ever ate, and he told me this was the secret to good scrambled eggs.

Leftover sausage he placed on a small plate in the oven. My father, when he visited, hugged his mother at the door, said hello to Mr. Samuels, then stooped to open the oven door, hoping there would be a piece or two of sausage waiting for him there. Usually there was. Sometimes also a biscuit to go with it.

THE FARM

Granddaddy built the house he and my grandmother lived in on his land, but across the highway from the farm proper. He built it with his own hands and for cash, paying for materials and labor as he built. It was a rambling brick ranch with a small but comfortable knotty pine-paneled den, a classic linear country kitchen with breakfast nook big enough for a small round pine table with lazy susan, a dining room, and a large gathering place kind of living room. Living room and dining room were rather formally decorated but used just like the rest of the house, especially when lots of family was there for a meal. The pantry was also large; it was mud room, pantry, laundry and back door foyer all in one. Washer, dryer, horizontal freezer, sink, cabinets and utility closet.

The freezer held the essentials of good eating including all parts of the hog. For me the freezer held something even more attractive, fudgesickles, a frozen ice cream kind of dessert on a stick. My grandparents made sure the freezer was stocked anytime the kids were going to be around. We could wipe out a box or more a day.

The house stood in a grove of tall long leaf pine trees. The trees offered protection from the sun in the summer and the cars and trucks on the highway year round. Since the highway was a long, empty two-lane road to nowhere stretching through the countryside, drivers tended to use an excess of speed when traveling between places. Sometimes these journeys came to a sudden end in my grandparents' front yard. If not for the protective pines, several of the cars might have graced the front door and living room bay window. It is never a good day when the sheriff and the ambulance park in your front yard with lights flashing. Rarely did my grandparents know the injured driver.

However, one of the dangers of living beside a busy highway – busy in the sense of high speed travel, not quantity of traffic – was being personally involved in an accident. For the longest time, the only family fatalities were dogs. My grandparents quit having any dogs because of the pain of losing them. One time they agreed to let our Boston terrier stay with them while we were traveling. When we returned, the dog was dead. I was sad, but not nearly so sad as my grandfather when, later, he lost his grandson, a real grandson.

Bryan lived next door across the dirt road. He was named for Granddaddy. And he was a couple of years older than me, but many years more experienced. Living on the farm, he had independence beyond what I, a kid raised in a town, could imagine at the time. Bryan had a go-cart. He raced the go-cart up and down the dirt road. Hardly anyone drove the dirt road because it did not lead to anyone's house; it only led to another dirt road and more farmland. Bryan loved to get up speed racing straight down the road, then turn the steering wheel hard and skid into a donut, pop his foot off the brake, onto the gas and spin away again. It was fairly safe to drive that way up the dirt road where he could see what was coming; the main risk was spinning off the dirt road into a ditch or the creek.

It was not safe to drive that way near the end of the road where it intersected with the asphalt highway. The cars and trucks that passed by on the highway were traveling fast and not expecting young boys in go-carts to spin onto the highway in front of them. This was true for the truck driver who hit Bryan.

Granddaddy's grief struck him deeply. He never said a word about it to me. I could see it in his eyes for many years though. The loss of a real grandson. I missed Bryan too, though not anywhere as deeply as Granddaddy did. And Bryan's father went kind of crazy. I could not understand that degree of grief and loss then; as a father now, I can.

Still, for the many years that the families were growing and the children were young enough to keep showing up for family gatherings, the farm and the house were wonderful places full of love and togetherness. Bryan was missed, but the love of the living and the happiness of the times we continued to share outweighed the painful memories and the grief.

Gatherings of the family felt like big time reunions. They were not reunions per se, just a good time for all to meet at the farm and enjoy an afternoon and evening together. We usually gathered for a southern dinner, the midday meal. Dinner was spread over big picnic tables in the back yard under the big oak where a swing hung. My grandparents served skillet-fried pork chops, pork roast or roast beef and, always, fried chicken. Fresh butterbeans, string beans and boiled potatoes with ham hock, mashed potatoes with gravy, white rice, corn on the cob, pickles and beets and collards or turnip greens. Rolls and white bread. Pepper vinegar, relish, chopped onions. Home brewed iced tea with lemon. Cake, pie, ice cream and, of course, fudgesickels. Dinner lasted all afternoon. And for supper we ate the dinner we had not consumed earlier. Some of the dinner was even better, later, at room temperature.

Even though my family was family only by marriage, the Samuels blood relations welcomed us and made us feel as if we were part of them. Of course, the kids didn't know to make distinctions. The parents did, but they were all still married to their first spouses at the time, so life was good, and everyone was happy. Later, divorce among Granddaddy's children and my grandfather's death would dissolve the familial affections. The kids grew older and stopped showing up for gatherings. Our affections dissipated like sunlight in front of an approaching storm. It might have been sad if it had not happened gradually so that all of us had a chance to adjust to the changes in the lives around us. But it was hard for Granddaddy because it was his family, his blood, his heirs.

When we were not eating or running around the house, we played outside. Sometimes swinging from the swing in the big oak beside the driveway. Sometimes wading the creek near the culvert, chasing water spiders, crawfish and minnows. Digging in the sandy bottom for small mussels. We ran up and down the embankment where the yard joined the dirt road.

Across the highway, the farm stretched hot and wide and full of opportunity. Woods framed the fields and sandy dirt farm paths separated the crops. Cotton grew just south of the house, tobacco directly across the highway. A few more tobacco fields were scattered about the farm, intermingled with cornfields. A solitary black walnut tree stood alongside one cornfield, a relic of times past when mules plowed the fields and needed to cool in the shade in the summer, or they would work themselves literally to death. The hogs had their own place just to the north halfway between the highway and Bob's Road to the east. Nestled against a large wood, the hog pen was a scene of noise and bustle. The hogs moved constantly, fed even more. They squealed and squawked all day, nosing into the feed bins, popping up the lids for a few snouts full before letting the lids slam shut. A cacophony of living, breeding swine. Snorting and snuffling, expressing the emotions of a wordless beast. This was the days of slopping the hogs, feeding them with the trash food no person or living thing would eat; the pristine, super sterilized production parlors had not yet begun to dominate the market. The time would come when Granddaddy would have been put out of the commercial pork business by such megalithic operations. By then, he no longer worried about the farm and farming.

Granddaddy loved hogs because he loved pork. He loved pork better than any other meat. Sweetmeats, souse meat, chit'lin's, sausage, roast, ham, chops, hocks, skin, ears and tails. He ate it all and loved it truly.

"Any part of the pig you don't eat, Granddaddy", I asked.

"Only the squeal," he replied, a twinkle in his eye.

Granddaddy once sent me home with a package for my mother. He loved my mother and knew her to be an excellent southern cook. Southern cooks need seasoning meat, so he sent a gift. My mother opened the crush of aluminum foil and shrieked.

"What in the world? Is this a tail? Why did he send me this? Was he just seeing what I would do when I opened it up?" she interrogated me as if I had conspired with Granddaddy to surprise her unfavorably with the back end of a pig.
"I don't know. He just told me to give it to you. I didn't ask what it was." I defended myself, but enjoyed the joke, if he had intended a joke.

My mother called him and asked why he had sent her the long curly pig tail.

"That's the best part to use for seasoning. I know you use ham hocks, but this is better. I thought you'd appreciate it. It's my favorite part for cooking with," he explained.

He meant it sincerely.

My mother accepted the explanation and tossed the tail into the pot with the fresh string beans she was cooking for supper. It tasted great to me, but probably only because I believed what Granddaddy said. Anybody else had told me that the tail of a pig was the best of anything, I wouldn't have swallowed it.

TOBACCO

My grandfather farmed a few hundred acres in rural eastern North Carolina, just outside the small town of Fremont. Fremont had a full block of downtown businesses, three banks and a couple of old brick tobacco warehouses that were used for storage and no longer served as a local market for the auction of tobacco.

That's how tobacco was sold at the time. And still is. A commodities transaction with the auctioneer pacing between flats of cured tobacco leaves, followed by a group of buyers, anonymous in their attire, dressed just like the farmers who paced just behind, listening to the auction bidding and comparing mentally the quality of the leaves being sold to their own farther down the row or across the warehouse floor. Quality is always somewhat subjective. Especially when the leaf is the same and the variation is in the color and moisture content. This stands in contrast to the auction floors of the big stock and commodities exchanges. Where they sell with a flurry of shouting voices, waving hands and confetti of order sheets, the tobacco method is steady and almost quiet. The auctioneer's voice is the only voice heard; others, buyers and sellers, whisper in the wake of the ever-pacing auctioneer. When a bid is accepted, the following farmers often reach into the bale and test the leaf between their fingers, lifting it to their noses to smell apart from the general warehouse aroma. Naturally, a good auctioneer is revered for being able to communicate clearly and succinctly the quality of the offering and the bids received. Personally, I never understood a word spoken in the rapid cadence of the auctioneers.

When engaged in the auction part of the warehouse process, none of the farmers really pay attention to the activity surrounding them. Forklifts scooting hither and yon, fetching flats of tobacco sold and replacing them with flats to be sold. Farmers parking their overloaded pickup trucks, tobacco bulging under canvas tarps and threatening to fall from the sides and off the tailgate, unloading their tobacco onto push carts (large wheel barrows) and pushing the unwieldy loads to the official scales where a ticket was issued with the certified weight. Pricing was a matter of cents per hundredweight. (Eventually prices climbed above a dollar and stayed there, but the price was still auctioned in cents with a dollar being 100.) And, most important of all, the exquisite fragrance of cured tobacco drifting through the warehouse like incense in a temple.

Flu-cured tobacco. The money crop that defined much of the South. Cotton and corn came and went, rose and fell on the favor of commodities traders and commercial demand. But tobacco grew and grew. People smoked and smoked more. Chewed and snuffed and puffed. Tobacco did not have multiple uses; it was purely a consumer product, a product to be consumed. And consumed it was, demand growing steadily into the 1980's. Then the lawsuits began. Tobacco was evil, and its producers more evil yet. The farmers stood mutely by as the tort lawyers and states' attorneys general engaged the major tobacco companies. R.J Reynolds, Brown & Williamson, Phillip Morris. As the settlements reached into the billions of dollars, more and more farmers saw the end of the market for tobacco. More and more shifted their plantings into food crops like corn and soybeans and, revived by a consumer yearning for things natural, cotton. Tobacco dissipated like a forgotten friendship, drifted away like the last survivors of a species mathematically doomed to extinction.

The ruins of tobacco barns stretch across the fields of North Carolina like ancient monoliths. Log-built in the piedmont and west, clapboard in the east. The design is uniform: two story height with two small vent windows up high and only two small doors at the ground for access to load the barn and check the curing. A low pitch to the roof. Sometimes two barns were connected by a shed under which the women who tied the tobacco leaves to the sticks could seek refuge from the stifling heat of a midsummer's day or the periodic late afternoon summer thunderstorms.

Inside the barn was strung a series of wide rafters. These began about five feet off the dirt floor (you had to duck under them) and continued in 3-4 foot increments to the top of the barn. The rafters were the racks on which sticks of tobacco leaves were hung. The tobacco was cured by heat from below. Originally, wood fires were built in small brick fireplaces on two of the outside walls. Wood was eventually replaced by gas. Gas could be controlled more easily, required less tending during the curing process, and resulted in fewer bonfires. Not surprisingly, the combination of a brittle wood barn packed with an inflammable plant heated by gas could create a spectacular fire. Once started, it was impossible to extinguish. No point calling the local fire department. For this reason, barns were usually placed at some distance one to the other. But I have jumped to the end of the process. First, the tobacco had to be picked.

Before the day of mechanical cropping, tobacco was picked by hand. Croppers walked through the fields of tall green tobacco stalks and picked the ready leaves, those yellowing evenly, tucked them under their arms until they had more than they could hold. Then they passed those bundles to the mule-drawn wagon following along behind them. The picking of tobacco was called cropping, and cropping was difficult and demanding work. The entire process depended on the speed and efficiency of the croppers. Until the croppers picked the leaves, no one else could begin their work. I recall waiting at the barn in the morning at the start of the day for an hour or so for the first wagon to come for tying and hanging. The quality of the cured tobacco also depended upon the skill of the croppers. Leaves that were still too green would not cure properly, no matter how much or how long the heat was applied in the barn.

Croppers walked between hot, humid rows of tobacco to break the yellowest leaves from the lower stalk of the plant. In the morning, as the sun began to burn the haze from the fields, the heavy green tobacco leaves sagged with dew. Wet sticky leaves garnished with an occasional snake and more frequently the bright green fat caterpillar called a tobacco worm the size of a big man's thumb. Leaves from the plants in one row extended to touch the leaves in the adjoining row. The croppers walked down this wet avenue until the sun hung in the summer sky long enough to dry the leaves and soak the croppers in their own salty, scratchy sweat.

The leaves ripened from the bottom up, so picking the largest leaves (and most valuable, as tobacco is sold by weight) required a tedious and back-breaking squat and lean to the ground, wrapping a hand around the base of a stalk, gripping the heavy leaves by their stems, wet with morning fog and dew, gritty with the dirt of the furrow, and breaking the stems from the sturdy stalk. The objective was to pick from a single stalk all the leaves that were ripe in a single twisting grip. Croppers began the day and the season with a deep stoop to pick the bottommost leaves. As the season aged and the lowest leaves had been picked, the croppers worked their way up the stalk. The leaves were knee high, then waist high, then chest high. And at each elevation, the leaves were a bit smaller than the elevation before. Thus, as the season lengthened and the croppers tired of the long toil to bring the tobacco from the fields while it was still ripe, the task eased, balancing the physical strain of their effort with the duration of the chore.

Once picked, the tobacco was packed neatly onto a wagon pulled through the field by mule or tractor. The wagon, when full, was driven to the barn where several women, loopers were always women, waited beside a stack of long pine sticks. The tobacco sticks were 5-6 feet long, stout and quickly became smooth through repeated handling and use. The looper laid a tobacco stick across two forked, vertical sticks, like for roasting a chicken over a fire. At her feet lay a ball of light cotton twine. A helper unloaded a neat stack of tobacco leaves beside her within easy reach. She tied a quick knot to hold the twine to the stick and then picked up a small bundle of leaves, looped the twine around the stalk end of the leaves, grabbed another bundle and repeated the process all the way down the stick, finishing the twine with another knot when she reached the end. In this way, the tier could quickly secure the leaves onto the stick in a way such that the leaves hung down from the stalks, but without having to be tied individually. A woman with experience could tie a full stick in about a minute.

The stick, now loaded with fresh tobacco leaves and weighing 10 pounds or more, was passed to a boy in the door of the barn. The door was small and low and thus could be entered only by ducking. So, the women passed the stick to the boy through the door. One summer, I was the boy. I received the stick, methodically grasping one end of the stick with one hand, then grasping the middle of the stick between the leaf stalks with the other. Pivoting, I turned into the darkness of the barn, a darkness sometimes cool and other times stifling. Raising the stick above my head, I released my hand holding the middle and pushed the stick as high as I could reach with my hand on the end. This was called poking up. High, almost hidden in the unlit darkness of the rafters, a hand reached down and grabbed the opposite end and lifted the stick from me. The hanger, as he was called, straddled the rafters sometimes 20 feet off the ground without protection (predating OSHA) and placed the ends of the stick across the rafter beams. In the meantime, I had returned to the door and received another stick. And the hanger was pushing the leaves of his stick lightly up against the leaves of the preceding one, careful to fill the barn without packing it so loosely that space was wasted, but neither so tightly that the heat could not reach the uppermost rafter to cure the leaves. This process was repeated literally hundreds of times until the barn was filled.

When the barn was full, we passed the word along to the farmer or his manager. The farmer (owner) or his manger would shortly come to the barn to check on the quality of the packing and verify that the barn was ready to be closed for curing. Those who cropped, tied, poked up and hung the tobacco had no role in closing the barn for curing. Spaced over the dirt floor of the barn were gas burners with protective flange covers. Each of these was lit and checked for proper flame adjustment. Then the doors of the barn were closed and latched. The drying process began. The farmer checked the barn once, maybe twice a day. In several days to a week, the tobacco would be completely cured and ready to be removed to a storage barn. At the storage barn, the cured tobacco was removed from the sticks and stacked until the farmer was ready to take it to market.

I never worked in tobacco (as the job is called) for my grandfather. By the time I was old enough to work in the fields or the barn, Granddaddy had ceased planting his own fields. He leased the allotment to one of his sons-in-law. He and I discussed the lousy timing, but we enjoyed other things by that time in my life, so it was never very important. We just knew it could have been fun for the two of us to have worked together so closely.

But I did help the older boys and the men load the tobacco from the storage barn to the truck for going to market. We piled the truck high over the cab until it teetered as if the whole arrangement might topple. The tobacco, though neatly stacked, bulged over the sides of the truck like a ruptured bladder. Once stacked to the point of failure, a tarp was trussed over it all and secured everywhere possible. Hemp ropes, soft from age and use, wrapped from grommets to truck fenders and back around and down behind the cab to the suspension on the other side. It was a bewildering web of rope and knots that seemed easier to cut to release than to untie. But the lines were taut and held the cargo into the bed of the truck despite its incipient proclivity to tumble free.

Since tobacco was a commodity, Granddaddy kept a close watch on prices in different markets, timing with some care the day of going to market with his leaf. Going to market was a grand experience for a young kid like me, too occasional to satisfy a young man's dreams of impending importance. Yes, even an old farmer like my grandfather spoke of market in a voice that intoned significance, moment and a seriousness that lies at the heart of all profitable commerce. It mattered to him. And, without exaggerating its meaning, Granddaddy let me know that it could be valuable for me to attend when I could. Thus, I relished the visits to his farm that coincided with going to market.

Market day began at 4:00AM for Granddaddy, 4:30AM for me. He rose, shaved, showered, dressed in clean khakis and a white long-sleeved shirt over a ribbed tank t-shirt, made coffee, then woke me. It was dark when I rose and dressed. Outside, in the pre-dawn light, a mist hung softly over the fields and silence enveloped our movements. Even though it was late summer, the damp air chilled me. I climbed into the pickup truck beside Granddaddy. He backed the overloaded truck carefully down the drive to the dirt road that ran beside his house. Then he clutched the truck into first gear, eased out the clutch and brought the headlights around to the highway, the direction of our departure. Looking into the long darkness of the highway, he made sure that nothing was emerging from the foggy road and pulled out slowly onto the asphalt. He shifted into second gear, and we were on our way.

Granddaddy pulled into a diner a few miles up US Highway 301, a major four-lane byway for north-south commerce between New York and Florida in the years before interstates. He bought a couple of sausage and egg biscuits for me, then proceeded toward the market of the day. Often it was Farmville, an hour to the east. Once it was Lumberton, a long, long drive south that ended after the sun was high into the sky and the fields quavering in heat. He rarely went to Wilson, the closest market. I do not know why.

Among a series of similar warehouse buildings clustered outside the town, Granddaddy would turn into one. Monk #1, Brown's #3, Knott's #4. The warehouses were the same from the outside but for the names painted on the empty walls. I do not know how he selected, though he always knew the people running whichever warehouse he entered. He pulled into the warehouse, blind in the sudden darkness, driving to one side where a couple of other farmers were usually unloading their tobacco. As I tumbled out of the truck, Granddaddy was off to his business. I explored the cavern of concrete floor, skylights, and stout wooden columns, delighting in the wonderful aroma of cured tobacco drifting throughout.

Tobacco is one of those things about which I wish, "If only it tasted exactly like it smells." Coffee is like that; as good as it can taste, it is never as fulfilling as the promise of its aroma. And, like coffee, the aftertaste of tobacco (smoke) is more revolting than you can imagine when enjoying its delicious aroma. So, in my innocence, standing amidst bales of tobacco in a vast warehouse, I savored the smell and dreamed of a perfection does not exist.

For the next few hours, as the truck was unloaded and the bales laid out across the warehouse floor to await the auctioneer and bidding of tobacco company buyers, I roamed the stark interior of the warehouse, listening to fragments of conversations among the other farmers and workers. The price of tobacco was a natural topic, but so were baseball, weather and gossip, the things discussed by people who want to be friendly without being friends, who want to talk as if sharing their lives without sharing anything that they would share only with a close friend. It was the talk of men. Men bound together by common toil and circumstances, men who faced the same challenges of working a field into a farm. I do not recall learning anything worth remembering, but I was a child and loved hearing what the men had to say.

Along the lines of tobacco bales stretching from one end of the open warehouse to the other, a cluster of men huddled in a group listening to the auctioneer like chicks around a hen. The auctioneer rambled and spat a staccato of bids and asks; men surrounding him fondled the leaf for texture and suppleness, the quality of its curing, listening without comment. Some of the men were buyers, others farmers. I never understood a word of what the auctioneer said, nor did I ever see a buyer make a bid. In a wordless pantomime of familiar looks and subtle nods, the auctioneer babbled ceaselessly, except when he almost paused to take a breath before declaring "Sold!" The farmers nodded among themselves with a few whispered comments about the quality of the leaf and the price just fetched.

Depending upon the condition of the market, the auction would be lively, the farmers excited about the prices. At other times, with prices so low they barely beat the support prices, the warehouse could be silent, dull, funereal.

By late morning, I had drunk a couple of colas and munched a pack of nabs or a bag of salted peanuts. I was hungry. Granddaddy eventually would have heard what he needed to hear and would declare the time of departure. It was forever a mystery how he decided it was time to go. He had not always sold his tobacco; I know because I asked him. In any case, I climbed back into the truck and onto the long bench seat beside my grandfather, and we drove out the large entry doors into the harsh and brilliant light of midday. We ate lunch in a diner just down the road. There was always a diner near the warehouse. The diner was usually so nondescript that I could never have guessed that it was open for business much less that food was served inside. But Granddaddy knew where he was and what he wanted. Fresh vegetables and maybe a couple of pieces of fried chicken. Not as good as we could get back at his farm but pretty good for a restaurant.

Back at his farm, Granddaddy parked the truck in the driveway, removed his boots on the back porch and ambled into the den. There, he turned on the TV (the channel didn't really matter), leaned back in his armchair (we called this the "red leather chair" because that's what my grandmother had wanted; it was some sort of vinyl, like naugahide), propped his skinny white sock feet on the ottoman, closed his eyes and fell soundly asleep. Mouth agape, he would snore peacefully for a half hour or so before waking completely refreshed and head out the door to work until dusk.

Growing tobacco was a difficult business. Price and price supports. Government protection, government interference, and government regulation. In many ways, it was like any agricultural crop. Good years, there was more leaf than the market wanted to buy so the price fell. Bad years, the price rose with the shortage of leaf, but there wasn't much to sell. It seemed a farmer was damned either way. Then there was the weather.

One summer, Granddaddy was hit by three hail storms in a month. The entire tobacco crop was ruined.

"What will you do?" I inquired.

"Oh I have insurance," he replied. "Truth is, I'll make more money than I would have harvesting it."

"How is that possible?"

"Well, I don't have the expense of cropping it, curing it or having to see what it will bring at market. I'll do okay."

And I knew it was true.

Another summer, Granddaddy's farm was smack dab in the middle of a drought. There was a general dearth of rain in eastern North Carolina that year, but his farm was having its own private drought. I visited a few times that summer and witnessed for myself how a promising afternoon summer thunderstorm would build in the distance, darken, then sweep toward the farm only to miss it by a mile or less. The farms all around would get a good soaking, but not Granddaddy's. It stayed dry as a Nebraskan dustbowl. The crops showed the strain as corn withered, crisp and brown leaves on the stalk, and tobacco leaves hung limply. I worried.

"Granddaddy, is there anything you can do to keep the crops watered?" I asked.

"We could put in a big irrigation system, but it only works so well and it costs so much we wouldn't make anything anyway." He looked down, sanguine. Not really worried, but with a bit of fatigue in his brow.

"So what will happen?" I wanted a better answer than he had offered.

"Jimbo, tobacco's just a weed; it'll be fine." He smiled because he knew it was true.

THE LAST SUMMER

The last summer that I spent with my grandparents began in the heavy humid heat of July. I had already worked a month for a highway contractor, driving a truck on a paving crew. The foreman appointed me the driver of the Pilot Car on my first day because I was one of only two on the crew with a driver's license (all the others had lost theirs due to driving drunk); the other man drove the truck with all the shovels, rakes, traffic cones etc. Mostly, I was bored senseless driving a Pilot Car (a pickup truck with a flashing sign that said

FOLLOW ME on the back, leading the not quite lost around the paving machine and road crew, driving from one flagman to the next and back again, more times each day than I could count). I learned from the paving crew. Most had worked hard labor all their lives and thought I was an idiot not to be going to college, and they told me so. Still, they were a friendly and helpful lot, always ready with a joke or a smoke. They were kind to me because I was the only one who could drive to a nearby convenience store for mid-morning or mid-afternoon soft drinks and snacks.

My last day in the paving business, I was helping fill some spots along the shoulder of a road we had just paved. I stood in the asphalt in the back of a dump truck and shoveled hot black oily asphalt over the high sides of the dump truck to the sand shoulders below. It was 107 degrees in the shade; I stood on 185 degree asphalt in the sun. Sucking down a tall Pepsi bottle filled with water every 10 minutes or so. The crew kept me hydrated.

When my grandfather called to see if I would be interested in cutting some hardwoods to sell as firewood, I said yes without even thinking about the fact that I had no chain saw or truck or anything else I needed to be in the firewood business. I just knew how great it would be to spend the summer with Granddaddy.

I went to the hardware store and bought the cheapest gas powered chain saw I could find (no start up capital). I bought an ax, a sledge hammer and a steel wedge. I figured I had covered the basics and was ready to tackle a tree.

Granddaddy was having some land cleared. A bulldozer was pushing all the trees into a massive hedgerow across the highway from my grandparents' house. That was my wood.

The first day, I slept in and Granddaddy took me over to show me the timber when he came in mid-morning. He picked up a piece of limb, asked for my ax and then shaped a wedge. Then he made another. I showed him my steel wedge and he nodded patiently.

"Just try these. Maybe use the steel one to get the split to open, then drive one or both of the wooden wedges into the log to split it all the way."

I said I understood and looked over the pile of timber that lay before me. Easily twenty trees, all oak and maple. Too scrawny for lumber and Granddaddy needed the land cleared because one of his other grandsons was quitting the banking business to come home to farm. I looked at the timber and thought, "This is great. I can knock this out in a week or so and then I'll make a lot more money than on the paving crew."

I said nothing to my grandfather except thank you.

He smiled and said, "Let's get started." And that first morning, I worked alongside him as we cut logs off the trees and split them. By lunch time, we had a neat pile, and I was feeling boldly energetic.

We stopped for lunch, walked back across the road to the house and stepped into the deliciously cool air conditioning where my grandmother had lunch waiting on the table. Ravenous, I ate everything in sight, fortifying myself for my afternoon sawing and splitting and stacking. When I finished lunch and my fourth glass of ice tea, Granddaddy and I retired to the den "to let our food settle". He fell asleep as he did most every day after lunch. I thought I would just close my eyes for a few minutes and then head back over to the timber.

I slept two hours.

When I woke a little past mid-afternoon, stupefied with sleep, tired and aching from the morning's cutting as well as dreading the sweltering afternoon heat, I kissed off the rest of the day thinking I would get started early the next day before the sun got up too high and heat choked the wood pile. Summer cutting firewood proved to be every bit as difficult as shoveling hot asphalt from the back of a dump truck. There is no easy money in hard labor.

MOUSE FLIES, SALMON,
And THINGS that GO BUMP in the LAKE

The year I turned forty, I indulged in a variety of commemorative activities. One event that was part of selfishly celebrating my birthday was a trip to the Brule River in northern Wisconsin to flyfish for steelhead, large rainbow trout that leave Lake Superior to spawn up the rivers. It was my first trip to the midwest, but the flat plains north of Minneapolis reminded me of North Carolina's coastal plains except that Minnesota forests are birch and spruce, moreso than oak and pine. I met a co-worker, Chuck, at the airport, and we headed north toward Duluth before turning east along Lake Superior. Autumn reds and yellows burst from the trees as rain showers rolled across the flat rural countryside. The emptiness of the farmland led me to wonder what it might be like to be caught on a lonely highway in a blinding blizzard like a scene out of the film, *Fargo*. Surely people keep emergency survival gear in their cars during the winter.

From what I could see from a distance, Duluth, Minnesota and its sister city, Superior, Wisconsin reminded me of West Virginia coal country, a land whose time and prime has passed. We drove east parallel to Lake Superior without being able to see the scope of its waters, then turned south to Brule River Classics where we met Bob, another co-worker, at the outfitter's camp where we rented a cabin. With a bathroom in one corner and a sink representing the sole element of a kitchen in the other, we stepped onto the limited flooring beside the doorway. There appeared to be a greater area of beds than floor, ample for three men who only intended to sleep. As soon as we unloaded the rental car, we embarked on what Bob liked to call "maneuvers", the search for local food and watering holes. The crossroads went by the name of Brule, and the Bois Brule River (Brule River in the compressed version of the name) ran through Brule

River State Forest. Bois Brule, literally translated, means "burnt wood"; however, it is also a term for the descendants of Native Americans and Europeans, especially French from Canada. Lake Superior was several miles north, but we postponed our visit to the lake in favor of scouting the state forest where we were scheduled to fish with guides the following day. We passed a pickup truck with a large dead bear in the bed. Wild country.

When we were driving out of Minneapolis, we had driven past the Mississippi River. The Brule has historically been the crux of the waterway that Native Americans, explorers, and the French voyageurs paddled in their 20-man canoes from the Canadian fur country across Lake Superior to the Mississippi. Very narrow at it headwaters, the Brule connected to the Mississippi via a short portage (less than two miles) to the St. Croix River, thus creating a continuous passage for trade from Canada south.

After a high carb breakfast of blueberry pancakes at Twin Gables, we met our guides and drove south to the put-in at Stonebridge where the Brule is only about 25 feet wide, three or four feet deep and crystal clear. Most of the river is fairly shallow with pristine, spring-fed waters. We had three fishermen in two canoes with one guide in each. Casting from a canoe was new to me, and it felt quite awkward to twist in my seat to cast the fly from behind my shoulder without hooking either Chuck or our guide. I was lousy at it, but Chuck managed to place his fly right beside the overgrown bank and land a 10 inch brook trout.

Fishing is called "fishing" and not "catching" because it is the act of fishing that brings joy to most fishermen. Catching is a nice complement, but the best parts of trout fishing are the outdoors, the wildlife, the cold water, and the meditative rhythm of casting a featherlight fly rod with a weightless fly at the end of the line, testing the appetite of the trout and trying to deliver an appealing fly within its reach. Trout are mostly conservative with their energy, so they rarely chase a fly, preferring to hover in the current and let the stream bring food to them. Naturally, when there is a large hatch of bugs, the trout can become competitive and greedy to gorge on whatever is emerging. Other than Chuck's brookie, we relaxed and floated with the current, casting without catching and eventually reached a lovely lodge with cedar shingle siding hidden in the woods on a small island named, logically enough, Cedar Island. A beautiful rustic arched bridge connected the island to the forest across the river. Just upstream of the bridge, a crystal clear pool five feet deep revealed 12-14 inch trout lazing in the current. With the clarity of the water and the shallow depth, we could not possibly fool the trout into taking a fly, but we tried for a few minutes, all the while enjoying watching wild fish ignoring an apex predator floating stupidly helpless above them.

Passing under the bridge, we entered a broad open pond less than three feet deep. At its outflow was a small rapid named The Falls, a pretentious and ambitious name for the fast riffles that slipped between two banks into a deep hole at an abrupt turn in the river. We were ready for more casual casting, so we pulled the canoes ashore and scouted The Falls as well as the pond upstream. One of our guides spotted a Chinook salmon beside a downed hemlock below The Falls. As we adjusted to the distortion of the ruffled flow of the river, we saw several others pushing upstream through the shallow rocky section. Our guides told us it was fine to try to catch them because they are an invasive species in the Brule and ideally should be removed. They also cautioned that the fish could easily weigh twenty to thirty pounds and might break our 4-weight trout rods.

Initially, I ignored the salmon and nymphed the fast water for brooks or browns. With no luck attracting trout, I decided to give the Chinook a try. Damien, one of our guides, suggested I use a big bright garish fly. I pulled out a chartreuse streamer, and Damien smiled. "That should work." The salmon was almost close enough to the bank for me to touch it, so I only needed a short length of fly line to flick the streamer into the fast water above and let the current drift the fly down. When the streamer neared the salmon's mouth, I slowed the drift. The salmon never shifted a centimeter. Damian advised me to put it on its nose, so I drifted the fly again guiding the path of the fly right to the salmon's lips. It gently pinched the streamer in its lips and set it to the side where the current swept it past the fish. I kept trying to position the fly where the Chinook would grab it. It would not bite. Then, just as I was about to quit my efforts, I must have succeeded in irritating it. The salmon swallowed the big streamer, and I set the hook, felt the weight of the fish and the hopelessness of trying to control it. Feeling the bite of the hook, even though it was barbless, the salmon thrashed and charged downstream for the pool and never slowed. I palmed the reel in an attempt to increase pressure on the line. Damian tried to block its flight with a net, but it shot down the river into a jumble of tree branches where the line broke, and the Chinook disappeared into the next lake. For a long ten seconds or less, I had connected to a freight train of a fish, thirty inches and twenty pounds of muscle in its element. It was brief but exhilarating.

The following morning, we returned to Twin Gables for breakfast. Bob had decided to meet one of the guides to explore some new water. Chuck and I chose to find our way back to The Falls. We had studied the topo map we had, and located a trail that would lead us back to the pond and the Falls. Leaving breakfast, we stopped at the gas station, but they were out of sandwiches. I asked if they expected to have any the next day, and they replied that they would be happy to make us a couple right then. Friendly people. We added a few beers and chips to the bag and headed for the backwoods. We mainly planned to cast for trout again, but I brought along my 8 wt. rod in case the Chinook were still moving upstream; with the larger rod, I might have a fighting chance of landing a salmon.

We hiked in on a trail that was clear but unmarked and mostly open second growth forest still recovering from a recent clearcut. When we reached the section of the Brule where we had seen the Chinook the day before, we looked into the small rapids but saw no movement. A blue wing olive hatch was rising off the shallow pond upstream, so we took turns sight casting to the small brook trout breaking the smooth surface of the water. The wading was easy with the pond only about two feet deep and the bottom firm. Some fish rose in open water while others rose around a fallen tree that offered more challenging casts. The day was overcast and pleasantly cool. We took our time with everything we did. I almost forgot that Chuck was somewhere nearby as I lost myself in casting and tying on new flies, watching the surface for rising fish, and listening to the sounds of solitude, running water and wind rustling the autumn leaves in the woods.

We saw only one other person all day, a real sport in a British driving cap with plaid vest who slipped through the pond in his red canoe with his Schnauzer stoically and obediently sitting in the bow. I imagined he hung a couple of matched Purdy's on the wall of his lodge, possibly the same one we had seen near the bridge. Both sport and dog ignored us with nary a glance or a nod much less a "Good morning" or "How's the fishing?". The sport did not scout the rapids, but ran them effortlessly and also made the sharp turn at the pool with calm, practiced expertise. He barely shifted his paddle as he steered his way through and into the next lake, whereas I would have been flailing my paddle wildly to try to avoid a capsize at the pool below The Falls where there was little room to maneuver. I envied him his time on the river of which he certainly had enough to master the most difficult section we had seen the preceding day.

The salmon never showed. Such is the way of life. What we expect often does not occur while what we do not anticipate can transform our day. Nevertheless, we caught and released plenty of small brook trout in the pond, so the fishing was satisfying even without the salmon. After long hours of weather changing from drizzle to blowing misty rain to sun bright on the little pond, we hiked back out through the cedar bog. We had worn boots on the hike in, and we had soaked them in the bog mud, so we kept our waders on for the walk out.

Back at the outfitter's, I added more blue wing olive flies to my box, and we bought a couple mouse flies each for the next day's steelhead fishing. They were quite realistic in size with deer hair for fur and a short piece of deer hide thong for a tail. As we left the shop, a cold squall blew through with high winds bending the trees like straight line winds from a tornado. We made it inside the cabin before a torrential downpour accompanied by thunder and lightning.

The three of us drove into Brule and ordered some burgers and beers at the Kro-Bar, a fine roadhouse that probably gets lively either late or mainly on weekends when most of the local folks are not working. Dimly lit with a long bar and a concrete floor and more dancing room than tables for eating, it reminded me of the juke joints I pass when driving rural roads in North Carolina, the kinds of taverns with one front door and few windows that you never see open because business begins so late and ends so early. We did not have time to check this place out when the action was hot since we were seriously fishing.

"Seriously" because, if you have traveled a long way to stand in a cold river and wave a long stick at invisible fish, you must be crazy or serious. We preferred to believe we were not crazy. Nevertheless, when you consider that we release everything we catch and, even if we kept what we caught and calculated how much we spent per pound to catch them, we could make a good case for crazy. On the other hand, walking through airports with long metal tubes protecting our fly rods and checking duffle bags stuffed and laden with waders, boots, vest, extra fly boxes, and plenty of gear we would never need, we looked serious and full of intent, our hats littered with old flies like tiny trophies.

All three of us piled into the rental car to drive to the spots where our guides said we would find steelhead, or at least salmon. Under blue skies, we stood on the rocky banks of the lower Brule, warm with a cooling breeze, and scouted the water. The river looked like old orangeade from the previous evening's storm runoff, and the turbidity should have improved our chances.

When water is too clear, fish can see the humans playing with flies and rods. Unless desperate, fish are not stupid. They cannot know that you plan to release them, and even a barbed hook must pinch a bit when it sinks into a bony fish lip.

No steelhead. No salmon. But we did land a few small wild rainbows, and Chuck hooked another 10 inch brook trout, a big brookie in our home waters in the South where most native brooks are 6-8 inches. Pleased not to be skunked, we had devoured a day testing every hole, riffle, and undercut bank we could reach with a fly line. We tried every fly in our collective boxes, dry flies and nymphs, floating and sinking lines. Still, we raised not one steelhead or salmon. Maybe the lake level had not risen enough to give the fish easy access up the river. After all, none of us really knew what we were doing. All of us had plenty of time on the water fishing for trout, but only Bob had ever fished the Brule for steelhead.

To ease the pain of our poor results, we drove several miles east to Iron River where we ate at The Spot. The food was ample and tasty even if underwhelming. The service was friendly and the view over Buskey Bay on the Iron River serene. We headed back to our cabin early so we could wake at dawn, skip breakfast and fish the early daylight hours. The challenge for each of us was who would fall asleep first. All of us snored. If Bob fell asleep first, Chuck and I were in trouble. Bob's snoring exceeded the combined volume of Chuck and me (with me the louder of the two) and rattled the cabin like a train running off its track and crashing off a cliff. Loud, continuous, no breaks for breathing. No rhythm either. Unfortunately, Bob usually fell asleep first, no matter what we did to try to keep him talking while Chuck and I drifted off. Mid-sentence, with the lights still on, Bob would snap on the snoring engine, and there was no respite. Goodness save the poor guy who woke in the middle of the night to relieve himself and have to try, once more, to fall asleep with Bob snoring. Chuck cheated; he knew that Bob snored horribly, so he brought the earplugs he used at the gun range. He also kept a bottle of scotch beside his bed. He shared the scotch with me but not the earplugs. Some things are not meant to be used by two people at once. I often read and write in my journal before going to sleep, but I could not focus on the words or concentrate on the meaning of the book I was reading. I could only wait until I was too tired to keep my eyes open.

Another morning with no strikes. When you fly from North Carolina (or Virginia for Bob and Chuck) to Minnesota and drive to Wisconsin, you make the trip because you expect fishing superior to that which you can find on your home waters. The grass is supposed to be greener. Of course, as adults, we should know better. I reminded myself that I do not fish to catch trout; I fish for the tranquility of standing in clean, clear, cold moving water, focusing on the drift of the fly line, the action of the fly, and hoping for a good strike followed by the excitement of playing a fish to the net. When I fish, I cannot consider problems or worry about anything mundane (root derivation "world"). I have tried just to test myself. During my worst times in the working world, I could not fret when I fished. Instead, I listen to the murmuring water, hear the wind rattling alder leaves, and see the sunlight electrify the reds, yellows, and golds of autumn. I savor the blue skies and fair breezes that soothe me as I wade or rest on a river bank.

When we rendezvoused for lunch, we detoured to the house of a local fly tier, Dick Berge. A retired schoolteacher, Dick's fly tying bench sat below a big window overlooking a lake. Wisconsin surprised me with the number of lakes scattered through the extensive forests, as if anyone could own a place on fresh cool water good for swimming or paddling in the summer. Dick was a delightful host and demonstrated tying some common flies. Having a tying bench with all the materials – feathers, thread, beads, hooks, scissors, and the vice, of course – at hand made tying much more convenient. Having a pleasant view no doubt improved the atmosphere of his work. Dick sells his flies, and we bought some for the rest of our trip.

We planned to fish the "mouse hatch" as our grand finale. We needed a moonless night so we would be concealed from the big lake-run browns and salmon (it was clear that the steelhead had yet to move into the river), fish in the thirty inch range. Clouds eased across the setting sun, promising conditions. Bob hired Keith as his guide for the night, and Keith said it was a perfect night for fishing the browns that eat mice swimming in Big Lake. Now, I can understand how a mouse might fall into a creek where a big-mouthed brown trout would scarf it up, but why would a mouse go swimming in a big lake at night? Skinny dipping? Swim meet? Whatever the reason, we had purchased our mouse flies and doused them heavily with floatant gel to keep the big fly on the surface, just as if the mouse was swimming. In my mind, I could only think that this was a joke, a cartoon, like a snipe hunt for Boy Scout initiation.

We arrived at Big Lake about an hour before dusk armed with both our trout rods and beefy 8 wt. rods for the trophies we dreamed of landing. We waded down the shoreline 100 yards to a small peninsula to dodge the soupy bogs along the shore. I first strung my 4 wt. and tied on a Royal Wulff Trude, one of my favorite attractors with a bright red body and white wings, that I hoped would be visible to a trout in the waning daylight. There was no evidence of a hatch and only occasionally rippling rings to indicate feeding fish. Although Chuck and I cast blindly into the lake, we mostly walked the shallows to scout the bottom conditions for firmness and obstacles such as fallen trees and boulders. Once the sun set and our vision expired in the moonless night, we would move only by feel, shuffling along the lake bottom as we eased into deeper water to shorten the distance we would have to cast and, hopefully, getting closer to our targets. On the other hand, being in water near our waist and stepping into a silty mire, sinking without solid footing, would be terrifying. Waders have a bad habit of filling quickly with water if breached, and the air trapped in the feet is the only buoyancy, so your feet rise while your body is turned upside down, your head forced down into the water where there is nothing for your hands to grab to right yourself.

The sun set, and all three of us switched to our larger rods with the deer hair mouse flies. In the lake, we could hear the sound of big fish breaking the surface. The hoot of a barred owl echoed from the far shore. Keith advised us not to panic if something huge ran into one of our legs while we fished in the lake. He said a lake run brown or salmon could feel like a monster when it collides with a human in the pitch dark of a moonless night. Oh boy. With those words of confidence, Bob and Keith paddled out to the middle of the lake to a channel near a weed bed. Chuck moved down the shore about 50 yards from me. The night was quiet and perfectly still. I could hear Chuck waving his rod through the air and Robin's muffled voice out on the lake. The rapids where the Brule entered the south end of the lake muttered, muted by the distance. I waded cautiously into the lake until I was almost waist deep.

Casting a large heavy mouse fly without being able to see the fly line or the fly or even the position of the rod, making all the usual casting actions by feel alone, disoriented me. I could not see to mend the line nor see how much line I had to lift from the water to backcast. Sometimes the cast collapsed around me, many loops of fly line falling over my head and shoulders in an impossible tangle. Although I knew that the line had collapsed because I failed to allow the line to fully straighten behind me on the backcast, I could not see the error, so I was never quite sure. More than once, my frustration tempted me to curse, but I maintained silence for the sake of the necessary stillness to tease the fish close to where we stood even though nothing was working. On the positive side, occasionally I could feel that the backcast had fully loaded the rod and my forward cast laid out the fly line gently across the still water. Then I could retrieve the mouse fly with subtle twitches that may have imitated a swimming mouse disturbing the lake. Again, I could see nothing, so I had no idea whether the mouse action appeared to a fish as a mouse swimming or a mouse drowning or even a big hook wearing a deer fur cape. In any case, I failed to attract a strike.

After one of my major tangles, I backed closer to the shore for safety and so that I could concentrate on unknotting the fly line without worrying that I might stumble into deep water. I heard a loud rustling behind me on the bank. Something big was coming out of the woods. A man? A bear? What else? My heartbeat accelerated as I fumbled to control my rod and line while simultaneously reaching with my left hand into my right side breast pocket for my small flashlight. I continued to fumble the rod and line as I tried to hold them out of my way so I could use both hands to hold the light and twist the head into the On position, point the light toward the noise and shield my eyes so I would not blind myself. If someone had been filming me, no doubt all of my motions would have looked spastic, a fool and his fear.

I managed to aim the light and saw that what was behind me was ... a deer, a doe. Not Sasquatch or a serial killer or even a hungry black bear (the least threatening of any except the deer). Her eyes shone bright as she stared into my flashlight. She was unafraid, unlike I had been, and casually splashed along the shallows as she moved down the shoreline away from me. I quickly settled down and returned to fishing, such as it was. I accumulated sufficient failed casts to seriously offset the successful ones, so I retreated to the shore after another half hour or so. Chuck soon joined me having had similar luck though not as many tangled casts. He too had heard the noise coming from the woods and asked what it had been. But he had remained in the lake the whole time. For protection?

We left Bob and Keith out in the middle of the lake, and Bob later reported that he had landed one brown, but it was not the monster lake-run brown trout he sought. All in all, the mouse hatch had been a bust. I recalled that Keith had said it was a perfect night to fish for lake-run browns and salmon. He had *not* said it was a perfect night for *catching* lake-run browns or salmon. Still, standing in a lake at night with no moon and no visibility for a point of reference or comfort had been exciting and unique, unlike any fishing that we did back in the South. The Brule, with its history, its wildness and crystal waters, will remain a fine diversion with great memories.

SLICKROCK: The Whole Story
Including Notes from the Blizzard of 1993

Prologue

A mile west of Robbinsville, we rounded a bend in the desolate mountain road, and flurries began to fall. Looking up toward the mountains past Lake Santeetlah, we watched as snow clouds dropped over the ridges. Snowflakes alternately drifted and swirled as we drove northwest along the Cheoah River where it followed a boulder-strewn bed from Santeetlah Dam to Calderwood Lake at Tapoco. We joked like teenagers about getting stuck in the snow as we climbed the Forest Service road to the parking lot at Big Fat Gap. Waiting for us at the trailhead was a handwritten sign:

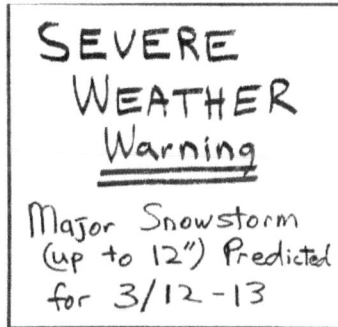

Facsimile of sign posted at trailhead

Joe declared, "This is crazy, We're crazy. I'm crazy for listening to you two."

"Come on. A foot of snow will be great. No trouble. Plus, we won't have to find springs for water," I replied. The three of us started up the steps at the base of the trail. "It's a hard climb for the first half mile, and it's uphill all the way to Hangover Mountain, but none of it is as bad as this first section."

The Hike to Naked Ground: Part One

It felt like a summit. We stood in the clouds and blowing snow, but the mountain seemed to fall away from us in all directions. We had stopped in the middle of the trail after a steep climb through a rhododendron thicket, a root-choked path that would be a drainage gully after a heavy rain. I pulled an energy bar from the pocket of my storm shell; the bar was too hard to chew, already frozen.

"This must be Hangover Mountain. The worst part of the hike is behind us," I remarked to Mark and Joe. We had climbed more than 2,000 feet in the past two miles.

"You said the worst was behind us an hour ago. Then we climbed this mountain," retorted Joe.

"Better keep moving; I'm getting cold." My fingers had stiffened in the few minutes that we rested, and my body began to chill. The cold penetrated to my bones, and my feet lost feeling, not good for relying on feel when hiking over uneven ground.

As we started down the trail, I tried to warm my hands. Because of numb feet and cold muscles, the downhill trail was almost as challenging as the ascent had been. New snow covered the ground lightly with no measurable accumulation. The trail was slippery over the decaying leaf litter that masked the trail at the end of a long winter. As my body warmed with the effort of hiking briskly over the slick trail, my hands began to warm. The warmth ignited an excruciating pain in my fingers, far more than I should have felt after a quick stop. The temperature hovered around freezing, but the wind chill near the summit may have been closer to twenty degrees. We pushed on toward Haoe Mountain and Naked Ground, the ridge at the head of the Slickrock Creek drainage that connected to Bob Stratton Bald.

Mark and Joe had been right; I had told them that the worst was behind us after the first mile of trail. Hangover Lead begins at the parking lot at Big Fat Gap with several steep wooden rail ties forming steps followed by a seemingly endless series of steep switchbacks. Finding a comfortable pace was impossible. Our lungs burned as we climbed the trail. The air was cool at the Gap with only a light breeze apparent. I wore only a t-shirt under my storm shell because I knew the uphill tramp would make me sweat. Snow fell sweetly, magical in the silent wilderness. It was good to be back in the woods, carrying a backpack and hiking with good friends.

First Attempt to Hike the Ridge Solo

Mark and I had tried to hike Slickrock for almost four years but never could coordinate our schedules. My fascination with the Wilderness began seven years before when I hiked in on Ike Branch Trail. I had gotten a late start and underestimated how far past Asheville I had to drive to reach the trailhead. Dusk was settling over the forest when I parked my car beside Calderwood Lake. With my two black Labradors, I hurried up the trail about a mile, stopping before dark so I could set up camp. As I was looking around for a patch of flat ground, a mountain boy approached from the woods. He carried a Winchester 30-30 rifle and was ambling off trail through the forest.

"Hey." It could have been a scene from *Deliverance,* so I opened the conversation to be sure he knew I was friendly and not afraid of an armed man in the empty woods. "Wha'cha huntin'?" I switched on my best good old boy mountain accent. It was not a true mountain accent, but it was Southern enough to hopefully sound like I was local.

"Bar," he replied, his response clipped and economic, wasting no breath while looking at my dogs milling about, my dogs that had done nothing to alert me to the presence of a stranger coming into our camp.

"Boar?" I asked.

"No, 'bar'," he clarified. Ah, "bear", I thought to myself.

"And hog." There is the "boar", I thought, again to myself. I did not want him to think I considered his accent was anything but perfect. Hillbillies can be a sensitive lot.

He was not much for conversation, but then suddenly turned his head as if he heard something off through the woods. "Gotta go. Brotha callin'." His quiet drawl sounded like he was drinking molasses as he spoke, as if speech needed only the mild vibration of vocal cords without the shaping of sounds in the mouth or the movement of lips.

I had heard not a sound, not a leaf twitch, not a whisper. And, quick as he had appeared, he was gone, disappeared into the forest with not a snap of a branch or crunching of the autumn leaves freshly scattered throughout. Although his departure comforted and relieved me, I knew he knew where I was camping, and he could easily return to the spot in the dark without a sound or a light or even the moon to guide him. Mountain folks know their country, their terrain, their terroir, their territory with no reliance on trails. Rocks and trees and swales from old creek beds give them all the landmarks they need. But autumn darkness had swallowed the forest early, and I had only two choices, camp and get some needed sleep or pack myself back out to my car.

I turned my attention back to the fallen tree trunk where I had set my stove. Before I could pull out matches to light the stove, my mind went blank. I suddenly did not know where I was or why I was there. I looked at the gear strewn around my feet and wondered what to do next. My thoughts outran my logic as I questioned why I believed that I had the skills to be alone in a wilderness area with sunset past, the darkness of night consuming the forest. Panic was climbing up my throat, then I inhaled a conscious breath and remembered I had been a Boy Scout and learned what to do living in the woods. Whew, that was close. I still have no idea what caused me to experience those moments of mounting fear.

Following the directions as best I could recall, I struck a match and struggled to get the troublesome stove to ignite. When finally lit, I boiled some gritty creek water and poured it into the package of dehydrated shrimp creole. After a quick dinner, I called the dogs into the tent and, leaning against an old spruce, tried to write before reading myself into a fitful slumber. Pitch dark impenetrable night surrounded us. Rain fell much of the night, muting any sounds that might have concerned me.

The next morning dawned foggy with a damp chill. Strong winds blasted the trees high on the ridge above. The roaring wind sounded like a winter storm, but only gentle breezes fell into the bottom of the cove where I had camped. I boiled a pot of water for oatmeal and tea, pleased to be starting my journey through Slickrock. Unfortunately, I had to stuff my tent into my pack wet from the overnight rain.

The dogs and I got on the trail and followed it upstream on a moderate grade to an unnamed gap, then turned east, level along the southside of the ridge at the northern end of Hangover Lead. Yellowhammer Gap appeared sooner than I expected. I checked my topo map and saw that plenty of uphill awaited me on the way to Big Fat Gap. I carefully set a steady pace, not too fast or slow, just one foot after the other to make the climb as even as possible. Then the trail took an abrupt turn with an even more abrupt increase in grade. Steps, or even a ladder, would have been appropriate. Fine with me, I thought. I generally prefer the direct approach. In no place did the trail skirt the ridge summit to soften the grade between dips and gaps along the ridge. The rising topo continued almost unbroken for more than two miles to Cold Spring Knob.

I hiked up and up. It felt more like mountaineering than Blue Ridge backpacking. As my lungs sucked harder and harder and my calves, knees and buttocks tightened to the point of cramping, I recalled a line of poetry I had once written: "the chest heaves, the lungs no elasticity... aching knees, as if mud bound in a thaw."

When the topo finally flattened, we took a break. Wind growled up the ridge, tearing through the trees. In fact, the only sound I could hear was the roar of the wind as it swept up from the Cheoah River gorge, one burst never dying before another rolled over it.

After straining my knees on the long slog up the ridge, and losing a liter of sweat carrying a pack that included five days of food for the dogs, the trail dropped precipitously down the north side of Cold Spring Knob to Big Fat Gap. As hard as the inclined trail was, the abrupt downhill to Big Fat Gap was even harder on my knees. By the time I reached the gap, I could hardly walk. While uphill hiking takes a toll on knees, a steep downhill is murderous. With every step, the knees threatened to fail and drop me tumbling out of control.

At the gap, I paused to evaluate my situation. I took a long break to rest and refuel and study the topo map again. I shucked my pack, ate more gorp, and sucked down more water. Rejuvenation eluded me. My body was exhausted as if I had already hiked two full days. As I reclined against the hill, I stared at the steep start for Hangover Lead across the parking lot from where I sat. From the parking lot, Hangover Lead began its southern section with a couple dozen steps heading up the contour of the ridge. Chilled from sweating, I pulled on my rain jacket to shield me from the ruthless wind shooting through the gap from the western side of the wilderness. With no canopy of forest to obscure the sky, I was able to see the sky clearly for the first time since beginning the hike the day before. The rain had not left for long. Referring to the map, I confirmed that the grade of the trail eased but never declined until after the summit of Hangover Mountain a couple of miles away. The half mile from Hangover to the summit of Haoe Mountain was comprised of a series of ups and downs along the ridge top. An uncomfortable realization seeped into my mind; I was not physically prepared for the challenge of the weeklong trip I had planned that would lead me along the ridges above the wilderness and back out the way I entered.

I decided I would be wise to abandon the hike. After months of sedentary office work and an inconsistent running routine, I was not in good enough condition to complete the circuit I planned, but I was determined to return. The short route back to my car would have been retracing Hangover Lead north to Ike Branch Trail, but I could not face the steep climb out of the gap up to Cold Spring Knob, so I decided to follow the easy downhill grade of the gravel forest service road. With all of its switchbacks, the distance would be longer but not as demanding on my aching body.

The dogs and I started a carefree stroll down the road. Hiking through late fall woods, the trees held plenty of autumn color despite leaf season having passed its prime a week or so earlier. My body remained painfully fatigued, but the downhill and switchbacks offered relief. At one point, I smelled a terrible stench like a garbage dump, the sweet, pungent, sour odor of decay. Not the decay of a dead animal, the stale rot of trash. I had heard that bears could smell that bad. Stopping, I listened carefully for any sounds in the woods before deciding that the bear, if that is what it was, had passed ahead of us and was on its way wherever bears go when they are out wandering.

We stopped for lunch across from a sign pointing the way to "Confederate Graves." An unmarked side trail led to the graves of two brothers who had fought in the Confederate Army. There was another grave marked but unidentified on a small wooded knoll which extended toward Bear Creek between two abandoned fields. I suppose there had been a homestead on the site many years previous. Folks tended to bury their kin close by.

The dogs and I relaxed in the grassy cemetery on the knoll, drank some water, and cooled in the shade, while I once again reviewed the map. Near the cemetery, a jeep track entered the forest. If I could find the entry point, the track eventually connected with a foot trail that wound along the side of the ridge and ultimately exited at Tapoco, the small village built by Alcoa Aluminum to house its employees when building the Cheoah Dam. It would be an ideal shortcut bypassing the forest service road as well as the highway. On the other hand, bushwhacking carries risks; you never know what conditions await you, and you are traveling an unused route. If you have an accident, you are very much alone. As I had experienced in Linville Gorge, short cuts should be avoided. Still, I mentally committed myself to trying the old jeep trail. After all, the dogs were with me.

A couple hundred yards farther down the road, I came to the Orr Cemetery which was marked on the USGS topo map. As I studied the map, I saw that I should already have reached the jeep track to Tapoco, so I backtracked keeping a closer eye on any sign of a track leaving the gravel road. After recrossing the bridge over Bear Creek, I looked into the woods below the road and saw an old overgrown jeep track.

My feet cramped badly as I started down the leaf-covered path. I was not positive that it was the correct route and was further confounded when faced with a choice of three trails or tracks after I crossed a rotten bridge. It had been many years since anyone had used the trail. Weeds, briars, and saplings choked the trail, and I again questioned whether I had made a poor choice of route. Even on the map, this was an area where it appeared no one traveled. If I became lost or injured, no one would happen by and help me out. No matter how loudly I might yell or whistle, no one would hear me on the backside of a ridge a thousand feet above the Cheoah River and a few miles from the highway. Any noise I might make would die swiftly in the thick woods. I was alone.

The trail tightened against the ridge face, one side straight up and one side steeply down to a cascading creek. The benefit to this was that I could not get lost on this section as the trail only went where I could hike. It had been cut into the side of the ridge long ago, so I could not accidentally wander off on an animal trail or some other imaginary path through the trees. Nonetheless, the longer I hiked in the dark shadows of the forest, the more solitude I felt, the more exposed. My feet hurt worse and worse, my left foot cramping every time the ball of my foot landed on a small rock.

I had always believed in the wisdom of having a backup plan, but deep in this unvisited woods, I had none. I had to find the way to Tapoco to be able to exit and return to my car. Sure, I could have backtracked, but I feared getting lost on the return trail since the route never looks the same when you turn around. I was glad to have the dogs with me. I could talk to them, and they never told me how foolish I was. The dogs lifted my spirits as happy companions. They thought nothing of getting lost.

As the sun dimmed in late afternoon, I thought about the practicality of setting up camp on the rough trail. I had what I needed though my water supply was low, and the creeks were far below me on the steep mountain face. As if checking the map would bring me closer to my destination, I reviewed it frequently. I had been hiking off the forest service road for almost two hours. I should have been close to intersecting with a jeep track that ran up the mountain to a reservoir above and behind Tapoco. Without knowing how clearly marked or overgrown that trail might be, I worried that I could hike past it without noticing just as I had first missed the jeep trail itself. But I kept moving, aching back and sore legs, famished, but determined to get out before nightfall.

And then I could see a cabin through the trees a hundred yards or so ahead of and below me. As I approached the resort, more cabins came into view, then a tennis court and an asphalt drive. I had reached Tapoco.

The Hike to Naked Ground: Part Two

My plan for the trip with Mark and Joe called for camping the first night at Bob Stratton Bald, a mile high grassy pasture with unbroken views all around. The Bald is just less than a mile from Naked Ground, the ridgeline above

Slickrock Creek drainage. I intended to wake early to photograph the snow-covered Bald, the blinding white of the surrounding mountain ranges, and the brilliant clarity of the winter sunrise. The forecast conflicted with my plans. With a potential blizzard rolling in, there would not be a sunrise, just a pale gray veil of snow falling in muffled silence. Because photography was not an option, we decided to camp at Naked Ground, four miles from the trailhead, for the first night. Another part of the plan was to drop into the Slickrock Creek drainage and follow the continuous series of switchbacks to the bottom of the drainage, then follow the creek until we intersected with the Big Fat Gap Trail. Having identified the trail out, we hoped to hike to Wildcat Falls, camp, and hike out of the basin Sunday morning.

The plan seemed feasible until we reached Naked Ground.

We arrived at Naked Ground about four in the afternoon and set up camp in a flat open space near where the trail should descend to Slickrock Creek. We could not find a sign for the trail north into the drainage. The snow fell quiet and steady. In four hours of hiking, four inches had accumulated on the ground. With a storm overhead, nightfall was less than thirty minutes away. We dropped our packs against a fallen tree, and all agreed we should camp there for the night and check the conditions in the morning. The snow was falling faster than the sign at the trailhead had forecast, so we acknowledged we might be abandoning our plans when we woke. Joe lit the stove for tea while Mark and I pitched the tent.

By the time the tent was erected, all of our gear was smothered in snow. While Joe boiled pasta, I dusted off the gear and passed everything except the empty packs to Mark inside the tent. By nightfall, we were sitting cozily in the tent with our bootless feet warm inside our sleeping bags. As we ate pasta and sipped hot tea, we discussed weather, women, and work, in that order.

My wife and daughter were at home in Atlanta watching the weather reports and wondering what conditions we encountered in the mountains. Before I left home, I had checked the probability of a rare decent snow in Atlanta because it would be my daughter's first, and I did not want to miss playing with her the first time she saw our yard covered in white. The forecast called for a slight chance of up to four inches but declared a snow event unlikely. My daughter's second birthday was just two weeks away.

Mark and Joe were both single. Mark's girlfriend was traveling in Florida; Joe was, as usual, between relationships. I had met Joe during my first year of grad school. He hosted and self-catered a champagne brunch at his apartment. His true dream was to be a chef, but his ancestry dictated otherwise. He invited several grad students from our department, none of whom knew each other very well. During grad school and the years that followed, we became the best of friends. Although we visited infrequently, I knew I could depend on him, a trust he had proven more than once. Mark and I worked together at a real estate company. I trusted him implicitly having known him almost as long as I had known anyone, including Joe.

Dinner complete, it was still early in the evening and snow continued unabated.

"I'm not worried about snow load. This Moss tent is designed to handle that. Nor do I think the wind will be an issue; even though the forecasts predicted winds in the blizzard could reach sixty miles per hour, the tent should handle it. And we have not had much wind so far anyway. The guy at the gas station said maybe a foot; no big deal." I tried to reassure. "Remember, even the sign at the trailhead said '*up to* 12 inches'."

We talked and talked as the flat darkness of the snowy night settled around us. We tried to sleep. The Wilderness was perfectly silent except for the occasional subdued rustle of leaves when the wind rushed down from the north, channeled up the basin onto the ridge and through the trees covering Naked Ground. Snow continued to fall.

The Blizzard

The blizzard began about two in the morning. At least that is when I awoke to the howl of wind rushing through the forest. The wind surrounded us. From the droning sky to the wavering treetops to slamming the fly of our tent, all the noise of the storm stirred together into one cacophonous rage.

Although we slept, we remained restless. Everyone pretended to sleep when they were not. Snuggling deeper and deeper into our sleeping bags, we fought the sound of cold outside by burrowing into the warmth inside. The tent seemed to be closing in on us. I pushed one arm to my left and felt the weight of snow against the tent wall. Without effect, I tried to push the snow away from the inside then finally crawled out into the storm and gloom to clear the snow from the sides of the tent. The blowing snow blinded me, so I worked mostly by feel. I held my watch to my face. It was 4:00 AM, and the snow had piled up to the height of my calf, at least a foot higher than when we turned in. I scooped a small trench around the tent fly before hurrying back inside.

"Everything is fine, but there is a lot more snow, a lot more than forecast. And the snow is still falling hard. We are in a blizzard for sure. We might as well plan to return to the trailhead first thing in the morning. Aside from the wind, the weather is not horrible, not too cold, but there is no way we can safely hike into the basin, so we should hike out the way we hiked in."

Mark and Joe concurred, and we all tried to sleep until sunrise, whatever it might look like.

At first light, a slight brightening of the dull gray pall of the blizzard, I stuck my nose out the back of the tent. Gray. Nothing but shades and gradations of gray. Trees were darker gray; snow was lighter gray. There was not a hint of sunlight piercing the cloud cover. Even the sound was gray, neither noise nor silence, just the constant murmur of the blizzard swirling around us. I took a photo. Muted monochromatic morning snow.

Once again the snow was deeper than when I had checked a few hours earlier. We discussed our situation and agreed that conditions were more serious than before. We considered waiting for the storm to break. The forecast, that we could now believe was more accurate than not, had called for the blizzard to last 24 hours. We would be trapped where we were until the next morning if we waited for a clearing. It was not a bad option. We had fuel and food and water. But we knew we were only four miles from the trailhead. The hike in had taken four hours, so the hike out, which would be mostly downhill, should not take more than six to eight hours.

We discussed the options for an escape route. Continuing into the basin, if we could find the trailhead north, and following Slickrock Creek seemed the shortest and most direct route. Would the snow along the creek be shallower than on the ridge? Or should we retrace the ridge trail? We would not be able to follow our tracks in due to the depth of new snow, but we had come that way so should find it more familiar than breaking new trail down by the creek. In truth, none of us had confidence that the creek route would have less snow than the ridge route. More importantly, we realized that our chances of rescue were higher if we stayed on the ridge where we might be seen from the air.

Nevertheless, rescue seemed unlikely. Given the amount of snow and the severity of the blizzard, surely any rescue would need to come by ground, on foot. And no one would attempt that during the storm when we were still not overdue. We had to extract ourselves. We had to get out that day. We had to get out by ourselves. No one could help us.

The stark and empty solitude of that last thought hit hard. All of us were concerned and anxious. We remained warm, well-equipped, had plenty of food, fuel, clothing, and winter rated sleeping bags. Still, we were very much alone, deep in a remote wilderness, the trailhead four miles away and seven miles from a paved road that connected to Robbinsville, the closest town at fifteen miles down the highway. Our only option was to return to the vehicles at Big Fat Gap where we had more gear and more supplies, then wait until the snow melted enough for us to drive off the mountain. It had been snowing eighteen hours straight, and the snow now reached above my knees. Even if we reached the trailhead, we would be stuck for days.

"Anyone there?" called a voice from outside the tent.

"A ranger!" Excited, I thought, if someone had managed to hike in, surely they could lead us out.

"Yes. Who's there?" I looked out the flap. A man and a German shepherd stood like shadows in the woods.

"Be there in a minute," I called while putting on my boots and coat.

I trudged through the snow and harsh winds to meet Dick and his dog Jester. Dick explained that they had camped at Stratton Bald, and the winds had collapsed his tent, so they had come down at first light. He was understandably shaken.

"I passed your tent on my way up last night. The storm is much worse than I anticipated so I wondered if I could hook up with you guys to help break trail. I know I cannot make it back to my truck alone."

"Sure. Where'd you park?"

"In Joyce Kilmer. I came up Jenkins Meadow Trail from the south."

"We parked at Big Fat Gap. But we'll give you a ride to Kilmer when we can get out. We have a couple of four wheel drives, but this snow is mighty deep."

"I have a case of beer in the back of my truck if you'd give me a ride over there."

"Sounds good, but we'd give you a ride anyway. Assuming we can get ourselves out."

Jester nuzzled Dick's leg, then curled up on the snow beside an oak tree and was quickly covered. I told Dick our plan to strike camp inside the tent as much as possible to keep our gear dry. Joe called out that tea was ready, and we gave a cup to Dick. He sat against the oak where Jester had curled and changed his socks, exposing his feet to the frigid wind so that his socks would be dry. His face was hollow and haggard from his experience in the storm overnight. I could only imagine what he must have felt, alone as his tent collapsed in the winds. It was obvious the storm had scared him.

The storm blew on. Snow and snow and snow, falling, swirling, smothering the landscape. The wind stiffened with increasing velocity. It slapped us like the hand of a hard and bitter foe. I stamped around outside the tent trying to keep my body warm as I passed packs inside to Mark and Joe for them to load. Other than cold feet and numb toes, I was doing pretty well and anxious to get moving. Once we began hiking, all of us would feel warmer. All of us would feel more in control of our fate.

As soon as Mark and Joe had loaded the packs, they crawled out of the tent and into the blizzard. We hurried to strike the tent, working so quickly that we tore stakes from the ground and ripped the tent fly in the process. It was past time for us to be gone from there. We stuffed the tent in my pack, strapped our packs on, and called to Dick.

"Look, it took us four hours to get here from Big Fat Gap, but now we have to break trail through deep snow. We need to plan on a longer hike out, say six hours at least, even though the trail is mostly flat to downhill."

It was after ten in the morning. Packing up had taken longer than it should have. With a late start, everyone shuffled swiftly through the snow as we headed for the trail. The trail was nowhere that we could see. We knew there were no blazes because Slickrock is designated wilderness area. The few trail signs we had passed were wooden and marked trail junctions. The short wooden posts would doubtless be buried in snow now. We studied the woods for evidence of a trail, any opening in the tree cover, any avenue of hardwood trunks, a pathway through rhododendron. Nothing appeared. We plodded single file through knee deep powder snow until it got deeper. The lead hiker broke trail, pushing aside as much snow as his mass could displace. The rest of us followed, the last man having the benefit of everyone else's busting trail. It can be a good way to conserve energy by sharing the burden among the group.

(None of us owned snowshoes. Few people in North Carolina do because heavy deep powder snow is rare; most often, the snow is wet and no more than a few inches deep and quickly forms a frozen crust. I later learned that even the local Sheriff's Department only owned one pair.)

We tried to follow the ridge by keeping the drop into Joyce Kilmer on our right, to the south. We weaved and meandered seeking shallower snow but found none. We walked on the tops of shrubs and low branches to avoid the deepest snow. Joe took the lead. We waded into thigh deep snow, then crotch deep. Thigh deep required a sustained effort; crotch deep was simply impossible as we could not muster sufficient force to push the snow aside. With dry powder snow, there was no resistance to support our weight or our attempts to push forward. We might as well have been trying to slog through a soupy mud hell in a Southern swamp, or even quicksand. Joe held his hiking stick in both hands stretched out ahead of his torso and kind of hopped on top of the snow. He started crawling on his hands and knees. The rest of us followed, breaking off small limbs to mimic his tactic. The sticks did not prevent our hands from sinking into the soft snow or our knees from sagging, but we muddled forward, partly by lurching over the surface.

The spastic motion of hopping with hands and shimmying to bring our knees and legs along worked better than trying to walk, but we were immediately exhausted. Worse, we sweated, inviting hypothermia. To make progress, the key was not stopping. However, we tired so quickly maintaining the odd contortions above the surface that we seized every spot that the snow might be shallower as an excuse to stand, walk, and wade. Each step into crotch deep snow threatened to hold me where I stood because I could not lift one leg high enough to clear the snow and lost my balance trying as I could not lift my second leg to carry me forward. Often I fell backwards as if knocked off my feet by my backpack. More than once I called Dick to help me stand back up from where I lay on my back below the snow like a turtle trapped on its shell.

He could pull me forward to bring me upright. Then I would spring onto the top of the snow and move in a quick scrambling crawl, breathing heavily, struggling to maintain my delicate and precarious balance on top of the powder, knowing that if I slowed, I would sink. Fearing that if I sank, I might not be able to recover, feeling that I might become trapped in a suffocating pit of downy snow.

Snow fell furiously in flakes and clusters, silent and deepening. The blizzard slammed the ridge, blast after blast of hurricane force wind. We pushed across the winds, hoods cinched close around our faces, noses numb. Much of the time, we could see each other yelling as if only mouthing the words. The winds swept sounds into the distance. When Mark turned to try to hear what I said, I saw a patch of translucent skin on his windward cheek. I said nothing because nothing could be done right then. But I knew that it meant the weather was taking a greater toll than we had yet recognized. We struggled on.

Pushing, crawling, digging, pulling. We walked on the low branches of mountain laurel and stepped on thickets of briars. Sometimes it helped; sometimes not. We tired. After toiling for a couple of hours, we stopped to drink water and chew energy bars we had carried inside our shirts to keep them from freezing. Our exhaustion was complete, our minds cloudy, our analysis unreliable.

Time and again impassable drifts or dangerously steep terrain blocked our chosen route. We tried to stay as close as possible to where we thought the trail should be, but snow completely altered the terrain we otherwise might have recalled and often obscured our view, so we repeatedly attempted alternate routes to dodge obstacles. We identified no landmarks from our hike in. It became difficult to remember where we had come from or remain focused on where we were heading.

"Where do you think we are? How far have we come this morning?"

"Let me check the map again. I'm pretty sure we have not reached Haoe Mountain yet."

The trail back to Big Fat Gap broke off the Naked Ground Trail at Haoe Mountain. There had been short markers there that showed the junction with Hangover Lead. No one doubted that the markers would be buried by now. The map was anything but conclusive. We were convinced that we had not passed the mountain because we had not sensed reaching even its moderate summit. Nor had we slipped around the summit or headed off down one of a few spur ridges that led eastward. Still, nothing was certain, especially with our increasingly confused thinking. We collectively retraced the topo lines, matched the compass to our direction, and remained unsure.

We muddled onward, shuffling, wading, and crawling up, down and across the ridge foot by arduous foot. Mark took the lead to spell Joe.

"Damn it, Mark. Find the shallow snow. Look for where the wind may have blown it thin. This crawling is too slow and tedious," I yelled, frustrated, not angry with Mark, anxiety surfacing.

Mark was the strongest of us. He broke trail until he was beyond exhausted. Joe alternated the lead when he saw Mark faltering. I had only my wool pants and gaiters to protect my legs, so I navigated. Dick was, as he had told us, unprepared for this much snow, so he kept to the rear with Jester. Luckily, Joe is compulsive and carried in two sets of shell gear. Who knows why? No backpacker I know would have carried so much extra weight. But Joe did, and Mark needed it as he and Joe continually broke trail.

Following the team breaking trail does not make the trail easy; it makes it possible. With the powdery snow, every displacement by the first guy quickly filled the furrow he cut almost full. The second guy got a small unnoticeable advantage, and even the last man in line still had to force his way through with tiring exertion. Meanwhile, the snow fell and fell. Wind whipped, slapped, pushed, and shoved. We tumbled and groped and crawled as best we could. The air and sky continued to be shades of white and dull gray. We squinted through eyes stung by blowing snow and eyelashes thickly crusted with frozen ice. My nose hurt, my temples ached, and my skin felt raw with the sharply penetrating winds of the blizzard's gusting winds. Although my hands would warm with the effort of clawing through deep powder, my toes were simply numb; no pain, no feeling at all.

Suddenly, a ten foot high drift blocked our path, the ridge falling away steeply to either side. We could only go over the drift. One by one, we clawed, scrambled, slid, and climbed to the top of the drift. Then Joe gave out.

"We need to dig in. Let's just dig in," Joe said flatly, his eyes focused on nothing, his expression empty.

I saw the fire disappear from his eyes. Exhausted, I watched him drop his pack. I turned to Mark. "Joe's in trouble," I yelled above the storm.

Mark replied, "Yeah, but we really need to press on. We've got to keep moving."

I agreed. We looked ahead for the next section of trail and found nothing passable. I went back to check on Joe. Dick was resting beside him on the downwind side of the drift, out of the howling wind as much as they could be. Snow continued to pile higher as the blizzard raged on. Joe's eyes were lifeless. Dick was too quiet, too pensive, withdrawn into himself. I could see all of us deteriorating, passing a tipping point beyond which we might not be able to help ourselves or each other, including me. Our exit hike had become far more severe than we expected. In the relentless storm, we remained exposed and cold and tired. We needed more than energy bars for fuel, a long rest, and a break from the weather.

It was four o'clock. We had been hiking five and a half hours and still were not sure where we were. We should have reached Haoe Mountain and started down Hangover Lead toward Big Fat Gap, but we had not yet found the mountain summit. We hoped we had just overlooked it as we slipped around onto the northern slope and connected with Hangover Lead without being able to identify it as such. But that seemed unlikely. Equally disconcerting was the possibility that we had overshot the summit and proceeded down the western slope of the mountain, a roadless area that would not lead us out.

Mark and I studied the map again. There was one section of the trail between Haoe and Naked Ground where the trail traversed a very narrow ridge where the ridge fell steeply to each side. In fact, we remembered hiking that section the day before because we commented on how stunning the view would have been if not for the snow and clouds. It had to be the very spot where we stood beside the drift. High winds updrafting on both faces of the ridge could have formed the tall drift we encountered. We argued that it could not be the same location because that section was only a half mile from Naked Ground. Surely we had covered more than half a mile in five hours. In five hours, we should have been within a mile or so of the gap, our destination. Together, we scoured the map and the topo lines for other patterns farther down the mountain that would match our location. Nothing.

"Joe, c'mon!, Let's get moving."

"No. We really need to dig in, dig a snow cave and wait out the storm," Joe reasoned.

"Snow cave?" I was puzzled. Although I did not have the experience digging snow caves that Joe had gained hiking in the Cascades in Washington state, I wondered to myself how we could dig a cave in fresh dry powder. "No, Joe. We keep moving and look for a good site for the night." I knew a good flat site was a dream as we had not seen any open areas big enough for two tents since we left our original site. "Joe, let's get off this exposed ridge. We'll find a good camp. We promise to stop at the first decent site we find, but we have to leave here now," I tried to convince him.

At that moment, Mark called from up ahead, "Over here."

Mark had ventured onto the ridge face and discovered an exposed area that had been partly scoured of snow by the winds hammering into the ridge. We eased out onto the crusty surface, an easy walk if we were careful with our footing so we did not slip, and traversed into deeper snow.

A large outcropping of rock topped the ridge, so we stayed below the crest, searching always for the shallow snow and careful not to wander too far away from the trail down the face of the ridge. Getting lost in the trackless woods of the creek basin could have been deadly. We stayed high because we were confident of finding our way back to the trailhead if we kept to the ridges; there was also the unspoken hope of positioning ourselves to be rescued.

Once again, we found ourselves in deeper snow. With the blizzard still blowing, deep snow was unavoidable. We were too tired to continue crawling. We were too tired to keep our balance as we sank into powdery snow above our knees. The invisible sun began to set, the forest darkening. Night would settle over us early in the storm. We needed to find somewhere to camp.

We continued below the rock formation at the top of the ridge, fighting with waning energy to cross the face. We could see that the ridge face steepened. To avoid the exposure, we would have to climb back to the crest through the deeper snow or risk a long slide down the steeper section of the face. Two poor choices.

"Maybe we can camp here."

"Where? There's nothing remotely level."

"We can dig a platform in the snow."

"Yeah. And build a snow wall to windward to protect the tents a bit."

"OK?" Everyone nodded though with little enthusiasm. Too fatigued to craft a different plan, all of us embraced this one. "OK. Let's get going. Our light is dropping fast, and this will take some work."

We dumped our packs uphill and started digging and pushing snow with sticks, hands and feet. The soft dry snow moved easily, but everyone was tired beyond their limit. We pushed and stamped, packing the powder as best we could, until we had a flat space just barely long and flat enough to pitch two tents. Though we thought nothing of it at the time, Dick tellingly positioned his tent with the entry fly facing away from us.

Joe dug a small shelf for the stove and began the laborious process of lighting the stove to melt snow for dinner, tea, and water. Snow dislikes boiling, so it first must melt enough to melt the snow above it. Making water from snow takes patiently feeding snow into the pot steadily as it begins to melt. A pot of snow yields about a quarter pot of water. Joe persevered to first light the stove in the cold and strong winds, then make tea and dinners before melting enough snow for water. The storm never abated.

Mark and I pitched our tent then helped Dick finish pitching his, the winds rushing up the ridge slapping the loose ends of our tents which threatened to kite away. Tent stakes were useless in the soft snow, and no one had any snow stakes, so we buried deadmen and tied a line to a small tree. The result was sloppy but secure. With the wind wall in place, we had decent shelter from the ongoing blizzard.

The tent offered good protection despite not being taut. All day we had struggled against the snow and steep terrain along with wind so strong that we expected it to knock us down. All physical effort had been challenging. No one could feel their toes any longer. Fingers moved stiffly and constantly ached with cold, nearly useless as anything but paws for crawling over the snow. Every two or three steps, we had had to catch our breath before pushing through the deep snow. Now we rested in the cramped gear-filled space of a poorly pitched tent, grateful that it seemed ten degrees warmer than out in the storm. We took pleasure watching the warm and moist steam of our breath rising and condensing into a frosty film on the inside of the tent.

We turned in early, alternating feet to head. It was my turn in the middle, my head at the back of the tent, my butt in a hole, and my back resting on packs and coats as if slumped in a recliner. We lit a candle for comfort, not heat. And then I slept, warm and secure between my friends, exhausted but safe.

Our Situation Changes

During the night, the blizzard passed. The winds eased but did not cease. When we woke at 7:00, we assessed our situation. Should we wait for the clouds and fog to clear so we could verify our position even though we would lose valuable travel time? Or should we rely upon our belief in where we thought we were, push on, and risk becoming truly lost? We all agreed that we must verify our position before we attempted to move. Although our camp would be almost impossible for anyone to spot, continuing without knowing our position would be more dangerous and, perhaps, deadly. Becoming lost was our greatest risk and our greatest fear.

Joe started the stove for tea and breakfast while Mark and I studied the map. From outside the tent, Joe reported that the weather remained overcast with occasional breaks in the clouds. He could not see Haoe Mountain or the ridge that Hangover Lead followed. But he saw small openings of blue sky.

All of our gear was damp or frozen. The condensation that had frosted the ceiling of the tent had shed onto the sleeping bags then thawed from our body heat. Mark's toes were hard and cold to the touch and slightly purple with the beginnings of frost bite.

In the gusting winds, Joe struggled for more than half an hour to light the stove. Mark and I called over to Dick's tent to see how he and Jester had fared the night. Dick replied that they had been okay during the night, but he was concerned about his feet. He also reported that his socks were frozen into his boots; he had already tried urinating on the socks to thaw them. I offered Dick a couple of heat warmer chemical packs rather than waste fuel melting water to pour into the boots.

Then Dick asked, "Does anyone know anything about frostbite?"

"A little. Why?"

"My toes look pretty bad, but I don't know if it's frostbite."

"I'll come over and take a look," I replied. Turning to Mark, I whispered, "This could be real trouble."

I pulled on my boots and maneuvered my way to the front of Dick's tent. I handed him the chemical packs, and he showed me his frozen boots and socks. It would be impossible for him to put the boots on with the socks frozen inside. I tried to rip the socks out, but they might as well have been glued inside. Then Dick stuck one foot out the tent flap. It was horrific. Raw, bloody patches with a blister on his big toe the size of his toenail, and the edges of his toes all a purple shade of black. Frostbite.

"Yep, they're pretty bad. Probably early stage frostbite. If you take care of them, you might prevent it from getting a lot worse," I downplayed the severity to try to encourage and not alarm him.

Meanwhile, Joe, with speechless determination, had finally overcome both the wind and the stove to boil water for tea and a breakfast of freeze-dried chicken and rice. He crawled back inside the tent to eat and warm his body and fingers, all numb from sitting on the snow and working the stove.

Mark, Joe and I reviewed our situation once more, this time in whispers so that Dick would not panic. We had to move if possible. We could not and should not move until we verified our location. We were concerned that the condition of Dick's feet and boots might prevent him from moving anywhere. We did not discuss what we would do if Dick could not hike. But each of us thought how scary it would be to leave one of the three of us behind to care for Dick. Whoever stayed would be handicapped by a person who could not help themselves. The two who tried to hike out would face the increased challenge of breaking trail without others to assist. If the two who left failed to reach the trailhead, the two who stayed might not be found before running out of fuel (therefore water) or food. As best we knew, we had made only half a mile in five hours, so we remained three and a half miles from the trailhead, at least four days' hike unless trail conditions improved.

Up to that moment, we had battled the snow which was mostly a battle of endurance. Given enough time, we thought we would find the trail and return to the cars at the trailhead. Given enough time, we would be able to drive the cars down the Forest Service trail to the highway with four-wheel drives engaged and moving cautiously around the frequent switchbacks. However, with Dick's frostbite, a new challenge emerged.

Did we have time? Dick's feet were in bad shape and would continue to worsen until we could get him out of the snow. Was having time sufficient? If Dick could not hike, one of us would have to remain behind to assist him. It was precisely the kind of unanticipated change that could transform a challenge into a tragedy. The two who went for the trailhead might succeed, but they would not be able to deliver or send aid or supplies to whoever stayed behind. Food, water, and warmth would slip away with the passing of time as the two waited for rescue. Even if two of us reached the trailhead at Big Fat Gap, we did not know if we could get the cars to the highway or if the highway was passable. There was no cell service.

What we knew was that we all should be okay if we stayed together. Leaving two behind would complicate our situation without improving our safety. Still, Mark, Joe, and I knew we faced the possibility of Dick not being able to hike or help himself. We could not leave him alone. For the first time, I felt true fear, the fear of failing, of not being able to retreat safely, of putting two dear friends into a situation that had taken a dreadful turn. I had a choking fear of losing what bit of control I believed I still retained.

For the first time I cried. As I tried to explain what time my wife expected me, I was overcome by the anguish and fear she would feel when we did not return. I also thought about my daughter growing up without a father and being too young to retain even memories of me. For her, it would be as if I never existed. Even though I was well, my wife would not know that and might easily imagine that we were trapped and dying or dead. I knew she would call for help; I did not know then that she had called for help the day before because the storm was so much worse than forecast.

(The forecast had called for "up to four inches" in Atlanta. More than eight inches closed down the city. Houses in neighborhoods near ours lost power, but for some reason ours did not. Before I left home, Beth had given me a casual fedora, mainly as a fishing and dayhiking hat. I decided to leave it behind because it would not be as warm as a toboggan. As Beth worried about conditions in the mountains and talked on the phone frequently with her parents as well as mine, Taylor periodically picked up the hat and said "Daddy hat." Beth hid her tears. Worried about our safety since the storm had exploded, Beth also wondered if she and our daughter would see me again. My mother made travel plans to be in Atlanta in case we did not get out of the mountains by Monday. She thought she should be with Beth if I was not coming home. Both Beth's father, Harry, and mine called the local sheriff's department urging use of helicopters and rescue teams. Each told the sheriff they were on the way to help. The sheriff dissuaded them. "You can't get here; the roads are closed. Even if they weren't, there is no way you could get into the backcountry. Stay home. We'll keep you updated.")

"Dick, are you having any luck with your boots?"

"I think the boiling water is working." The chemical packs had failed, so Dick lit his own camp stove and boiled water. He used a lot of fuel, but he thawed his socks and boots.

"Well, I guess I better head out and see if I can see any landmarks to confirm our location," I said to Mark and Joe. "I'll only be gone for 15-20 minutes. I'm going to try to backtrack to the knife-edge trail where the big drift was. Then I'll try going past the camp and up to the ridge crest."

I retraced our trail from the previous afternoon, hoping that the packed tracks would make hiking easier and faster. Our footprints were visible, but I still sank to my knees at every step. I was breathing heavily after less than fifty yards, my body weary, aching, and sore from the prior day's effort. Then a cloud lifted, and I could see into the creek basin, the bottom of the wilderness, the stark black tracing of bare trees over the brilliant white of sunlit snow 3,000 feet below. The sight was at once inviting and comforting, as if there was indeed a way out of our cold trap. I turned back toward camp, looking up and above the ridgeline hoping to catch a view of the Haoe summit. It should have been close. As I scanned the distance, the clouds dissolved once more, and there it was, Hangover Lead, the ridge down to the trailhead at Big Fat Gap. It felt near enough to touch though it was not. Quickly, the clouds obscured everything again. The ridge disappeared, and I almost questioned whether I had imagined what I wanted to see. I felt certain I had seen the ridge, but it had been too brief to study it.

Turning back toward camp, I retraced my steps and passed the tents as I climbed to the ridge above us. It was steep, the snow as deep as any we had crossed. I moved from tree to tree as much as possible. I slid over a fallen oak into the branches of a large mountain laurel then waded over to a shallow patch at the base of a rock formation on the ridge crest. There was no clear path, no obvious trail. But it seemed the only way passable. I returned to the tents.

"OK, let's pack up. I saw Hangover Lead. We are exactly where we thought were. We made maybe six-tenths of a mile yesterday, and we definitely have not passed Haoe Mountain summit."

"Could you see the mountain?"

"No, but Hangover Lead ridge looked fairly close."

"Could you find the trail?"

"No. I scouted to the top of the ridge. It'll be tough, but I hope that we can find the way once we reach a group of rocks at the crest. The trail has to be there even if we cannot see it under the snow. I'm sure there are no other options. The ridge gets steeper just past our camp, so we have to get off this face and climb higher."

"Dick, can you travel?"

"Yes, I think so. I know I don't want to stay here. Have you got an extra pair of dry socks?"

"Yeah, and you should put your feet in baggies too. Your problem is that you don't have gaiters or anything to prevent snow filling your boots at your ankles. You need to do all you can to keep your feet dry, plus the baggies will give you a vapor barrier that'll keep them warmer."

We began to load our packs. It was cold in the shade of the north face of the ridge. Occasionally, the clouds would break and a touch of blue sky appear. Everyone was anxious but excited that we would not be waiting in our tents. Packing with stiff, cold, aching fingers hurt and also was frustratingly slow. We hurried to strike camp because it was past 1:00, and we had only a few hours to hike if we made camp before sunset and nightfall. We knew that we could not make it to the trailhead that day, but we wanted to get onto Hangover Lead far enough that we might make the descent the next day.

Just over three miles away once we passed Haoe Mountain, the trail would be largely downhill. With the blizzard past, we counted on being able to double our pace. If we crawled in straight lines instead of seeking shallow patches of snow, we should accelerate our progress. We knew the plan was a long shot, but we chose to believe it was possible.

It was nearly 2:00 before all of us were packed and ready to hike. We edged across the steep face and began to climb. Following my morning route, we scrambled over and through trees and limbs until we reached the rocks at the ridge crest. It looked like a dead end. Jester bumped into Mark and almost bumped him off the crest. The drop into Joyce Kilmer was precipitous; climbing out at that spot would have been impossible without climbing gear. It was enough of a close call to remind all of us how suddenly our situation could change to one of desperation. The incident illustrated clearly how tenuous a line we held between safety and tragedy.

Joe scurried up the snow bound rocks and shouted back a muffled "C'mon." One by one, we lurched onto the rocks in a nearly desperate surge of energy and pulled ourselves through the snow. Joe was crawling under the branches of a rhododendron thicket.

What a breakthrough! Finally, we stood atop the ridge and could identify the trail. The snow remained too deep to hike casually, but it was beautiful, pristine, and stretched across a small summit woods. We held a straight line crawling toward Haoe Mountain. When we paused for water and trail mix, we thought we heard the thumping rhythm of a helicopter far to the west, but we could see nothing because of the trees. We pressed on.

Joe then explored an opening in the woods to the north and discovered shallower snow where we could actually walk for a short while. Knee deep, it offered a needed reprieve from the strenuous crawling of the previous hour. Joe's route led us over the Haoe summit proper until we connected to the trail north to Hangover Mountain. Although the trail signs at the junction were buried, we could see clearly the ridge that ran north to Hangover. The trail cut through a rhododendron hell and dropped steeply into Saddle Tree Gap, another solid landmark from our hike in. We plunged and slid through the hip-deep snow toward the saddle, laughing in the sun like happy skiers heading for the lodge under clear blue skies.

As we rose toward the other end of Saddle Tree Gap, the snow was the deepest we had encountered. At the top, we found a broad open area near a couple of small trees where we had a view of the wilderness to the west including the Slickrock Creek drainage below and the ridge opposite us in Tennessee. We noted that our site was also a good place to be seen if anyone was searching. Although we had been moving for only an hour and a half, we agreed that we should stop and take advantage of a good camp. The route toward the summit of Hangover Mountain was soft deep snow and thick with trees. We needed to dry our sleeping bags and eat a good meal, regain some energy for the next day. If we had continued, we knew were not likely to find a good flat open campsite, we would not be in the sun, and we would not be easily seen. We had decided that rescue needed to be an option.

For thirty minutes, we tramped around the site packing the snow so that we would have a soldi platform on which to sleep and move about. We hung our sleeping bags over the small trees to dry in the late afternoon sun and light breeze. It was about 20 degrees, but the sun was warm, the air clear and dry. We pitched the tents and organized our gear. Joe gain took the lead melting snow for water, tea, and dinner. Mark slipped into his sleeping bag to try to warm his feet. We heard helicopters across the wilderness again but still saw nothing.

Our spirits improved immensely. A fine camp. Good visibility. Spectacular view over most of the wilderness. A bright winter sunset over mountains blanketed with deep snow and forests frosted like a fairyland. Our progress had been better than before. We had covered half a mile in less than two hours. At that pace, the trailhead could be less than ten hours away, a long day. It was possible to reach the vehicles the next day.

Joe had melted three liters of water and rehydrated two dinners when he ran out of fuel. We tried to start Dick's stove to melt more snow for the morning, but his stove would not light. Among the four of us, we had four energy bars, a couple pounds of trail mix, and four bagels. But we could no longer make water, and we would enjoy no more hot meals. We had enough food and water if we reached the trailhead the next day, but only if. Water would be our first problem. With the depth of the snow, making a campfire with wood was not an option. We could not find dry tinder or kindling or any sort of dead wood, all of which was deeply buried.

Nevertheless, all were relieved to be off the north side of the Naked Ground ridge and into the open, into the sun. We were certainly not lost, and we had finally had a taste of progress. With sunset, temperatures dived below freezing. I woke at 2:00 AM shivering in my bag. It was below zero Fahrenheit. I tightened the drawstring at my shoulders, tucked my face inside, curled my knees, and hoped for warm sleep before dawn.

A Cable from the Sky

We woke with the sun. It was 2 degrees.

Mark had slept with the bagels in his sleeping bag to keep them thawed, so we had warm bagels with honey for breakfast. Hot tea would have been ideal, but the bagels beat oatmeal. Mark gave a bagel to Dick and turned around a couple minutes later to see that Dick had dropped the bagel on the ground in front of his tent. Mark was irritated that Dick made no effort to preserve what energy he might have left. Plus, we lacked a surplus of food considering the strenuous challenge that faced us.

Morning was glorious, the sun warm and golden over the mountains to the east and the surrounding snow brilliant once again under blue skies so clear and deep you half expected to see soft points of starlight piercing through.

We promptly started striking camp. Mark and I both told Joe and Dick that we were committed to make our way to the trailhead and cars by the end of the day. It would be difficult to cover three miles in deep powder following a ridgeline with no trail through the rhododendron thickets. But we were unwilling to consider anything less. We emphasized our resolve by explaining that, if we even thought we were close at sunset, we would continue hiking into the night despite the risk. Camping would be our last option.

Dick responded, "If I don't get out today, I will lose some toes." We knew he was probably right but said nothing. He was depressed enough.

"OK. Let's get moving."

"I'm still unable to put on my right boot. I've tried everything except boiling water since we do not have a working stove." Dick looked worried and a bit desperate. As he pushed his foot into the boot, his heel failed to clear even the top edge of the ankle collar. It looked hopeless to the rest of us.

"Just keep trying. We have to get started. We have lots of ground to cover today."

"What's that?"

Everyone stopped to listen. Far to the west came the soft muffled flutter of a helicopter. We scanned the distance, raking the opposite ridges with our eyes, straining to see the source of the sound.

"There, just to the north beyond Stratton Bald!"

A solitary helicopter swept south along the ridge just above the trees.

"Look. There's another one. And another behind that one."

We were ecstatic. Each of us was secretly relieved that we might be rescued but too cautious to assume that the helicopters would pick us up.

"Do you think they are looking for us?"

"I wonder if anyone else is out here."

The helicopters cruised the ridge line, circling and obviously searching.

"What should we do? Signal them?"

"We must signal them. They might be looking for us. Even if they cannot pick us up, we need to let our families know we are alive."

The sun still lay low near the horizon, so anyone in a helicopter who looked in our direction would be looking into the glare of the rising sun.

"How can we attract their attention?"

"Wave your coats. And I have a signal mirror in my emergency kit." Clustered together in the open area on top of the ridge, our arms flailed as we tried to capture the reflection of the sun in the signal mirror.

We do not know what worked, but it only took a few minutes before a helicopter spotted us, turning suddenly nose down and racing toward our position on the gap. Another followed quickly behind, then another.

The first helicopter circled above us until the second, with a red cross, arrived. The second hovered over the ridge thirty yards to the south and dropped a crewman down a cable to the ridge. We could see he was a short man and tried to warn him with hand gestures that he was going to land in an area of drifted snow the depth of which would exceed his height. We waded over to him.

"We're here to take you out. Another storm system is moving in."

"Good. All of us are in pretty good shape except for one guy's toes. He needs attention soon."

The crewman looked past me, then turned and said, "But we cannot take the dog."

"Bullshit! The dog has to go with us. He can't survive out here. What's the problem?"

"We just don't have any way to haul him up."

"We'll think of something, but we have to take him with us."

"OK."

Dick could not, fortunately, hear the exchange. I knew I would never leave my own dog behind, and I was sure Dick would refuse as well.

The helicopter had moved away while we talked. The crewman spoke into his helmet microphone and called the chopper back into position overhead. As the downdraft from the blades buffeted us, a cable lowered the rescue seat, a "penetrator". We shouldered our packs in readiness.

I motioned to Joe to step over to me. "You first."

The crewman jumped past me to retrieve the seat from the drift where it landed. As I extended my hand to help the crewman out of the drift, he yelled to me, "Quick! Now, get on!"

I did not want to be first. I wanted to make sure everyone got up safely, especially Jester. But I was the one closest to the seat, and the Air National Guard was not wasting time. What we did not know at that point was that they had many others to rescue from the backwoods. The crewman struggled to secure a strap around me and my pack. I was unbalanced, my heavy pack pulling me backwards. Once he clipped the safety strap behind me, he had to yell to be heard above the thwacking of the helicopter overhead. "Hold tight. Keep your legs bent under the seat. Make sure they are bent under the seat." I would have appreciated a longer discussion about how the seat worked, what I could expect as I rose up the cable to the chopper, preferably the entire owner's manual so I might feel prepared. No time.

He signaled the helicopter, and the cable tightened. As the seat cleared the snow, I swung into the branches of a small tree. The cable continued to rise, and I tried to push the branches aside without releasing my death grip on the seat post. I bounced off one limb, and the cable lifted me into another. With my left hand, I grabbed the swivel at the top of the post where the cable connected so I would have use of my right hand. Suddenly, my left hand thumb was pinned between the swivel and a limb, the cable still rising, smashing my thumb. For a brief moment I hoped the crew could see how my hand was pinched and might adjust the lift. Nope. Painfully, I snatched my thumb free fearing that it was badly crushed inside my glove, expecting a surge of blood spreading across the glove any moment. I hugged the seat tightly with both arms as the seat broke through the last of the limbs and swung into the top of another tree. I hung snagged in the top of that tree for a moment before breaking loose and starting to spin.

The spinning of the seat accelerated once I broke free. Faster and faster. Rising and spinning and rising and spinning. I could not focus and closed my eyes. The speed of the spin blurred the ground below. I tried not to think but began to feel scared that I would fall. Out of control, I wanted to return to the ground and start again. How could I stop spinning? I needed to be able to see where I was and where I was going. I tried again to open my eyes and instantly felt nauseous and disoriented. The weight of the pack coupled with centrifugal force from the spin pulled me away from the seat post, and my arms weakened with the effort of holding tight. I tried to look away from the ground and focus on the mountains around me but felt sick and feared losing my grip, feared I could hold on no longer, began to consider what falling from a several hundred feet would feel like (of course, I had no idea of our altitude; I just knew everything below looked small). The seat continued to rise; the spinning never stopped, never slowed. I thought about the relief of letting go and falling into the snow, but I held tightly and tried to stop thinking.

After a couple of minutes that seemed like half an hour, the downdraft from the blades of the helicopter washed over me, and I knew I was close. Then I worried how I would cross from the seat hanging on its lifting arm to the helicopter as we hovered hundreds of feet in the air.

The cable stopped. The spinning stopped. I turned to face the open door and the crewman sitting there to swing me in on the pivoting lift arm. He reached past me and closed the door. I was safe.

What Followed

One by one, Joe, Mark and then Dick, holding Jester inside his pack in front of him on the rescue seat, were lifted to safety. The helicopter flew over Big Fat Gap, our trailhead destination. We saw nothing but flat white snow; the cars were completely buried.

The Air National Guard flew us west to the hospital at University of Tennessee-Knoxville where we were the first of more than 150 hikers that they pulled out of Slickrock Wilderness and the adjacent Great Smoky Mountains National Park. No one measured how much snow fell in Slickrock. Mount Mitchell, farther east but almost seven thousand feet high received 52 inches.

Mark and Dick were treated for frostbite.

The hospital staff graciously allowed Jester to stay with Dick while he was in the emergency room. When they moved Dick to his hospital room, they moved Jester to the helicopter hangar where both nurses and crewmen cared for him inside a warm kennel. Hospital staff also called in a veterinarian and fed Jester hamburgers. Jester recovered from his mild hypothermia in a few days. The hospital released Dick in a wheel chair after a week, but he had to be readmitted to hospital when he returned home.

Dick spent ten more days in the hospital before returning home still in a wheelchair. He lost all of his toenails. Doctors performed skin grafts on his toes. It was a month before he could walk.

For Joe, Mark and me, our toes remained numb for the next several months. The skin on our toes, fingers, and nostrils sloughed continually for a couple of months. Fortunately, the translucent patch on Mark's face during the blizzard never presented a problem.

Mark and I tried to fly back to Atlanta, but the flights did not leave until evening, and we were both anxious to return, me to my wife and daughter, Mark to his girlfriend. Realizing that we could drive home faster than fly, we rented a car and departed for Chattanooga. We had heard rumors that Interstate 75 between Chattanooga and Atlanta was closed but did not believe it until we reached the outskirts of Chattanooga where the motels were full despite being without power, and the interstate itself was a parking lot of cars and semis trapped by the storm. Some of the people had been trapped on the interstates so long that the National Guard was dropping food and water from the overpasses. We calculated the math quickly, called Mark's girlfriend (she had not cancelled our flight), and hurried back to Knoxville to catch a plane.

At the airport, I stripped off my underlayers, the smelliest of my clothing, and stuffed them in my pack. We boarded the jet and found our assigned seats. A young woman had the window seat on our row, I had the middle and Mark the aisle. I tried to ignore my malodorous contribution to the seating row; Mark was almost as aromatic, but he was farther from the window. Mark leaned forward while making sure the young woman could hear him and asked me when the doctors said I could bathe again. We both actually felt sympathy for her, but there was nothing we could do, and we were cracking wise as the jet backed away from the terminal.

The Asheville airport was closed due to the blizzard as was Interstate 40 from Knoxville east, so Joe flew to Charlotte to stay with his sister before continuing to Asheville aboard USAir. Because the Asheville airport remained closed the next morning, USAir offered Joe and the other passengers an immediate departure on a ground flight. Sooner sounded better, so he accepted. As the bus departed the airport and pulled onto the interstate, Joe realized, too late, what a "ground flight" is. Adding insult to injury, by the time his bus reached Asheville airport, the airport had reopened and his original flight would have landed.

Two weeks passed before the three of us could return to Big Fat Gap to recover the cars, a week for the snow to melt and a week for the Forest Service to clear more than a hundred trees that obstructed the seven miles of forest service road. Mark and I drove around to Joyce Kilmer to check on Dick's truck. An old hemlock had fallen across the adjacent creek and crushed the truck cap over the rear bed. The case of beer was untouched.

Several months later, as autumn settled over the wilderness and the trees shed all their leaves, Mark and I returned to Slickrock and hiked to Naked Ground to retrace our return route. We could not find the campsite on the north face of the ridge, but we located the camp site in Saddle Tree Gap even though it was nearly unrecognizable. The shrubs on which we had hung our sleeping bags to dry were in fact the tops of trees. And the trees we recalled were more than twice the height we remembered. We realized that the snow in the gap must have drifted 10-12 feet deep during the blizzard. Scouting the route, seeing the ridges without snow, seeing Hangover Mountain without clouds, we admitted to each other that we likely would not have made it back down to Big Fat Gap. The forgotten and invisible obstacles were greater than we had thought.

It was 2001 before I learned the full scope of the storm named "the Blizzard of 1993", "the Superstorm of 1993", and the "Storm of the Century". My father-in-law stumbled onto the National Geographic documentary of the storm on the TV and called us. In addition to the snow in the mountains, storm conditions affected every state on the east coast. The winter cyclone produced the lowest pressures ever recorded inland. Homes on both the Gulf coast and the Atlantic coast were destroyed by high winds and storm surge. Reportedly, 270 people died.

My Final Attempt

My original objective when I first decided to hike in Slickrock was to complete a ridge-top circuit of the Slickrock Creek basin. In 1997, I planned to take one of my dogs, Ranger, and complete the circuit from Naked Ground past Bob Stratton Bald and down to Slickrock Creek then out to Calderwood Lake. It would make the circuit a three part adventure, but that was fine with me. At least I would close the loop on a dream.

In order to avoid backtracking miles of trail, I hired a retired Forest Service ranger to give me a ride from my car where I parked it once again beside Calderwood Lake to the trailhead that would lead me up the south face to Naked Ground. Jim Burchfield had been with the Forest Service for 32 years and had cut many of the wilderness trails. His father had worked for Alcoa at the Cheoah Dam (the one from which Harrison Ford leaps in *The Fugitive*, leading Tommy Lee Jones to comment that Ford's character had done "a Peter Pan").

Jim was quiet but proud of his years with the USFS and protective of the wilderness. He urged me to hike the Joyce Kilmer loop trail through a rare remaining cove of virgin timber with poplar trees 400 years old and more than 20 feet in circumference. On the way up the rough road to the Wolf Laurel Trailhead, Jim detoured a short way to show me Swan Cabin at Swan Meadow. The rustic cabin offers no amenities (no power or running water); it is truly a wooden tent, providing only shelter. Nearby are an outhouse and a spring. At the time, it rented for $15 per night and could accommodate ten people. Jim encouraged me to reserve it during the spring when the meadow came alive with wildflowers.

A couple miles farther on FS 81, we came to a dead end turnaround. I put a dog pack on Ranger so he could carry his food, then shouldered my pack and said farewell to Jim. Ranger and I started up the trail. The day was cool but delightfully spring with trees beginning to bud and, down low, wildflowers popping out with fresh colors. We hiked casually up the switchbacks, taking our time with plenty of day left to reach the Bald. When we reached the trail junction with Bob Stratton Bald Trail, the sun seemed to light Naked Ground to the east, so I stopped to look around, to see if I recognized any landmarks such as our blizzard camp site. Among the open hardwoods, there was nothing distinctive, and I did not want to take time looking for the Slickrock Creek trailhead that we never found when we stopped during the blizzard. In the years since our adventure, I had told the story to plenty of people and relived the experience with each retelling. This hike was for me to continue what I began a decade earlier. I did not want to revisit or reevaluate the blizzard. When the Stratton Bald Trail intersected with Haoe Lead Trail, I realized that Naked Ground was not lit by sun, it was lightened by clouds blowing over the ridge on a stiff northerly wind. The trees were frosted with rime ice (hoar frost), a magical winter wonderland, especially on the Frazier firs.

Along the trail west to the Bald, we encountered some fine views over the wilderness basin and beyond into Tennessee. Ranger and I quickly selected an open area facing north on the meadow to set up camp. As soon as the tent was up, I stripped off the cotton short I had foolishly chosen to wear while hiking and stuffed it into a zip lock to prevent it making other dry clothes wet (the next morning, it was frozen). I switched into polypro and fleece and pulled windpants over my shorts. Although the wind on the Bald was mild, it created a wicked chill nonetheless. I fired up the stove and brewed a cup of tea that I enjoyed while walking around the open bald taking photos of the views of ridges and mountains stacked in rows for miles to the horizon. After soup and dinner, we retreated to the tent where we could avoid the wind and mist of blowing clouds. Ranger curled up close beside me, and we slept well if a bit chilly.

The meadow sparkled with frost just as I had imagined on our 1993 trip. Bright mountains ignited with the fire of sunrise. A gusting breeze chilled us more than the 20 degree air temperature. I fed Ranger, chewed an energy bar and sipped on hot tea while I struck camp. We started down the trail about 0915. Although it was not bitter cold, the ground was frozen hard enough that my boots refused to grip, which worried me facing a day of steep descents and inclines along the ridgeline. Of course, the knee-wrecking down sections added to my cumulative pain. Even Ranger had some tough moments as he climbed and slid over fallen trees that he refused to bypass.

Without pushing too hard, we held a good pace and made better time than I had planned. We set out with only one liter of water so I knew we needed to reach Big Stack Gap Branch Trailhead as early as possible. Cruising along the ridge with Slickrock Wilderness (North Carolina) to my right (east) and Citico Creek Wilderness (Tennessee) to my left (west), the trail held the high ground for the most part, meandering among old growth hardwoods, spruce, and poplar. With open woods along the ridge, views across the basin were frequent, and I stopped regularly to take photos. Ranger kept pace, and I hoped he would alert me if we neared any bears. Citico Creek is a bear sanctuary. We were hiking in early spring, and bears might easily be hungry after winter hibernation. I did not forget that neither Ranger nor Sika had alerted me to the mountain hunter on our first trip into Slickrock.

I expected we would need to stop for lunch before reaching Big Stack Gap Branch, perhaps at Glenn Gap or Harrison Gap. Unfortunately, with no trail junctions to mark our progress, one gap blended into another as I enjoyed the hike and the views and the solitude until we came to an intersection with a trail rising from the west. I consulted my map. And it was good that I did. I needed to take a trail due east that I had failed to notice. Fodderstack would go to Big Stack Gap, my intended destination. I realized I had hiked much farther than I thought. Without knowing how much ground I might cover, even downhill, I anticipated that I might only reach the trailhead for Big Stack Gap that day; instead, I was going to reach Big Stack Gap itself by lunch.

We stopped for lunch at a large open site with lots of sun. A fallen tree created a good bench, and there was a fire ring. It was tempting to camp there for the night, but it was only midday, so I dropped my pack, lit the stove, fed Ranger, and enjoyed a leisurely break. We had a good view down the ridge through open woodlands. All was quiet except for the sighing of a light wind swirling through the leafless hardwoods. My heavy pack and fast pace had left me fairly damp with sweat. With sun and a light wind, my synthetic clothing began to dry. I wanted to strip off my shirt and pants, but the wind and altitude were still wickedly cold. Ranger was getting old, so he was quite tired when we stopped and curled up to nap after eating. Both of us rested before setting off down Big Stack Gap Branch Trail toward Slickrock Creek. Two hours later, we had replenished our water supply and made the first two of nine fords across Slickrock Creek, the second of which passed threateningly close to the upper cascade of Wildcat Falls. To wade the swift creek, I removed my boots in favor of sandals (Tevas) with grippy soles.

Slickrock Wilderness had been mostly logged in the early twentieth century. Small gauge rail carried the timber from the upper reaches of the drainage down along the creek to the Little Tennessee River (until Alcoa built Calderwood Dam and flooded the river). The trail along Slickrock Creek was what remained of the old rail bed, a corduroy of dirt where the rail ties once lay. The rails are long gone as are the small bridges that crossed the creek whenever one side of the ridge fell too steeply to the creek to support a railroad. That did not make the trail easy to follow. There are no blazes in wilderness areas, so hiking along the creek was fine so long as there was a trail. But more than once the trail vanished on a steep slab of rock that was soon vertical. Continuing would have required rock climbing gear. When this happened, I had to backtrack until I could find the hint or suggestion of a path on the opposite side of the creek, then wade through small rapids and a rocky bottom to cross. The cold creek was refreshing, and Ranger, a Labrador, was eager to get wet with me.

Not far below Wildcat Falls, we found an enticing wooded camp site beside the creek with just enough sun to help dry gear. On the banks of the creek, moss covered the rocks; the small valley bottom was shaded, cool, and damp with rhododendron and ferns heavy between the trees. It was 60 degrees just before sunset. I pitched the tent and then dried my feet which were cold and shriveled from creek crossings. Slickrock is known for good wild trout fishing so I pulled out my fly rod and fished several pools from the Falls on down past my camp without any luck. Fortunately, I love fishing more than catching. I savor the solitude, the meditative nature of rhythmic casting, the magic of tossing a nearly weightless imitation of a small insect or larvae to temp a fish that often seems smarter than its predator humans. Catching is a pleasant reward, but I would have released any trout caught in those sacred waters anyway.

After dinner, I sat on a rock leaning against a fallen tree trunk and listened to the music of the creek while drinking my tea and writing in my journal, Ranger asleep at my feet.

With the temperature in the tent a bit warmer than outside, Ranger slept well. At 0700, I placed the stove just outside the tent fly and boiled water for oatmeal and coffee. The ridge above me lit with the sun peeking over the eastern ridgeline. I had expected the ridge to block the sun until later in the morning. Because it reached the creek early, I decided to postpone hiking and wait for the air to warm and some gear to dry. I fished a pool downstream at the next ford. Too early and cold for a hatch, I cast for a while over deep crystal clear water until I hung my fly in a tree. When I retrieved my line, I discovered that the flyline had broken just below the nail knot. Despite my confidence that the line would hold the small fish I expected to find in the creek, I packed up the rod and struck camp.

I changed into shorts, tied my boots to my pack, and strapped on my Tevas with the hope of avoiding two footwear changes for each of the remaining seven fords. The next two fords were only 0.4 mile apart; assuming the trail continued to follow the old rail bed, I would have easy walking in my sandals.

I missed the first trail that broke to the right and uphill. Having crossed a deep ford through fast water, I failed to locate a track on the opposite bank of the creek. Looking back across the creek, I spotted the trail downstream from where I stood, so I forded back to where I started and found where the trail descended to creekside. I located the next ford without error and stopped to change into boots for a 1.4 mile leg to the next ford.

Most of the trail followed old rail bed, but much was narrow, rocky, and exposed above the creek. Footing was a constant concern with a heavy pack. At times I would think I had lost the trail only to realize that it continued across the boulders alongside the creek. In other words, there remained no visible track in those sections. Also, had the water been high, the rocks forming the trail would be underwater, the trail invisible, and too slippery to cross safely if wet from rain or fog. The fords were mostly pleasant though sometimes deep and swift. My hiking stick helped me on those crossings. Ranger was in his element, and, despite being tired, he handled the water easily. The day warmed nicely, so even the cold mountain stream was more refreshing than cold.

We reached Lower Falls, a spectacular transparent emerald green pool, just before 1300. The bank of the creek below the falls was a field of large boulders eighty feet to the water, too rough for either me or Ranger to make the scramble down (or back up). So we sat in the middle of the trail with a perfect view of the pool and falls from above and slightly downstream. I dreamed of retuning with mask and fins to swim the pool with color and clarity like the tropics. We rested in the sun and ate a leisurely lunch as the falls droned from the splashing of its cascade with a background of soft winds in the tree tops. Only one ford and 2.8 miles lay before us. We were nearing the end of completing my circuit, closing the loop on my dream. Still shod in my sandals, I hoped that the trail ahead would let me complete the hike without changing into my boots.

What I expected after the final ford was rail bed all the way to Calderwood Lake, then open woodlands with a soft footpath back to the trailhead. My guidebook (Homan's) described the trail as "undulating easily". Nothing in a wilderness area is easy. Once we crossed the final ford, we found the most challenging trail yet. As we had already experienced, trees fall in the wilderness, and trails are rarely, if ever, maintained. This is not the Appalachian Trail with its legions of volunteer Trail Runners scampering over the ridges to clear paths for through-hikers. The trail clung to the side of the ridge as if leaned there for only a moment. Narrow sloping paths high above the creek offered poor footing over slabs angled almost vertically, the exposure serious and unavoidable. On the other hand, wildflowers lined the trail; the small purple and yellow irises were stunning with brilliant color while appearing too fragile to be wild. A break in concentration could result in tripping over a loose rock or root. Ranger tumbled twice trying to clear fallen trees. Both times his slid downhill on soft loamy soil and landed in tangled brush. He needed a hand from me to climb back up to the trail. For both of us progress was unnerving and exhausting, though for me oddly satisfying. I was closing on the end of my loop.

When we passed the junction with Ike Branch Trail, we paused to commemorate finally completing the circuit we began more than ten years before. Ranger (and Sika) had joined me for that first attempt to hike the ridgeline. I had finally finished what I started and seen what I wanted to see, land worthy of the term "wilderness". On this trip, we had not seen another person in three days of traveling miles through the forest, past waterfalls, and along a pristine fast-running creek.

We crossed a sketchy, weathered, and shaky bridge into the woods above Calderwood. A relaxing hike in the shade ended the trip without drama. I had had more than my share of that in Slickrock and celebrate the memories.

SEA

SAILING to JAMAICA

PROLOGUE: MY FATHER'S STORY

My father was out of town at a business meeting when one of the men told him the following story.

*   *   *   *   *

This kid is walking along the dock in Beaufort and meets two guys from Bermuda who have stopped for provisions before leaving for an open ocean passage to Miami. The kid starts talking with these guys, and they tell him they are delivering a sailboat to Jamaica. The kid says he has always wanted to sail offshore, and they ask him if he wants to join them; they just lost their third crewman and needed a third.

The kid says he wants to go, then calls his parents, tells them where he is leaving their car parked and says he will call them whenever they next stop at a port. The parents ask about the Bermudans; he tells them their names are Earl and Paddy and the ship is named *Eliza* out of Connecticut, bound for Miami before crossing to Jamaica by way of the Bahamas. Then he is gone.

It is two days before the parents hear anything; they are relieved to receive a collect phone call from Southport. Their son has laid over there for a couple of days and needs clothes and all the things he did not have with him when he suddenly decided to jump on a boat when he had only gone to the coast for the day to surf.

The parents throw some clothes, books and a camera into his backpack and drive a few hours down to a marina near Southport.

When they arrive at the marina, they begin looking for their son, but do not know where the sailboat is berthed or what it looks like. They walk down a dock looking into the companionway of each boat for their son.

"Mother! Father!" The son waves to them from a few boats down the dock.

The parents look, and there is their son sitting in the cockpit of a white-decked, blue-hulled ketch with two black men; one short, trim and athletic, the other almost six and a half feet tall, big like a pro football lineman. They try to keep the shock they feel from showing on their faces as they hurry to the boat and embrace their son.

"Hi! This is Earl, and this is Paddy." The son introduced his shipmates.

"Hello. Pleasure to meet you." Both men responded with warm sincerity in British accents.

*   *   *   *   *

"O.K., so what happened then?" my father asked the teller of the tale.

"I think the kid ended up sailing to Jamaica, had some trouble with a bad storm off the Bahamas, and then flew home."

The teller of the tale paused. Then he continued, "But can you imagine how the parents must have felt seeing their son for the first time since he called to say he was sailing to Jamaica with two strangers? Can you even imagine?"

"Yes, I can," responded my father. "The story is about my son Jim."

Beaufort, North Carolina

"Mother, I'm going down to the beach today. I'll stop by Beaufort on my way and talk to some shrimpers about work, but then I'm going surfing near the Point."

I threw my green Birdwells into a small red daypack with a water bottle and some wax, strapped my surfboard onto the rack on top of my father's station wagon and headed for the beach. The sun was just beginning to rise as I turned off the highway onto the country road that winds through bucolic farmland. A cool summer mist lay lightly on the fields, and the sky was perfectly clear. A great day to be in the water! As every surfer heading toward the beach does, I hoped for good waves.

The drive was peaceful; I enjoyed the solitude, the green fields of corn and tobacco stretching down long rows to clusters of dark woods, the small towns of Trenton and Maysville draped in Spanish moss, the black water creeks disappearing into lowland wilderness. It was only an hour to the coast, and there was rarely any traffic on the back roads. At most, I sometimes passed a tractor or two and a few farmers piddling along in their pickups, studying the land and their crops. A few miles before Maysville, a car approached. As it drew close, an arm emerged from the driver side window and a fist turned thumb up, a universal symbol for "Surf's up!" As the car passed me, I recognized a friend from Swansboro. I waved and immediately thought about skipping the visit to the fishing docks in Beaufort.

But I had an obligation to my parents to make an effort to find a summer job. I had postponed my first year of college and lived south of Morganton on a friend's land near Casar and the South Mountains for several months, then returned to Kinston in the middle of a recession to try to find work. After a semester studying welding and (separately) art at the local community college, I landed a part-time job as a maintenance man at a local motel. They were desperate. My technical skills extended no further than the changing of light bulbs and the removal of broken bed frames. When they insisted that I clean the pool with toxic muriatic acid without any protective gear (respirator, full coveralls, gloves, etc.) because it was cheaper to have me and the dishwasher do it than it was to hire people who knew how to work with the acid safely, I quit.

The recession dragged on. I looked for work, but there was none to be found. I had always wanted to work on a shrimp boat, so I regularly checked the docks for openings. Nepotism was the first rule of hiring among the captains. You had to be related by blood to one of the Downeast families, a Styron, a Midyette, or Guthrie, Lewis, Davis, Nelson. Still, they were friendly and polite when declining my inquiries.

So, to Beaufort I went. It was mid-morning when I parked beside the docks on Front Street. The water of Taylor's Creek rippled lightly with a soft morning breeze. Seagulls drifted overhead, chattering and scanning for schools of baitfish. Across the channel on Carrot Island, a few wild chestnut ponies grazed.

It was midweek, and the streets were empty. I strolled along Front Street and admired the row of stately, elegant 19th century homes that faced the water. Formerly homes to merchants and whaling captains during Beaufort's glory as the largest whaling town in North Carolina, many of the buildings needed renovation; still, they were magnificent. Along the waterfront, the old chandlery and warehouses were being adapted into restaurants and gift shops.

The docks were still dirty and worn, stained with diesel fuel, bird guano, fish scales and dried offal. As I walked onto the dock, I did not see any shrimper's outriggers. But, approaching the water, I spied the masts of a small yacht; it was low tide, and the deck of the boat itself was several feet below the dock. As I reached the edge of the dock, a short, athletic black man tried to lift himself from the deck. I offered my hand. He waved me off, saying something about being in good enough shape despite his age to climb up by himself.

His accent caught me by surprise; he was British. Living the South, I had never heard a black man with a British accent.

"Where are you from?" I asked.

"Bermuda," he replied.

"Where are you headed?"

A second, larger man jumped up to the dock. He could have played pro football; six and a half feet tall, probably 350. And the biggest, friendliest, happiest smile I had ever seen.

"We're taking this boat to Jamaica," the second man declared proudly. "Name's Paddy." He extended his hand.

"Mine's Jim. So how long have you been out? Where have you come from?"

"We left Elizabeth City yesterday, but we started in Connecticut."

Paddy and I chatted for a while as the captain, whose name I learned was Earl, arranged for provisions. They had left Bermuda a month earlier, flown to Canada for a holiday, then down to Connecticut to pick up the ketch. The boat had been purchased by Louis Mason (scion of the northeast Masons), who owned The Runaway Bay Club west of Ocho Rios, Jamaica. Earl owned a marina in Bermuda and had met Larry there. Paddy ran a charter boat out of Earl's marina. Larry had purchased the boat sight unseen and arranged for Earl and Paddy to handle the delivery.

Neither Earl nor Paddy had ever navigated offshore on the east coast before (the relevance of which I cannot fully explain since they both lived on an island in the Atlantic Ocean), so they had followed the Intracoastal Waterway (ICW) all the way south from Connecticut. Earl was trying to learn celestial navigation through a correspondence course as they traveled. Paddy was skeptical that the knowledge had taken root with Earl.

They were planning to leave Beaufort with a course offshore that would let them sail the most direct route to Florida, a course almost due south if they could avoid the northward rush of the Gulf Stream. They expected to save a few days sailing by getting offshore, reprovision in Miami, then cross southeast along the western edge of the Grand Bahama Bank to round the eastern end of Cuba. They were beginning to get anxious about finishing the delivery so they could return home to their businesses and families.

Earl returned and said to me, "So, do you want to sail to Jamaica?"

"Are you kidding!" His question came so quickly and casually that I was sure he was joking with me.

"No. We fired our other mate and put him ashore in Elizabeth City. He was a friend of ours, but he was doing too much whining about how badly he wanted to get back to his girlfriend. And we will need another crewman offshore."

My mind raced. Yes, yes, yes, I thought, but then remembered my father's car, no spare clothes, no toothbrush, nothing. Yet, I could not say no.

"I don't have my passport with me."

"I don't think you need one as an American travelling to Jamaica, probably just a driver's license or something. But anyway, we can find out before we get there, and we could drop you in Miami if we found out you needed the passport," Earl replied.

I did not want to refuse. Sailing a delivery to Jamaica... how could I NOT go? But it was not practical. I needed to return the car and get all the things I needed to travel for a few weeks.

"When will you leave, 'cause I need to take my parents' car back home; my mother could bring me back. It would take three hours or so," I explained.

Earl shook his head. "We need to leave within the hour."

Part of me was relieved. He had let me off the hook by giving me no option. I was disappointed, but it was still a good story. I had had the chance, but the logistics just did not work out. I could repeat the mantra: if only they could have let me take the car home, if only I could have planned for the possibility, if only....

"Well, I guess that's it then. I can't go. I sure would like to, but I need to return the car and get some gear, money, books, you know, a toothbrush and everything."

"Oh well. Maybe we will find someone else before we leave or pick up another crew later. Best wishes."

They each shook my hand, smiled and then dropped down to the deck of the boat. I watched as they ducked through the companionway into the cabin, then I turned and walked back across the dock to my car.

As I drove out of Beaufort and headed for the beach, my mind kept churning. I should go, but what could I do with the car? What about clothes? Books? All the other stuff I would need? All what other stuff? Did I really need a lot of gear to sit on a sailboat with the bow slicing through warm blue waters driven by balmy tropical winds? I needed a bathing suit and maybe a t-shirt; the thought hit me like a flash. I have what I really need. I could buy a toothbrush and a book. But what about the car? I could just leave the car. Yes, I could leave the car. Call Father, tell him where I parked it and lock the keys inside. No, he would not go for that because then he and Mother would have to drive to Beaufort just to pick up the car; they would have to leave after work and get home late.

But how often does anyone get the option that I was just offered? This is the stuff of dreams. A true adventure. The kind of opportunity that I would die for if I heard someone else telling the story. And how could I face a lifetime of having made an excuse NOT to go? I could drown in phrases beginning with "if only". What makes an adventure is the unknown, the surprise, the ill-prepared nature of the pursuit, the spontaneity, the willingness to take the risk, to accept the fact that the outcome is neither controlled nor assured.

I knew then that I must go. If it was not too late. I turned at the next corner and hurried back to the dock.

"Earl, I want to go! Have you found anyone?"

"No. We've been busy stowing everything."

"Look, I need to call my father and see if he will let me leave his car here. If he will, I am going to buy a few things at the drugstore across the street, and I'll be ready to go. OK?"

Earl laughed at my excitement and my plotting, "Sure, that's okay. But we need to leave in about 15 minutes, so hurry."

I found a pay phone at the chandler's shop next door and called my father at work. With nervous restraint, I told him what had happened, what my plan was and attempted to make it all sound like the perfectly reasonable and logical idea that it was not. After asking a few relevant questions like who the two sailors were, where they were from, was I really comfortable sailing away with two strangers, and what was the name of the sailboat, he agreed to let me go. I was almost as shocked as I had been when Earl asked if I wanted to crew with them.

I thanked my father with continued restraint so that he would not realize how surprised I was or how doubtful I had been that he would agree. He might have changed his mind. Or he might have decided that he needed to consult my mother. And I knew she had too much common sense to be persuaded by the sheer adventure of it all; she would have convinced my father that this was the ill-conceived plan that it truly was. But at the same time, I also knew that she would want me to have the kind of adventure that the voyage might become; and she would want to know that I would return safely from the journey.

I bought a toothbrush, toothpaste and the book *Alive*, the story of the Andes airplane crash survivors, not even thinking about the potential foreshadowing. I had with me a bathing suit, a towel and the jeans, t-shirt and sandals that I was wearing. I did not consider how I would get by with no more than a few dollars for the next several weeks.

"I'm ready," I announced in a loud voice from the dock, my throat tight and my stomach knotted with anticipation.

"Come aboard!"

I hopped onto the deck and stepped down into the cabin. Paddy showed me my berth in the bow beside the sail bags. I dropped my daypack and turned back into the saloon, not really knowing what to do or say next. Filled with disbelief at what experiences lay before me, I surveyed the saloon, the gimbaled galley stove, the portholes, the charts laid across the dining table. Then I noticed the motion of the boat rocking ever so gently, but rocking nevertheless, a motion never present on land. And I felt a lightness in my stomach, a brief twinge of fear; was I going to be seasick? Then Earl called me up on deck to tend the dock lines. We were ready to embark. For the moment, I forgot about the feeling in my stomach.

We motored down the channel past Radio Island into the turning basin for the Morehead City port, then cut the engine and set sail on a starboard tack, the bow rising into the swells rolling through Beaufort Inlet. With Fort Macon to starboard and Shackleford Banks to port, we could see the diamond black and white pattern of Cape Lookout lighthouse clearly as we veered south into the deep green open ocean. We immediately settled into the easy rhythm of the ocean swell, and Paddy announced that it was time for lunch.

My voyage began.

Beaufort to Miami

The sea rolled gently under the bow as we sailed offshore, but within sight of land. As Paddy and Earl oriented me to the various lines and gauges, tools and hazards of *Eliza,* I looked up to see familiar landmarks, seeing them for the first time in several years from five miles offshore, looking back from a place which I usually looked toward, leaving behind all that was familiar.

Paddy was jovial, lighthearted, and talkative. Earl also liked to talk, but was more taciturn and suffered spells of serious cynicism. Paddy just laughed at Earl's bitter moments; they had been friends for 20 years, so Paddy got away with making light of Earl and his carping. While Earl seemed the more intellectual and technical of the two, Paddy was filled with the wisdom of common sense and practical application. Earl committed himself to celestial navigation, precise and mathematical, with complex tables and scientific formulas; he would hang his reputation as a captain on accurate calculation and proof of position. Paddy would navigate by dead reckoning; he was quick to understand the relevant landmarks on the coastal charts. And, when there was no coast, he felt his way across compass points, current, drift, and apparent speed. He logged our daily progress in his mind, tracking our course over the charts without the need of noon sextant shots. He always knew where he was.

Eliza was a thirty-five foot Dickerson ketch with six tons displacement. She wore a white deck and navy blue hull; the hull had a hard chine (I later learned this as we slammed hard into waves, instead of slicing into large seas). An attractive, classic wooden yacht, but with no special features to distinguish her, she was solid and tracked fairly well with a shallow draft keel, but she would not win races. Her interior was comprised of a saloon with starboard settee and convertible dining table to port. There was a forward V berth just past the port head. The galley was conveniently located just at the foot of the companionway steps to starboard, where the crew on watch could reach down for a cup of hot tea in the pre-dawn chill.

Eliza offered few modern amenities. The dinghy was fiberglass with a 5-hp outboard that did not work. She had only a CB radio, no VHF; the radio barely worked. None of the sails was self-furling, and *Eliza* carried no self-steering gear. We contrived self-steering the old way, by tying off the spoked wheel to the aft mizzenmast. She did, however, boast the basic gauges for wind speed, boat speed and depth below keel. At the time, few pleasure boats were equipped with LORAN or any sort of satellite navigation system, nor was *Eliza*.

My first night in the bow berth I slept poorly, but rested well. I could not help but listen to the sounds of the sea rushing past the hull, the clank and slap of rigging and sail, the soft breathing of the wind. I reveled in the noise of being afloat, of travelling by wind over water. Tired and sore from my first day as crew of a small yacht, I also was too excited to miss anything. Paddy woke me for the 2 to 6 watch. I crawled up the steps to the cockpit and said goodnight to Paddy as he disappeared into the pitch darkness of the cabin. I felt very alone.

I surveyed my world. Waves and swells, only partly visible in the moonless night, lifted and splashed the boat. I could feel the pull of the sails and the dampness of the salt spray hanging on the wind. In the extreme distance, I made out the darkest edge of my world, the horizon, where the brightness of a star-dusted sky collided with the total blackness of the sea. I thought I could distinguish all the stars in the universe; never had I witnessed such a sky. I paused to be sure that the sky was not in fact smothered in stars, that there were constellations beyond the cloud of Milky Way that draped over the night.

Alone, I settled into my first watch at sea, absorbing all that I could hear, feel, taste, or see. Alone, my confidence began to emerge as I gripped the wooden wheel, occasionally checking my course by the compass's red night light, feeling the course by the motion of the boat over the swells and the tracing of the mast against the sky. I was alone, but in no way lonely; the boat was my friend, something at once new and familiar, a relationship of mutual care and responsibility. The night passed quickly into my first dawn at sea, another new world that carried all the wonder, excitement and beauty of coming home after a long journey to a place that is different but again familiar. Of course, the change was all in me.

At sunrise, when Earl came on watch, we tacked back toward the coast and began to estimate our location, trying to match towers and other landmarks on shore with our charts. We were off Topsail Island, having made less than 60 miles in 15 hours (I would learn this speed was about average); the loss of directional mileage due to tacking at night was greater than I had anticipated (because we did not tack often enough). We eased through another pleasant day of clear skies and moderate breezes as we sailed south, searching for Cape Fear inlet and the channel into Southport; Earl had decided that our progress offshore was too slow, so he wanted to return to the ICW for a while. The landmark for the inlet was Bald Head Island with its nineteenth century lighthouse, now defunct. We would know we were close when we recognized Frying Pan Shoals, one of the three great hazards on the North Carolina coast (the others being Cape Lookout Shoals and, of course, Diamond Shoals off Cape Hatteras).

I have seen and fished the shoals off Lookout, but not Hatteras, the deadliest of the three capes, Graveyard of the Atlantic. I had seen Lookout's shoals from my father's fishing boat. Those shoals were avoided easily enough; you just motor up toward the choppiest water and look for the bottom; when you can see it, you are too close and back away outside the roughest water. I had no fear of Cape Fear or its Frying Pan shoals; I knew that we would simply look for a change in the swells of the ocean, the small, random whitecaps of short, steep, breaking waves. Then we would need to tack toward deeper water and just miss the outer reach of the bar that extended twenty miles from the outer islands. I was still ignorant of the ways of sail. The wind and sea are gods; they are not always gentle gods.

We recognized Bald Head while still north of the inlet and made way for open sea, close-hauled on a reach, trying to yield as little distance as possible while gaining depth away from the shoals. Because we could see Bald Head, we should have realized that we were no more than eight or ten miles from shore, well within the twenty mile reach of Frying Pan's shallows. The wind freshened. Toward land I detected a faint tracing along the clouds, the slightest hint of a squall. I pointed to the line, but neither Paddy nor Earl took any interest. They believed it was just a cloud. We studied the depth meter closely, switching from fathoms to feet. The depth held anywhere from 26 to 31 feet, so we had plenty of water. Ahead, we saw the water begin to churn, the waves steepening with occasional whitecaps. Was it Frying Pan? We disbelieved what we saw because persuaded ourselves that we were sufficiently distant from the Shoals. Eyes scanned depth meter, waves, then clouds, constantly reviewing, evaluating, seeking affirmation that *Eliza* was safe in her depth and outside the reach of the Shoals. I still thought the clouds over land were threatening; they seemed to be approaching quickly and moved contrary to our breeze.

Suddenly, the depth dropped from 27 to 21, then 19, then 16, and 13.

"We're running over the Shoal!" someone screamed.

But we could not reverse our course. 11 feet, then 9, then 7. (We needed 4 feet for the keel plus the height of the waves.) We bucked wildly in the rough water that seemed to surround us without warning, steep waves rising, lifting the bow as the stern sank, the pull of the water seeming to seize *Eliza* in its grip. We were losing steerage as we mired in the maelstrom of confused seas. The squall line became clearly visible, a black-edged cloud rushing toward us from the west, heavy rains dropping in metallic gray columns, the shore behind the squall now lost behind a curtain of torrential rain.

"Paddy, look!" I pointed to the squall. "It's what I thought it was."

Then the wind slapped us with a cold snap of its fist, wind and rain mixing with the spray of waves lifted and thrown with all the wild fury of an unrestrained sea. It was as if Neptune himself rose beside our boat, scooped a mighty handful of ocean and hurled the cold gray waters into our faces.

In my initial fear, I just wanted to start the engine and power out of the danger. But we were making headway and soon found ourselves in stormy seas, but past the shoals, sailing briskly in the aftermath of the squall. The rain passed, and again we could see the coast and the lights of Oak Island and Southport, so we turned toward the inlet, grateful the storm had left us behind.

It was dark by the time we entered Cape Fear River approaching Southport. The buoys and channel markers were difficult to identify despite having charts of the area. Although a couple of the buoys were lit, none of the entry markers were. In the darkness, the lights of the town confused our eyes and obscured the navigation markers. We missed a sharp bend in the channel and immediately ran aground on a falling tide. As *Eliza* listed further and further, we resigned ourselves to a long uncomfortable night waiting for the tide to rise again so that we could grapple her off the bar. Once the tide rose and lifted us from the sand, a passing fisherman tossed us a line and pulled *Eliza* back into the channel, and we continued to the marina in the dim, red light of sunrise.

After a shower at the marina, I called my parents.

"Where are you?" they asked.

"Southport." I replied, a bit nervous, excited, and anxious. I had been overwhelmed at times during the prior two days, but did not want them to know it or hear it in my voice.

"You've been sailing for two days and only reached Southport?" my father questioned, somewhat incredulous. Father had never been a sailor, so he only knew how fast a power boat could have reached Southport.

"Yep." I tried to explain the effects of having to tack away from the coast at night and avoiding Frying Pan, but then changed the subject. "I was hoping you might be able to come down and bring me some clothes and other stuff I need."

"You know we want to see you. Just tell us what you want us to bring."

A few hours later, as Earl, Paddy, and I rested in the cockpit, I looked up and saw my parents walking down the dock. I called to them, at the same time wondering how they were going to react to meeting my black shipmates. Introductions went smoothly; I know my parents were as charmed by the British accents as I had been. I spent the afternoon with my parents, telling them everything I had experienced in the previous two days. They were visibly reassured that I was safe and travelling with trustworthy gentlemen. After dinner, they drove home. The next morning, Earl, Paddy, and I departed Southport and motored down the ICW. It was the first of many hot, still, and humid days of listening to the clattering engine instead of the wind, of smelling diesel fumes instead of salt air.

South of Southport, the ICW passes through open sounds between the outer islands and the mainland. The channel cuts through shallow waters marked by shoals of marsh grass, the black mud of which is exposed at low tide and smells like the primal ooze where life began. The channel is generally too narrow to permit sailing and tacking, so a motor is essential though tiresome.

Still, the scenery was nice enough to alleviate some of the tedium of listening to the motor droning its monotonous racket.

As we entered South Carolina, the open water ended, and the channel followed what appeared to be more of a canal than a channel. I called it Root Beer River for the flat brown murky color of the water, but its name is Little River. The canal had been cut through a rough and overgrown swamp with dull water and air as still as death itself. Hot, lifeless, stifling. A haven for all that torments us. Bugs, stinging insects, snakes, and worse. In the miserable heat of a mid-summer day, I could not imagine the ecological beauty hidden behind the tangled screen of vine and scrub. We suffered through, dreaming of shade and cool breezes, blue water and fresh air.

By late afternoon we were docked somewhere near North Myrtle Beach beside an old junk-style yacht. We each drank a cold beer and enjoyed the slightly cooler air of early evening before locking ourselves in the cabin behind the porthole and deck hatch screens. The whine of mosquitoes after sunset was continuous. Sleep was hot and elusive. I lay sweating on my clammy berth, wishing for the slightest movement of air that never came. Dawn was heavy and humid but offered the illusion of cooler air until the sun rose over the trees and the baking resumed.

The next day was worse. Hotter, more humid, as still as roadkill two days dead. We muddled south down the colorless channel, seeing nothing but tidewater marsh and swamp, breathing engine fumes, sweating every drop of water we drank and more. Having endured a nearly endless day under a scorching sun, we anchored for the night in a small cove off the main channel. There was no land in sight, only still brown water, brown marsh grass, and the smell of decay. None of us could eat. With the setting of the sun, the droning mosquitoes surrounded and besieged our tired ship. We suffered another long restless, claustrophobic night hiding behind small screened portholes. We listened to the insects buzz and prayed for the blue seas with fair winds offshore.

By midmorning the next day, we discovered signs of civilization, a dilapidated fishing dock. We had reached Charleston. Without pausing to explore the pleasures of this historic seaport town, we motored across the harbor, past Fort Sumter and back into the ocean.

How glorious and refreshing to have returned to open ocean. The maternal roll of the swells, the seductive caress of the wind and the complete liberation of the senses unfolding to a boundless horizon. Our spirits rejoiced. We were sailing!

A few days of good peaceful weather followed.

Then, the first afternoon off the coast of Florida, a big squall with thunderstorm formed over the mainland and swept to sea with a leading edge that was arched in the angry curve of a shelf cloud. The winds rocked, rolled, and tossed us mercilessly, threatening to rip our sails from the masts before we could reef them. The fury quieted within the hour, and we sailed relieved into nighttime. First dolphins. A pod of five joined us, playing off the bow wake and seeming to reassure us that the storm was gone.

Night and the next day were again peaceful sailing under clear skies and pleasant winds. But, again in the afternoon, the same kind of storm formed and rushed seaward to thrash us. The scenario repeated for another two days until we yielded and decided to seek shelter on the ICW again. We needed provisions anyway, so we entered Ponce de Leon Inlet beside its magnificent nineteenth century red brick lighthouse. The water was clear, and we were fascinated by the stunning electric colors of the large jellyfish that floated beneath us.

Thus began a long journey of motoring the canals of the Florida ICW. We watched coconuts drifting by and eventually interrupted our boredom by making a game of catching them with a bucket as they slid along the hull. More afternoon storms, but the wind and rain did not bother us in the quiet and protected waters of the ICW. The only events that broke our tedium were the periodic drawbridges that opened only at predetermined times, so we would wait as long as an hour for the next opening. At night, we docked or anchored. Titusville near Cape Canaveral, Vero Beach, Fort Pierce, Jupiter, Palm Beach. Endless canals lined with boats and sea walls. None of us wanted to be sightseeing tourists. By the time we reached Fort Lauderdale, I was ready for some action.

At Fort Lauderdale, we discussed our next move. Crossing the Gulf Stream takes some planning to avoid being swept northward in its current while trying to make a landfall on the western side of the Bahamas. Neither Earl nor

Paddy wanted to lose the time it would take to stop in the Bahamas, clear Customs, and be distracted by the sights. So, they decided we should plot a course that skirted the southern edge of the Grand Bahama Bank, a massive sandy shoal extending west of Andros Island 25 miles or more that varied in depth from 0 to 25 feet. They wanted to provision in Miami, then sail open water without landfall from Miami toward Andros, turning south and east to pass north of Cuba and then through the Windward Passage between Haiti and Cuba before turning southwest for Jamaica. They estimated a week of hard sailing if we had good wind.

I met a gentleman topping off the gas tanks for his daughter in her 21-foot center console outboard, the *Little Damn*.

"Where are you headed?" I asked.

"My daughter's running over to Bimini."

"By herself?" I queried. It seemed to me a long way for a teenage girl to go alone.

"Oh yeah. She'll be fine. It's a clear day. And it's only 60 miles; take her four hours at the most."

That close, I thought to myself. I never realized that the Bahamas were so accessible. Sixty miles and I could be in another country, a tropical island paradise (I had not yet seen the islands, so I had my dreams). These people could run over for the weekend. I began to regret that Earl and Paddy were in such a hurry to reach Jamaica. Maybe they lived on a tropical island, but I had yet to see one, much less visit one. I wanted to go, but I had no vote. They had been away from home for more than a month and were increasingly anxious to return.

We motored down to Miami and docked in the municipal marina beside a city park in the middle of what appeared to be downtown. The three of us walked into the city, grabbed a greasy burger at a lunch stand, then wandered through the streets listening to the Latin culture overwhelm things English or American. Earl wanted to go into a K-Mart, so we browsed through as he looked for batteries or something. Then, over the crackling speaker, a blue light special was announced...in Spanish. Somehow it all felt too foreign, too isolating. My mind disconnected; I was not in Florida, I did not know where I was. I could not understand the people or recognize the culture of the streets. What was supposed to be familiar was strange; I had wandered too far. I began to worry that I could not return to the place where I began, could not find the park, the marina, or anyone or anything that would connect me with my past, my own culture, my homeplace that I did not know I had left.

I hurried along the sidewalk looking for anything that I might recall. It was hot; there was no longer any shade. The stone walls of the buildings, the concrete of the sidewalks, the asphalt on the streets all conspired to magnify the heat, the humidity, the unbreathable hotness of air that lay deathly still in the middle of the crowded city. I needed space, color, room to walk and air to breathe. I looked for the park and eventually saw trees, palm trees, green fronds waving gently on fresh breezes against the pure, rich blue of a perfect sky. Then I saw the water, its blue also a reflection of the purity of the sky. I began to relax, to recover, to feel no longer lost or alone.

I wandered about the park, enjoying the shade, the breeze, the sights. I met a young brunette who worked in an art gallery. She discouraged me from trying to get my art (large macramé wall hangings) placed in a gallery. Just not what galleries looked for in Miami.

A gentleman sporting a long gray ponytail approached me where I was sitting on a bench in the shade. He made casual small talk before propositioning me. If I wanted to be his boyfriend, he would cover my expenses and give me a Rolex like his. He flashed his wrist for me to view. Being openly gay had not migrated to North Carolina, and this was even before the revival of South Beach. He seemed nice enough but could have been a serial killer of the Bundy type for all I knew. Engaging but ultimately murderous. When I politely declined, I hoped he would just wander the park seeking another target, and he did.

I headed back to the marina to see if Earl and Paddy had returned from their shopping spree. They said their money was running low, so provisions would be less than exciting for the next leg of our voyage. I thought they meant less steak, not less food. Earl and Paddy returned an hour or so later. They were snickering about having purchased some Instant Grits.

"Do you really eat grits?" they asked. "We heard that you people from the South like grits."

"Sure. They're good. Though the instant grits are not as good as the kind that cook for a while. Best with sausage and eggs, but I've eaten them alone. Kind of bland," I replied.

"Good. Once we are at sea, we want to see you eat some," Earl dared me.

We stowed the provisions, food for the week Earl was convinced would get us to Jamaica, and motored out the channel toward open sea once again. Motoring alongside massive cruise ships that rose above us like skyscrapers, Earl plotted a course aiming farther south than we wanted to go, but allowing for the northward drift of the Gulf Stream. When we cleared land, we set sail as the sun began to settle its warm evening glow over a rolling ocean. I was excited but also a bit nervous as I thought about being offshore for at least a week. I was excited that the next landfall would be our destination, Jamaica.

Miami to Jamaica

About 10 that night, I woke when *Eliza* suddenly began to dance wildly, the water jumbled and irregular, the motion lacking any rhythm. What felt like an approaching storm was only the Gulf Stream, the powerful ocean river flowing north from the Gulf of Mexico along the eastern seaboard of the US toward Ireland and the British Isles. I went back to sleep.

Next morning, more clear blue skies and gentle swells, fresh, clean air. Looking over the side of the boat, I thought I could see the bottom of the ocean. I checked the depth meter; 60 feet. I could distinguish coral heads as dark spherical shadows against the brightness of sand lit by sun on a cloudless day through the clear blue tinted sea.

"I can see land. There," Paddy pointed east toward the horizon where we could just see the faintest tracing of white beach broken from the sky by a similar tracing of darkness that was trees.

"Is that Andros?" I asked.

"Yes," affirmed Earl.

Paddy shuffled a bit and looked toward his feet, "Maybe. I do not know though. We drifted a lot crossing the Gulf Stream last night."

"Not so much," disagreed Earl. "I allowed for a couple of knots. That fellow at the marina said the Stream had not been running so fast lately."

"Well, it sure seemed to get choppy for moving so slow," I chimed in, not really knowing what I was talking about, but having a reaction that was strong enough to justify expressing an opinion. After all, I had experienced currents before. Maybe I did not know the Gulf Stream, but I knew that, when a tide flowed fast enough to create severe chop, it was moving more than a couple of knots.

Earl shook his head in emphatic disagreement and as evidence that he was a captain with a crew that just did not understand. We took turns with the binoculars scanning the island for landmarks that might help identify it as Andros or another island. If it was not Andros, we had no idea which it might be because Andros is a long island that forms the eastern boundary of the Grand Bahama Bank. Earl had set our course to track the eastern edge of the banks, so he wanted the island we could see to be Andros.

Paddy was the first to know. "That is Bimini."

"Impossible. Look at the chart. We would have to have missed our target by 90 miles," Earl argued.

Earl traced his logic and intended course across the chart for our benefit. What he said made sense. Except for a couple of assumptions, unfortunately, the two key factors: speed of current and speed of boat. While Earl assumed two to three knots of current, he also assumed that *Eliza* would be travelling at five to six knots. When I had awakened in the night, we had been travelling three to four knots because the wind had diminished after sunset. Paddy nodded his head. Earl had failed to adjust his course when the boat speed fell below five knots. With a current flowing northward at four to five knots and a boat speed of three to four knots, we were simply floating in the Stream, making a course to the north faster than we were crossing. Earl should have started the engine when the boat speed dropped below five knots.

Earl remained stubbornly unconvinced of his mistake until we could see the seaplanes landing in the Bimini harbor. Then he just as quickly decided, without explanation much less discussion, that we should clear Customs. So we sailed for the marina dock and tied up.

The Customs officer was a caricature of a third world government official. He was stiff and neat and starched and aloof. His speech was curt, his facial expression unrevealing; he treated us with polite suspicion. His office was on the second floor of a powder blue cinder block building beside the marina. The office had a ceiling fan, but no air-conditioning. Most of the light came from the few windows behind his desk.

"Why have you come to the Bahamas?" he asked.

"We are sailing to Jamaica, delivering a sailboat," replied Earl.

"How long do you plan to stay?" the officer queried.

"We really plan to be headed south from here."

"Do you plan to stop again on another island?" the officer continued, as if not quite believing Earl, and not understanding why we had stopped to clear Customs in Bimini if we were not planning to stop in the islands again. I did not understand either; nor do I think that Paddy understood. But there we were, politely submitting ourselves to interrogation by a bureaucrat who would have preferred not to be bothered, but who, having been bothered, was going to be as thorough as his disbelief dictated.

We sat in his office while he paced through the required questions with Earl, never lifting his head to acknowledge our presence much less commit even the smallest act of friendliness such as a smile, I began to think of the situation from his perspective. Two black men with British passports travelling with a long-haired young white American on their way to Jamaica who have stopped to clear Customs in a country where they do not plan to stop again. Why? Drug runners? Still, if we were smuggling drugs or planning to, why stop? Why engage a Custom officers? The only rational conclusion may have been that we were idiots.

He had a point. I just did not understand why he did not simply make his point, throw us out of his office and send us on our way. We were being foolish or silly or superfluous or stupid, and if he had half a brain, he would have told us to stop wasting his and our time and hit the water.

We returned to the boat and motored out the channel into the midday tropical heat. The sun glared off the silver slick still water of the bay, amplified by the blinding white of the sand bottom. It was humid and oppressive. There was not a breeze worth mentioning as we rounded the point and headed south for deep water, the noise and fumes of the engine making it seem only hotter.

The days that followed were so hot and still that each one simply melted into the next. We drifted nearly becalmed over the Grand Bahama Bank, seeing nothing in the air, nothing on the metallic sea and nothing below the crystal surface of the ocean except trackless acres of sterile white sand. The depth varied from as much as 15 feet to as little as 6, barely enough to float us. Occasionally, we would glimpse a shadow darting out of vision; sharks. And once, but only once, I could bear the heat no longer and jumped overboard into the water; but the water was no cooler than the air. Paddy was the first to spot the five foot barracuda hovering off the stern, waiting, patiently observing as I floated beside the boat, both of us listless in the tropical heat. We ate a smaller barracuda Paddy caught.

Meanwhile, Earl had been perfecting his noon sighting. With the flat calm, he could not have had an easier horizon to find with the sextant. He pulled his navigation tables up into the cockpit beside him and began the excruciating process of calculating our position.

"There!" He had completed his calculations. "I know exactly where we are." He was full of self-assurance despite, or because of, his many errors over the preceding days and weeks. He had unshakeable certainty that this position was correct, that he had overcome the earlier mistakes and arrived at the careful and precise location of our little ship in its place on the globe.

Paddy and I looked over Earl's shoulder to see the magic spot on the chart that represented our position on the planet. What we saw was the dark blue of deep water; the depth showed more than 100 fathoms; we were floating in barely six feet, a single lonely fathom.

"Earl, you're wrong again." I could not restrain myself. Was it the heat or my own natural impudence? I do not know, but I know that what I said, I had to say. I could no longer remain silent in the face of his egotistical incompetence. I needed for him to have to face the truth of his error, to confess the inadequacy of his effort, to admit to me and Paddy at last that he had no idea how to navigate, that he was lost and that we would all be better served by relying upon our collective dead reckoning.

"No, this is where we are," Earl pointed to the spot on the dark blue of the chart.

"You are positive?" I challenged him.

"Yes. Of course. I checked my calculations three times. They are right this time," his voice revealing his anger at being questioned by his crew.

I went for the kill. "Earl, what is the depth at our location according to the chart?"

"Looks like 100 fathoms (600 Feet)," he responded.

"Come here Earl," I gestured to the port side of *Eliza*, irritated that he was not willing to recognize his mistake. "Look down there." I pointed into the water. "Well, what do you see?" I asked smugly.

"The bottom," Earl said.

"Then how could your position, which shows us to be in over 100 fathoms of water, be correct?"

"I am sure I am only off a couple of miles," Earl replied in an attempt to make a plausible excuse.

"Then look to the western horizon. Do you see any change of water color? Do you the dark shadow of deep sea? No, you can't because we are over the Bank many miles from deep water," I lectured.

Paddy interrupted my tirade to say, "We need to get off this bank. We need to get to deeper water."

"Why?" I asked. "We're making little headway, but there's not likely to be more wind to the west. And besides it will take us off course; we will lose time."

"I know, but I think we must quickly get to deeper water and away from this shallow bank. We probably should motor away now," Paddy continued.

"We are not starting the engine and using what little fuel we have," Earl asserted. "We may need it later, and we have nowhere to refuel."

"Paddy, why the urgency?" I asked. I knew that Paddy was not excitable. He would not overreact. But I did not yet understand the source of his concern.

"If we get a storm over these shallows, the waves will be steep and very rough. If we have only six feet of water and a four-foot chop, we will be bouncing the keel off the bottom and could literally break the boat. Besides, if we were to wreck, we have only this little dinghy for the three of us; the motor does not work, and Andros is more than 20 miles away. In heavy seas, I think we would capsize before we could reach shore in the dinghy."

I knew Paddy was right, but did not feel the same sense of urgency. I lacked his blue water experience. We set a course due west seeking deep water.

After an hour or so, the depth had reached 25 feet. Paddy was mildly relieved. We continued west, however, searching for the 100 fathom water.

Just before sunset, we saw a line of clouds to the south. Paddy suggested that the clouds might have wind so we steered toward them.

In a half-hour, we could see the wind ruffling the water in front of the clouds. Earl hurried on deck to reef the main. Then it struck! A dry squall. Our soft breeze from the south instantly became a howling wind from the west. We turned to run a close reach on the starboard tack. It had been so long since we had a fine wind that we ran where it would take us the fastest. South. We intended to run with it while it lasted, thinking that the squall would blow itself out in an hour or less. But it raged on. We sailed hard with the mainsail under a single reef, heeled twenty-five degrees to port, the hull beginning to slam into the disorganized seas. The ocean turned dark and gray and dismal. The sky thickened with darker and darker clouds, and the clouds seemed to fill with an anger of their own, as if they wished to extinguish light itself while they merged with the sea and vanquished our horizon.

Suddenly it was night, pitch black, a wild and angry gale screaming through the rigging.

"This looks like it is going to last a while. Let's close her up, and everyone in the cockpit. Sails down. We may need to trail a sea anchor." Earl and Paddy agreed that this was more than a squall. Night had caught us before we made deep water; but we still had only twenty-five feet under the keel. "The water's deep enough not to wreck the boat, but it is going to be a rough and uncomfortable ride."

With our storm jackets and life jackets on, all three of us sat in the cockpit holding wherever we could while the boat leapt and jolted through random and chaotic waves of six to eight feet height. Surrounded by blackness, the ocean merged with the sky, waves visible only when they broke into whitecaps. Rain slashed sideways through the air, slapping our hands and faces, whipping through the bare rigging. The wind roared; we yelled to each other to be heard above the noise. The wind speed indicator showed gusts consistently exceeding fifty-five knots.

It was a week later when we learned that a tropical depression had swept through the Bahamas leaving much damage.

As the wind subsided to twenty-five to thirty knots late that night, we set a course to the southwest, again trying to get off the Bank and into deeper water. The seas softened into long swells of ten to twelve feet over the ocean by morning. It had been a long night for all of us, and I had finally collapsed in my berth a little before dawn. After sleeping for a few hours, I returned to the deck. The day was fabulous, the sky swept clear by the storm, the seas big but friendly, and the ship sailing confidently across the sea. As we rose out of a trough, I scanned the horizon and the heavy seas that surrounded us. Not a boat in sight, but there was an island, and we were only five miles or so from its shores. I could see the brilliant white beaches, the lush green of its palm trees. Then I realized I was looking due south. I was looking at Cuba.

"Is that Cuba?" I asked rhetorically. Neither Earl nor Paddy had been paying much attention.

"Oh no," Paddy said quietly, thinking to himself what we were all thinking. We were in the wrong place, too close to Castro's Cuba, a country that still occasionally seized yachts and crew without justification. A country still an enemy of the United States with a full embargo that crippled the island country's small economy despite assistance from Soviet Russia.

"We need to get away from here."

And we did, tacking back to the northeast, carried quickly by the remnants of the storm winds.

For the next few days, we tacked and tacked and seemed to make little progress. Earl persisted believing his celestial sights, while Paddy and I conferred on dead reckoning. Earl thought we were making good progress to the southeast; Paddy and I were even more convinced that our tacking was taking us too far to the north and south and not far enough east toward our destination, Great Inagua and the Windward Passage. We ran low on food and, more importantly, water. We were content not to eat much since it was oppressively hot, and we were not active. But the shortage of water concerned us. We did not have a watermaker nor had it rained since the storm.

The days and nights that we spent on our unintentional oceanographic survey of the pool of water that reached between Cuba and the Bahamas all merged into one memory. Beautiful days with fair winds and gentle swells; soft, balmy nights with star-dusted skies that I studied endlessly during my night watches. Between occasional scans of the horizon for shipping traffic, I lay in the cockpit, steering by the mast and stars and marveling at the depth, the majesty, the sheer wonder of infinite space that lay above me. I had never before seen the number of stars that I saw there, every one a sun and none close enough for any human to ever reach in a lifetime. I relaxed in the pleasure of complete awe.

Paddy and I continued to doubt Earl's navigation, if you can call his errors anything other than wasted effort. Our water shortage was soon to be life threatening; we needed to find a harbor. Based on his noon sight, Earl gave me a course for my night watch. The easterly bearing seemed to carry us too far north, but Earl believed it would bring us to an island by the following midday. I disagreed but kept my doubt to myself as Earl retired to his berth, and I began to sail south of the course, almost southeast. Yes, a small private mutiny.

After a couple of hours, I thought I detected a change in the horizon. I could not be sure. It seemed like a hint of light, a weak glow that appeared only as a difference in the blackness of a spot on the horizon. I steered a little further south. Every five minutes or so, I stood up for a better look at what might lie ahead. There seemed to be something, an apparition or suggestion, but I worried I might just be trying too hard to see something that I wanted and needed to see, that I hoped to see. Still, I continued with the more southerly course, rationalizing that I could return to my original course later if my vision proved to be fantasy.

An hour later, I was sure. I could see the sweeping light of a lighthouse. I woke Earl.

"I see a lighthouse." I knew there was no lighthouse on the bearing he had told me to sail.

What I actually *saw* was not so much anything identifiable as it was a spot of haze, brighter than the black ocean night surrounding it, that I believed was a lighthouse, a point of reference associated with land and the possibility that we would no longer be quite lost somewhere northeast of Cuba.

"Where?" Earl asked.

"To the south," I replied.

We pulled out the charts for the area. The only island with a lighthouse anywhere close to where we could have been was Great Inagua. Earl thought we were too far north to see Great Inagua, but the position was consistent with where Paddy and I thought we must be. I sighed with silent relief as Earl agreed to steer directly for the island. Earl meanwhile pulled the harbor guide for the entry directions. It sounded like a tight channel, and the guide said it should not be attempted at night. But we were desperate and tried it anyway. We needed the safety and implied security of being tied to land. It had been ten days since we left Bimini. (Unknown to me, my parents had begun to worry about not hearing from me.)

The next morning, we woke inside a small man-made harbor lined with concrete sea walls fully protected from the open sea. Paddy went in search of a Customs officer. Here we go again, I thought. When he returned an hour later, he had found a bar, but no Customs officer. First things first; we were hungry and thirsty, and the bar addressed both needs efficiently. Of course, what I did not know at the time was that Earl and Paddy were out of money. They had expected Jamaica to be the next landfall after provisioning in Miami, so they did not save any of the cash they had from the boat's owner. Even water was going to cost money on Inagua.

While Paddy was checking out the island, I was scouring the charts. I looked at the progress marks going back a couple of days and laid the straight edge on the course that Earl had told me to steer the night before. Had I continued on that course, we could have sailed past the Turks and Caicos Islands far enough north to miss them entirely. Instead of landfall in Inagua, we would have been in the Atlantic heading for Western Sahara with no way to plot our position.

Next day, an eighty-foot Burger aluminum yacht docked ahead of us in the little square harbor basin. They had stopped in Inagua due to trouble with their desalination water maker. The crew let us enjoy their air-conditioned saloon since the owner was not sailing with them. As I met other sailors, most of whom had moored in open water off the town proper (near the bar), I discovered that virtually everyone had made an unplanned stop at the island due to one problem or another. Great Inagua was no one's destination.

Soon after the Burger docked, a local boy drove up in a garish powder blue Chevy Nova; the hood ornament was a big Peace symbol reminiscent of the American 60s, hippies, and Woodstock. He introduced himself, "Hi! I'm the local pusher, mon." We almost laughed he was such a caricature of himself. But we composed ourselves and tried to act as if we were taking him seriously. We seriously declined his offer of illegal drugs, though I believe he only had a little marijuana. Not missing a beat or an opportunity, he offered his taxi service, but again we refused; town was only a quarter mile away, and we were able-bodied and broke.

Except for Matthewtown itself, the island was undeveloped and uninhabited. The backcountry is over 500 square miles of scrub land that is home to wild boar and not much else. Lake Windsor (or Rosa now) lies 12 miles long and supports the largest flock of flamingos in the western hemisphere. The houses in the town were quaint and colorful remnants of 19th century British colonial occupation, stucco and brightly painted with tropical greens and yellows and reds with wooden shutters. At one end of the main (only) street lay the marina, at the other the lighthouse, a blindingly white squat old lighthouse built in 1870 and still shining to the horizon to bring weary sailors to shelter. I climbed the neatly painted black circular stairway to the top for a view over the island. A small white mountain on the north side of the island caught my attention.

"What's that?" I asked my guide, Matthew (named for the disciple), the 21 year old keeper of the lighthouse.

"Salt," he replied.

"A mountain of salt?!"

"Yes. See to the right of the mountain. There. The long dark canals. Morton Salt draws sea water into the canals, lets it evaporate, then scoops out the residue." He explained that Morton was the biggest employer on the island and had built an airstrip to fly in its managers. The salt itself was shipped by barge.

Matthew was a bright young islander who was soft-spoken, articulate but reserved. He was proud of his lighthouse and proud of his responsibility for it. He seemed to enjoy showing me both the lighthouse with its antique Fresnel lens and the island, almost all of which was visible from the lighthouse. Matthew pointed to the southern shore of the island. I could see that the water there was shallow, the water mottled by sand and coral. He told me that Spanish cannons had been found on the shallow flats and that there were caves on the shore where people believed treasure was probably still hidden. In response to my query, he said very few people ever came to the island to dive for wrecks or treasure.

I also met a local philosopher, Mr. Theo Farquarson, 84 years behind him and many more ahead, a lover of life who rides a bike everywhere. He advised me: "drink milk and live as long as Methuselah," "live and let live," and, commenting on my ponytail, "in my day, boys who tried to look like girls were called 'sissies'!" We both laughed. He was a kind old man and meant no harm.

The residents were delightful, friendly, always smiling. We made a habit of lingering around the After Work Bar, the source of conch fritters, cheap beer, and cheaper rum. One night we rowed out to an anchored trawler to listen to someone we met sing and play guitar. A crescent moon glowed overhead, spotlighting the calm waters, darkened by occasional passing clouds, leaving moonshadows. I drank orange drink rather than beer most of the time since we had not yet received money from Mason to purchase provisions, including water. I swam with the local children, hiked across the rocky beach and collected shells. One day, we gathered on the beach to push a trimaran into the sea.

Over the next couple of days, as we tired of conch fritters for breakfast, lunch and dinner, Earl hocked almost everything off the boat. First the dinghy, then the dinghy's outboard (which did not work anyway), then his watch and the CB radio (also useless to us). He placed calls to Mason, but Mason was not in the mood to send more money. Tired of bar fare, Paddy and I jumped at the offer of fresh fish. A couple of kids had speared a large amberjack; the kids had speared other smaller fish, but they did not want the amberjack; they said it was "pisin", poison. Paddy acknowledged that reef fish can carry ciguatera but assured me that he ate amberjack in Bermuda.

Paddy laughed and said they were just scared of the fish because it was big, an island superstition. He said he liked amberjack and ate it all the time at home in Bermuda. I knew that amberjack caught off the coast of North Carolina had wormy flesh, but Paddy assured me this fish would be good. We fileted the fish and found no worms. Then Paddy fried it in the skillet, and we devoured a couple of plates each. It was a delicious change after days of conch fritters.

It only took an hour for nausea to strike; I was drinking a beer in cool air-conditioned comfort on the Burger when I began to feel so lightheaded that I could barely stand. I returned to *Eliza* and crawled into my berth. The rest of the long night was an endless cycle of dehydrating diarrhea and vomiting as my body tried to cleanse itself of the poison. In the morning, Paddy asked "The Pusher" to give me a ride to the local clinic. I almost blacked out when I stepped from the boat to the dock.

The clinic was clean, pale yellow and empty. I waited only a couple of minutes to see the doctor, an East Indian who had been educated by the British empire and was thus obliged to provide his services in an unserved place such as Inagua. He spoke little and administered a sulfa medication of some sort and sent me back to the boat. He thought I would feel better in a few days.

Before I got food poisoning, I had made plans to sail with a couple of Brits on their trimaran, *Whiskey Jack*, hunt wild boar with a guide that "The Pusher" knew, and hoped to find a day to snorkel off the south shore where the cannons and treasure might hide near a secret cave. Instead, for the next four days, I slept and rested and tried to regain my strength. I had little appetite, and fried seafood was sickening. Likewise, fresh water was expensive, and beer was not good for rehydrating.

I was still frail when we set sail from Great Inagua bound for Jamaica on the summer solstice. I feared I would be seasick, but settled into the rhythm of the swells comfortably. Earl and Paddy had bartered enough to acquire food and water for about five days. We hoped the next leg of the voyage would be no more than three days, but needed some margin against unfavorable winds.

The first couple of days were filled with steady trade winds and clear skies. When I came up on deck on the second morning, we were just off the coast of Haiti in the Windward Passage rolling over long, gentle swells. I was glad we were not within sight of Cuba lying to our west.

As I sat with my morning coffee, I heard a loud whoosh somewhere off the stern of the boat; I looked, but saw nothing. A few minutes later, I heard another, louder, whoosh; again, I turned to see what had made the sound, but again I saw nothing. I mimicked the sound for Earl and Paddy, and then realized it must be a whale. The next several minutes dragged slowly as we scanned the waves hoping to sight the whale when it surfaced. Then it did! Not more than thirty yards to port, a thirty-five foot gray whale surfaced for a quick exhale and breath, then swam onward parallel to our course. Though it was a brief encounter, it was truly awesome to see and hear a creature of such size, especially in the ocean.

As we cleared the headland of Haiti's northern finger, we steered southwester. We did not want to approach any closer to Port au Prince. The capital of Haiti was socially and politically unstable, and foreign sailors were vulnerable to attack as well as seizure of boat or person. We carried no weapons, so we thought distance was our best defense. By sunset, the winds had fallen to a quiet breeze, and we were making less than four knots.

I came on watch at ten. The air was still. The sea reflected the stillness so perfectly that every star shone from the water as well as the sky, and you could not see where the heavens ended and the ocean began. We drifted as if floating through space, sparkling silver stars above us and below. Mesmerized, I lay back in the cockpit and studied the infinite suns that spread over me, seeming close enough to touch, but too distant ever to reach.

Paddy had cautioned me to keep an eye out for sudden thunderstorms before he sank into the darkness of the cabin. Although my fascination with the sky absorbed me, I sat up to check the area for shipping traffic every few minutes. About midnight, I spotted a soft flash of light out of the corner of my eye. I watched until there was another, followed by more. The flashes were lighting a huge thunderhead several miles (possibly dozens) to the south. At first, I thought to wake Earl or Paddy. But then I waited as I watched the fireworks of lightning bolts shooting down to the ocean and flashes illuminating the cloud from the inside. I heard no thunder, and there still was no breeze. The light show continued until Earl came on watch. Then, just before dawn, a rain squall finally struck, but the winds were light, so Earl did not call us to reef the sails.

Dawn of the third day out from Inagua, we were anxious for landfall. It had been over three weeks since we left Beaufort, two months since they left Bermuda. We were three men on a small boat, ready to reach our destination. Paddy began extolling the good taste of Red Stripe beer. All three of us dreamed of good food, nothing fried, fresh vegetables and fruit and all the water we could drink. By midmorning, a good breeze had developed. By midafternoon, big seas had joined the wind. We were sailing hard and as fast as *Eliza* would sail, about six knots over long eight to ten foot swells with the crests blown off. We hoped the high winds would deliver us to Jamaica by nightfall, and all kept a serious land watch throughout the afternoon until sunset.

Sunset without making landfall was gravely disappointing and more disheartening than any of us had expected. We knew we must be close, but we also knew it might be two more days. The voyage had delivered us to our collective point of exhaustion. Too little money, too little food, difficult weather, and unreliable navigation had stressed us all. We were ready to be ashore, *Eliza* safely moored at Runaway Bay Club.

When I came on watch at ten, the sea was as still as the night before. We were barely drifting. By the time Earl came on watch at two, there was a touch of a breeze, just enough to keep the boat moving forward. I fell asleep quickly, still tired from my illness.

When I woke the next morning about 6:30, I crawled out of the cabin and stumbled to the stern for my morning ablutions. As I was zipping my jeans, I turned to ask Earl if he had seen anything during his watch. When I looked up, I was shocked and instantly overjoyed to see that we were coasting along the shore of Jamaica less than a quarter mile offshore.

"We made it! Are we really there?"

"Yes, it's Jamaica, but we still have to find Runaway Bay. Paddy, bring Mason's directions." Earl unfolded the map, and we began to look for landmarks that would indicate Runaway Bay, landmarks that might or might look the same from offshore. Mason's directions did not make much sense, but we thought they might make sense once we saw a reference point. Of course, the directions did not include a lat/long position that we could mark on a chart. The directions were the narrative a driver might give a lost car. There was no defined mileage, just "look for this" and "look for that". Palms lined the shore atop a layer of volcanic rock interrupted rarely by a simple house or two.

Despite having no idea where we needed to land, we remained jubilant and relieved to have arrived off Jamaica. We enjoyed sailing quietly along the coast studying the coral shore, the rocky sea bottom and the lush tropical forest. We saw neither people nor signs of people. There were no harbors and few lights until we reached a well-lit location near dusk. We thought we must have found Runaway Bay, and we turned into the harbor. We were wrong. Unlike interstate highways, the sea is not littered with locational signage, so one place can look much like another from the water. The sun had set, and night was settling over the sea so we headed away from land while still looking for Mason's landmarks.

(A few days later we identified the mystery harbor as Ocho Rios, one of the places Mason had referred to in his directions.)

We could not find Runaway Bay in the dark, so we continued down the coast. It was the middle of the night when we dropped anchor in Montego Bay. Paddy was determined to go ashore even though we had not cleared Customs or Immigration and could not legally leave the boat until morning. I went with him. It was quiet in town, but we were happy to simply walk around. We met a couple of working women who quickly took an interest in Paddy. Paddy turned on his charm and the threesome began talking trash to each other. One of the women grabbed herself indiscreetly to emphasize her point, and Paddy just laughed. When he turned his pockets inside out to dramatize his point, she laughed too.

Epilogue

The conclusion of our voyage was anticlimactic. Customs boarded *Eliza* mid-morning and performed a thorough search. I suppose we still looked untrustworthy, neither yachtsmen nor perhaps even sailors, more like vagabonds. Earl contacted Mason by phone to let him know we were there, but not quite there. In the meantime, a fierce wind arose from the east, the direction of our intended sail. Also, the anchor chain had wrapped itself around a large coral head thirty feet down and could only be freed by someone diving to the bottom to unwrap it. Earl cut the anchor line, leaving for local salvors the anchor and chain at the bottom of the bay.

Earl also convinced Mason that it would take at least forty-eight hours for us to tack into thirty-knot winds back to Runaway Bay. Mason agreed to pay a sportfisher to tow us back. Six hours later, replete with lobster sandwiches, we had been towed to *Eliza*'s new mooring off The Runaway Bay Club.

Mason gave us a hero's welcome, Bloody Marys all around and sent us to our own private bungalows before we joined his friends, guests from the U.S., for cocktails and dinner. The wives from New Jersey wanted me to visit them and meet their daughters. One husband, who worked for Union Carbide, suggested that I apply for a job in their Ocean Research department. Another friend recommended that I join the Navy as a diver. I think everyone was trying too hard to be sure it was a memorable party. I was too tired to care, so I just smiled and nodded my head. Only food and sleep interested me.

Mason invited me to stay as long as I liked and to drink as much Red Stripe (or whatever) as I wanted; literally the keys to the cooler. With his driver, I rode to Kingston to take Earl and Paddy to the airport. We stopped at a restaurant in Ocho Rios where one of the rivers spilled over a waterfall beside the bar. In Kingston, they sat me between the two of them for fear that this solitary white boy might otherwise be attacked as we drove through town. Kingston, unlike Montego Bay, was rife with crime and poverty. Houses had bars on the windows, and shops conducted business through holes in fence screens. The rough and depressed streets we drove through the city did not detract from the beauty of the Blue Mountains through which we crossed the island. Still, I felt safer with Earl and Paddy on either side of me until we reached the airport and said our farewells, knowing we would not likely see each other ever again. For the weeks we sailed together on a small boat, we had become friends; they had been good shipmates.

After several days of lobster sandwiches, long leisurely swimming in the pool, and trying to climb coconut trees, I knew I was ready to return home. Mason's secretary made my plane reservations and made sure that he paid me the wages I was due (it slipped his mind). I cleared Customs in Miami; the officer gave my backpack a couple of good pats, then winked, smiled knowingly and said, "Have a nice day." He seemed certain (probably due to my long hair), but amused, that I was hauling ganja, but my only legal violation was bringing back more than the allowable amount of dollars. I trusted a stranger to carry my excess.

Two months later, I finally started my fragmented college career at the University of North Carolina at Chapel Hill. When my parents arrived for their first visit a few weeks into the semester, they entered my dorm room looking sheepish, as if they were hiding something. I asked what was on their minds, and my father handed me a postcard. It was from Mason; *Eliza* had dragged her mooring and sunk, and he needed a captain for his new boat. He wanted me to return as captain of the *Eliza II*. I considered the offer for several days before declining; I had lived my dream of sailing to a tropical paradise. I stayed in school. For a while.

The EVERGLADES
And The TEN THOUSAND ISLANDS

For my fortieth birthday year, my first selfish celebration was a January seakayaking trip to the Everglades and Ten Thousand Islands area of the southwestern Gulf coast of Florida. I asked Joe, my dear friend from grad school, to join me, thinking he would enjoy the trip as much as I expected to. We had hiked sections of the Appalachian Trail together, survived the Blizzard of 1993 in Slickrock Wilderness, and I knew he had paddled mountain whitewater, albeit in a cheap dime store raft (against my advice) out of which he promptly tore the bottom on a river rock and then nearly drowned. Nevertheless, he would be a good companion.

We flew into Ft. Myers, Florida on ValuJet, the cheapest airline flying at the time. We had a few hours to wait before connecting with our Nantahala Outdoor Center guides, so we decided to drive out to Sanibel Island if we could find an inexpensive car rental. At the rental counter, I asked, mostly tongue-in-cheek (and laughing inside), if they had any cars for rent by the hour. Indeed they did. Surprise, but I did not show it. So, for $1.09 per hour, Joe and I drove off in a brand new $20,000 (at the time) Mitsubishi station wagon with full leather and power package, including a sunroof. The price struck us as downright silly, and we chuckled most of the way to the first seafood restaurant we found after crossing the bridge to Sanibel, the Lazy Flamingo.

After lunch, we drove over to Captiva, passing Ding Darling National Wildlife Refuge, named for a Pulitzer-Prize winning editorial cartoonist who blocked the development of a significant mangrove swamp on Sanibel. Both islands were attractive enough for Joe, a North Carolina mountain boy raised with disdain for all things Floridian (as in the mountain vernacular "damnFloridians" (or the alliterative version), the two words connected as if one), to admit that the islands would be a pleasant place to visit.

Our guides wasted no time having us select a seakayak that "fit" (which only meant that you could get in and get out without assistance, not necessarily with grace), describing how supplies would be divided among the group, explaining how to load the kayaks, and then delivering us to our lodging, the 19th century Rod and Gun Club in Everglades City. The Club sits beside the Barron River, furnished mostly as it has been since opening. Entering the front door, we stepped straight into old Florida, a place that remained wild into the late 20th century. Mounted in the hallway were an alligator, an alligator skin, a bobcat, an otter, a wild boar head, a matching pair of tarpon, a huge largemouthed bass, shark jaws, deer antlers, and of course a couple of antique guns. A bear posed growling atop an old phone booth with a working pay phone that had been built into a corner once the telephone had been invented. Surrounded by the Everglades with its panthers, alligators, uncountable birds, and even more numerous mosquitoes, the area is famous for its freshwater (brackish) fishing among the mangroves and saltwater fishing in the Gulf. [Note: This trip predated the widespread invasion of exotic species such as pythons and boas large enough to consume the alligators and deer.]

The Everglades area is also infamous for preserving the Wild West after the west was no longer wild. Rumrunners, dope dealers, smugglers, murderers, law breakers of all kinds have sought refuge hiding in the dark swamps and meandering creeks, rivers and bays that course among the Ten Thousand Islands, a string of barrier islands and mangrove swamps that extend along the southwest coast of Florida where the freshwater from the Everglades meets the saltwater of the Gulf of Mexico and creates the rich brackish soup that supports a variety of marine life such as fish, crabs, and shrimp. Over a period of thousands of years, the Calusa natives and their ancestors created much of the high ground in the swamps by piling oyster and clam shells into mounds that remain dry even during hurricane storm surge. Shards of their pottery lie scattered on Gulf beaches. The Calusa also relied on chickees, wooden platforms on stilts or pilings that created a livable surface above the murky water.

Chokoloskee, just beyond where we launched our kayaks, is a massive example of the shell mounds built by the ancient people who occupied the region. A quarter square mile in area, the island is 20 feet above sea level. After a quick, on-the-water tutorial in handling a seakayak, we paddled up Turner River and stopped at the first mound we approached. We could see the old cistern from Turner's homestead through the mangrove thicket. Continuing upstream another mile, we turned into a small creek that connected the river with Mud Bay. You cannot find many place names so honest. True to its name, the bottom of Mud Bay was a sucking soft gray silty mud that absorbed the blade of your paddle if you stroked too deeply. The silt spun off the paddle blade in a light gray cloud at each stroke.

Another creek carried us from Mud Bay to Cross Bays, a pair of similarly shallow, mud-bottomed ponds past which we entered a wider tributary that opened into Sunday Bay. We planned to camp on Sunday Bay Chickee, a modern National Park chickee with two platforms bridged together with a portajohn in the middle, on the northern edge of the bay. I paddled up to the chickee. With low tide, my head was below the platform, so I had to stand in my kayak to climb up. No problem, I thought. I held my paddle alongside the hull of my kayak and pushed on the throat to hold the kayak in position, to stabilize it so I could stand. As I pushed on the paddle, it never stopped penetrating the bottom of the bay. Just as with Mud Bay, the muddy bottom seemed to have no bottom. We later learned, after the crash of a ValuJet in the Everglades, that silty mud reaches from four feet to more than twenty feet deep above the limestone that forms the Florida sponge, the bedrock as it were. Adrenalin surged through me briefly as I realized that, if I fell from the kayak, there was literally nothing on which I could stand to extract myself from the water.

I called to Joe, and he pulled his kayak beside me so I could jump onto the chickee. Lying on my belly, I could reach my gear as Joe pulled everything from my kayak and passed it to me. We repeated the same process with everyone and then secured our kayaks to the pilings and enjoyed a cup of tea in the cool air and golden sky of the setting sun. Our guides prepared dinner and offered the box wine used for the sauce to whoever wanted to drink the cheap stuff. Joe and I did not hesitate. Somebody needed to dispose of the weight.

It had surprised me that we were not swarmed by biting bugs. The guides told us that summer in the 'Glades was completely unbearable, and even rangers did not enter the inland sawgrass marsh then. Instead, we enjoyed the flight of ospreys carrying fish to their nests, a few ibis perched in the mangroves, and fish breaking the reflective surface of the bay. Night seemed the clearest most of us had ever seen with the Orion Nebula visible to the naked eye and the sky dusty with millions of stars, suns spread throughout the universe and spanning thousands of light years. Most of the group pitched tents for privacy even though the chickee had a roof on each end. The still of the night was mostly silent though broken occasionally by leaping fish, bird calls, and at one point, the splashing of a larger animal nearby. We slept well despite the chickee swaying whenever someone strolled to the portajohn.

Everyone rose with the sun for breakfast. Luckily, the tide had risen, so the kayaks floated near the platform height and made for easy loading. Heading south across Sunday Bay, the skies were overcast, but the wind pushed us from behind, carrying us toward Oyster Bay and Huston Bay where we detoured around Last Huston Bay by taking an unnamed river to where it met Chatham River. Paddling was peaceful and quiet, and even as a group, each of us could appreciate our solitude. We reached the Watson Place at Chatham Bend for lunch and made camp before exploring the site of Earl Watson's legendary homestead where he paid his help after harvest by killing them. Remnants of the homestead included foundations, a couple of cisterns, a cauldron mounted on bricks for cooking sugar cane and a solitary threshing machine. No evidence of the cane fields remained as nature has reclaimed all the open ground except the one acre camping site behind the dock that the park service periodically mowed. Left on its own, the swamp would take it all back.

I had expected that the Watson Place might haunt me with its bloody history. According to Peter Matthiessen's series of novels beginning with *Killing Mr. Watson*, Watson was cruel, greedy, and prone to murder as a certain solution to some of his problems. He took advantage of his remote land, his sugar cane "plantation", to attract desperate people, some broke, some on the run from the law, to work for him. When the harvest was in, the sugar cane boiled into syrup and sold, time came for him to pay his workers what he owed for their labor. He reportedly killed more than one of them, dropping the body in the river on an outgoing tide or burying the body on one of the many Gulf islands where the sand is easy to dig, and few visitors ventured. We laughed about how many bones we might find if the old farm was not overgrown and the former cane fields impenetrable. Time and hurricanes should have uncovered anyone buried near the homestead and bleached the bones of those left to fertilize the fields. But none of us was sure how much of a joke it was. Watson was only charged with one murder, Belle Starr, reputed friend of outlaws such as the James Gang in

Oklahoma. Still, the residents of Chokoloskee tired of Watson's violence and collectively ended his life when he visited the island one day, without giving him an opportunity to list his victims.

One of our guides, Jim, led an afternoon sortie down the river to explore a small tributary stream. At its mouth, the stream was about fifteen feet wide, but red mangrove choked the banks and reached over the water. The width narrowed almost as soon as we entered, so we floated single file with insufficient room to turn our kayaks around. At several spots, the branches hung so low we had to lean back onto the rear decks of our kayaks to get under them. At high tide, we could not have paddled under the branches, and the tide was rising. The soil smelled of rot and decay, a pungent fecundity of marsh land. Claustrophobia hovered in the thick , soundless tangle of mangroves. When the branches scraped our decks, and we could paddle no further, we had to back out. I reached a small opening in the mangroves and tried to turn my kayak around like a three point turn in a car, but it became more like a dozen point turn as the long kayak pushed against the banks of the narrow stream, and I tried to make space that did not exist for a turn I should not have attempted. As I maneuvered back and forth, I peered into the shallow tannic water beside me and spotted a small alligator about two feet long in barely a foot of water. A cute little dinosaur that I was thrilled to see. Was its fourteen foot mother lying patiently on the streambed below me, hanging casually near the bottom with the confidence of an apex predator? How deep was the stream? I could have used the length of my paddle to measure the depth of the water under me, but that might have antagonized any large reptile resting there. Careful not to work my paddle blade too far down (in case mother was there), I kept sound to a minimum as I twisted the kayak to exit. I alerted the person behind me that I had found a place with room to turn around and then paddled for the open river.

Back at camp, as the sun fell below the tree line, I sat on the dock to read and write in my journal. A flock of ibis with long and elegant curved bills and white feathers winged past low and close enough for me to hear the wind beat of their wings. Then I heard a loud splash, dolphins playfully swimming upstream. Soon, another flock of ibis, a hundred or more, whirred noisily up the river. Around the dock pilings swam shrimp, crabs, catfish, and mullet. The swamp was alive, rich with a diversity of wildlife. Just before dark, a raccoon wandered through camp and crawled across the cauldron.

Despite listening to our guides recount the Watson legend as we sat around the campfire before turning in, we departed the Watson Place without encountering any ghosts or spirits and caught the slack tide as we paddled the river toward the Gulf. Halfway down Chatham River, we rafted up for a water break. Relaxed in our boats, we could enjoy the pelicans perched in the trees along the bank and the osprey young peeking from their nests of big sticks. Another overcast sky kept the day comfortably cool while we enjoyed an unhurried paddle to the open end of the river, the horizon over the Gulf of Mexico, our first taste of open water. When we cleared the mouth of the river, we angled southwest toward our next camp, Mormon Key.

The white crushed shell beach was littered with conch shells making it painful to walk barefoot. Some of the conchs bore a hole near the top that showed someone, (the Calusa?) had extracted the meat. Pottery shards from the days of the Calusa occupation of the islands, blackened by having been baked in fire, contrasted sharply with the sun bleached shells.

Everyone unloaded their kayaks and ate lunch on the beach with a chilly breeze coming off the Gulf. Several of us then paddled over to New Turkey Key, a nearby island that was also unoccupied. When we passed the southwest end of Mormon Key, we crashed into a hard wind. Between the wind and the whitecapped waves that the wind created, the passage was more demanding than our paddling of the two previous days.

Cactus grew on the island among the thousands of clam and conch shells and healthy stands of both red and black mangroves. After wandering around the island and taking photos for an hour, we set a bearing for Crab Key, a larger island across the bay back toward Mormon Key. Due to the wind and sea conditions, all of us did not reach the island at the same time. As we waited, we heard splashing near the shore of the island. Dolphins were playing, surfacing and leaping in the shallow channel between Crab and Mangrove Keys. I paddled quietly toward a small pod near the shore. Without scaring them, I hoped for a closer view and some photos. Still 30-40 feet from where I last saw one surface, BANG. One of the small dolphins had rammed my boat from the side, rocked me almost off balance, then slipped under and sped away so fast that it drew a furrowed wake. Fifty yards away, it was still swimming fast, and my adrenaline had not slowed either. Jim spotted a roseate spoonbill near me while two dolphins played near Donna, our other guide, and Mary. The dolphins jumped, turned, and frolicked with such passion it may have been foreplay (or more). Playing within ten feet of Donna and Mary, one surfaced between their two boats and looked shocked to have come so close to humans. But they never ceased swimming near us even while we shot photos.

Dinner followed my saltwater bath in the Gulf, then we joined a couple who had built a driftwood fire up the beach from our camp. Donna read a chapter from *Totch* (about whom more later), a local fisherman and legend who starred in a couple of films and smuggled tons of marijuana without getting caught; meanwhile, we dipped pineapple chunks in chocolate sauce. Joe was a hit with his recitations of Byron and "Jabberwocky". We fended off a raid by an aggressive raccoon before turning in. With our tent just ten feet from the water's edge, we hoped no sudden storms or spring tides would wash higher on the beach. Even a minor rise in water level would have flooded the tent because the beach was so flat. The Gulf lapped gently along the shore where we could see phosphorescence sparkling in the small waves.

The Everglades have attracted more than its share of characters, all with tales to tell, myths to repeat, legends to live. Mr. Watson, mentioned earlier, was a mean sort of character. Totch Brown was the opposite. A hardworking hunter of alligators from a young age, he waded the thin waters of the Everglades even when the mosquitoes swarmed so thick you could barely breathe, ever watchful for the panthers and various venomous snakes and spiders that also lived in the mangrove swamps or the inland sawgrass marsh, until the government outlawed killing gators. He was a commercial fisherman, a business which the government complicated and constrained by constantly introducing and changing arcane laws that made it difficult for an honest fisherman to make a decent living. Like other fishermen in the area, to better provide for his family, Totch began smuggling marijuana, the "square grouper", by the trawler load from South America. The Ten Thousand Islands, with its myriad and confusing channels, creeks, rivers, bays, and waterways, provided the perfect conditions for evading the law. Locals like Totch knew the tides and the shoals, the hidden places in the mangrove thickets, and on which islands large cargoes of illegal imports might be stashed for distribution by others with fast boats and shallow drafts. Even after the feds raided Chokoloskee by blocking the sole road in or out and arrested more than a dozen smugglers, they never caught Totch. As with other outlaws before him, the feds indicted him for tax evasion. Joe found a signed copy of Totch's autobiography in Ted Smallwood's Store on Chokoloskee, behind which the good folks gathered in 1910 to end Mr. Watson's violence and now operating as a museum.

Overnight, gleaming stars filled the night sky on Mormon Key except during a series of brief pre-dawn showers that rained just enough to create the perfect white noise for sleeping. From Mormon Key, we paddled the next day to Gun Rock Point, a small cove cluttered with mangrove roots and fallen trees, for a short break before crossing open water to Duck Rock. There is no rock at Duck Rock nor were there any ducks. Duck Rock was a short thin, kidney shaped pile of treeless sand that barely clears the surface of the Gulf at high tide. The plan had been for lunch until we arrived and saw there was no room to land the kayaks much less anywhere to sit or wander. We continued on to Pavilion Key, much longer than Duck Rock with a strong stand of vegetation running down the middle. The northern end of the key, where Joe and I decided to camp, was narrow. Both ends of our tent fronted on water, and the breeze swept across unimpeded.

Camp established, we ate lunch, then several of us jumped into the clear Gulf water for the closest thing to a bath we would get for another 48 hours. Looking west into the Gulf, beyond the horizon, was Texas. The brackish waters of the mangrove swamps was a few miles to the east. Four of us slid into our kayaks and paddled a relaxed circumnavigation of the key to enjoy the wildlife and scenery. White pelicans (unlike the brown pelicans we have in North Carolina), oyster catchers with their long red beaks and overall coloring reminiscent of puffins, great white herons, blue herons, and ospreys crowded the bushes and shoals around the island. In the crystal water, we watched as we slipped over sections of reef with scatterings of tropical fish schooling along with a small nurse shark, and a lonely star fish. As beautiful as the water was, there was more to see in the air than in the sea while the tide floated us along effortlessly.

As the sun set over the Gulf with stunning and vibrant colors, we gathered driftwood for another fire. Highs during the days approached eighty, but the nights were wonderfully chill. Sweaters and fires. The perfect island atmosphere. Dinner was salmon gumbo. All our meals had been tastier than anyone expected on a long camping trip in the backcountry where few of the ingredients can be fresh. Jim and Donna promised to share the recipes but cautioned that what is delicious after a day outside paddling a kayak or hiking a beach may not be as tasty as the same dish prepared in the clean comfort of your home kitchen. Of course, they were right.

We woke to yet another clear sky morning with light fog lifting. It was a layover day. We would remain camped on Pavilion Key until we packed the following day for the last paddle back to Chokoloskee. As Jim walked past our tent, he asked if he could get some help hauling dish water from the end of the island. When we reached the end and began to fill jugs with water, a dolphin cruised into the shallows and then charged through the water with sufficient speed to raise a foot high wave. It turned and twisted, stopped, lurched, stopped and charged again. Although we could not see what fish it was chasing, it was successful and swam away calmly back into deeper water.

We paddled most of the day, first around the key, then past Duck Rock to the mangrove shore near Gun Rock Point. The sun glared out of a clear sky over calm clear waters, and we cruised lazily along the shoreline taking photos and climbing fallen trees before heading back out to Pavilion Key. We had been camping enough nights that some people began to tire of "roughing it". I missed my wife and daughter because I had been away from home for almost a week. But I did not feel a homesick type of yearning. Family (and work) aside, I could have stayed until the biting bugs returned for summer.

We rested beside another driftwood fire on the beach while we ate dinner and watched another sunset over the Gulf. Who could tire of such beauty? Jim reported the forecast for our last day: scattered thunderstorms and winds increasing. He suggested an early departure to catch the rising tide back to Chokoloskee. So we rose before the sun and packed our kayaks in a dense fog. Visibility was less than a hundred feet, so it was not easy to keep the group within sight of each other. As the sun began to burn off the fog, we could see a hundred yards or so as if we were paddling inside a clouded bubble. We took a break on an unnamed mangrove key and then watched Crate Key, followed by Rabbit Key, emerge from the fog as we coasted easily. The islands were faint, shadows enclosed in a veil of mist. With the wind at our backs, we slipped swiftly across the sea and reached Rabbit Key with its pristine beach so early we decided we would not stop for lunch and continued on past Lumber Key to land on tiny Turtle Key with its small beach and some fallen trees that were ideal for sitting and eating.

Jim, making sure we remained on schedule to ride the tidal current that would carry us back to Chokoloskee, kept lunch brief. We had covered five miles in a few hours, and we had five miles ahead of us. Jim cautioned everyone to keep sight of him or Donna as we would begin to navigate through some unidentified channels to ride the tidal currents. The currents could be swift, so it would be easy to miss or not recognize a "marker" where we should turn. Away from Turtle Key, we passed between a couple of mangrove islands and began to see how the current flowed through invisible channels like a river. Soon the current pushed us faster than we could paddle. We used our paddles just to keep the bows of our kayaks pointed forward while the currents provided the power.

Overhead, an osprey circled, and we could hear its chicks crying from the nest, a piercing shriek above the otherwise quiet river. The osprey stalled midair then dived into the water. Rising without prey, it flapped its wings a few long beats and trembled hard as if shaking the water from its feathers then dived again. We watched the osprey repeat this several times before it lifted into the air with a small fish in its talons. As we floated out of sight of the osprey, we heard the breathy exhale of a nearby dolphin with a large dark cut on its dorsal fin. We followed along floating on the current. As we rounded a bend in the channel, everyone was surprised to see Chokoloskee less than a mile ahead. Speeding homeward on the wind and current, we had traveled five miles in less than an hour. Within a few minutes of landing our kayaks, a squall caught us in the open and drenched everyone completely. But we were at the end of our journey with hot showers and a farewell seafood dinner waiting at the Rod and Gun Club back in Everglades City.

CRABS in the SURF

No matter how much time you spend in or on the ocean, there are many creatures you may never encounter. I recall that Jacques Cousteau had traveled the planet for decades before he saw a whale shark at sea. I have never seen one. But in the time I have been in or on the ocean, I have seen many different types of fish, innumerable dolphins, hundreds of migrating eagle rays, one humpback whale and more than a few sharks.

During a hiatus from college, I moved to the Outer Banks of North Carolina, the wild protrusion of narrow sand islands that stand between the mainland U.S. and the arctic. Although most of the area is now very developed, mansions strung along the beach and a house tucked into every small stand of woods, when I moved to Duck, the cottage we rented was less than a mile from the end of the road, and the end of the road was fenced and gated.

The beach was a couple blocks from our cottage. It was September, so the water was not yet cold, but the beaches were empty. Tourists flee after Labor Day. With the sun warm and high, Jack, a roommate who waited tables at a linen tablecloth fancy restaurant at night and pretended to be a novelist during the day (he mostly slept), agreed to join me for a swim. We walked barefoot up the empty street and over the low dunes to a flat wide beach where there was no one in sight.

The waves were small but I intended to bodysurf. I strolled into the ocean and waited for a good wave then dove under the breaking crest. The water was refreshing. I stood up and waited for the next wave and dived through again. When I rose from the wave, I raked my hair away from my face and could feel sand. While it was common to end up with sand in your hair if you landed in the shallows at the edge of the shore, it was not usual for the same to happen in the deeper water. I dived into another wave partly for fun and partly to rinse the sand from my hair.

When I stood, I heard Jack screaming "Shit! Shit!" and hurrying out of the water. Before I could even ask him why, I felt pinching in my bathing suit, in the tenderest of areas. "Shit! What the hell!" I hurried after Jack as fast as I could wade through the water. On the beach, we both stripped as quickly as possible, tearing our bathing suits off our legs. The pinching in my crotch did not stop after I shed my trunks. Then my scalp started to feel pinching as well.

With no way to rinse off whatever was tormenting us, we dashed naked back to the cottage where we stood under the outdoor shower and also sprayed ourselves with a hose to thoroughly rinse every hair on our bodies. As the pain subsided, we examined the rinse water and saw the culprits. Crab larvae. Clear, the size of a pin head. Voracious beasts I had never encountered or heard about. The ocean close to shore must have been full of the swarm. The ocean remained off limits for a while.

[Note: There are other tiny irritants that can torture you when swimming in the ocean. One source is called sea lice, the larval stage of a Thimble jellyfish or other types of stinging creatures. They have so far avoided me, and I do not look forward to the same experience I had with crabs.]

SHARKS and a SARCOPHAGUS

We were staying in a lodge high in the cool air of Mauna Loa on the big island of Hawaii, a bucket of firewood outside the door to feed the woodstove inside in the cold nights. During the day, my parents attended a seminar, and I entertained myself by hanging out on Hapuna Beach, a public beach, or hiking on the hot black lava flows. At some point, I heard that there was a catamaran that sailed people offshore to an area where they could snorkel the clear blue waters.

I love sailing and being in the ocean, so I signed up. Halfway to our destination, the guide was instructing everyone about safety and such when he said that anyone who had a SCUBA certification could dive if they liked. They had a divemaster aboard to guide us. Count me in!

The divemaster briefed us on the dive and told us to take our time clearing our ears. No one would be left behind. He also cautioned that we might see sharks and should keep our distance. They would not bother us. Naturally, as the youngest in the dive group, I had trouble clearing my ears and had to return to the surface before heading back down.

We were diving in 30-40 feet, and I could see that the group had just left the first stop which was an open cave. The divemaster had paused at the opening, so I swam up beside him and peered into the darkness. Out of the black depth inside the cave, a shark emerged gliding toward me. Fascinated by the elegance and ease of its motion, I held my position, and another shark emerged. Both were black tip reef sharks about six feet long. The divemaster suddenly turned and noticed I was right beside him. I do not know why that concerned him, but I could sense urgency in his eyes. Maybe we were too close to the sharks. Maybe he was scared that I would get scared. He signaled me to follow the rest of the group, and I left the sharks peacefully guarding the cave.

Once I caught up with the group, we swam together as the divemaster led us to a moray eel, some lobsters, and plenty of colorful reef fish. When I learned to SCUBA dive, I immediately loved the freedom of being able to breathe underwater, never having to surface for air, the closest humans can come to feeling like sea creatures with their three dimensional freedom of movement.

Our dive time passed too quickly as we swam among the volcanic reefs. We approached our final stop, a formation called "the sarcophagus". Despite having been briefed by the divemaster on board the catamaran, when I saw others in the group disappear into a black rectangle in the ocean floor, I was spooked and felt a bit claustrophobic. Where did the hole go? How would I find my way out? I was one of the last to swim up and hover over the empty rectangle. I looked down into the hole trying to see some source of light, a bottom for reference, anything, and there was nothing but a pitch black void. I told my logical self that there was no danger; everyone ahead of me had done it, and I said to myself "what the hell" then exhaled to sink into the hole.

As I sank past the lip, I could see only dark rock walls. I saw nothing below me. But I continued to fall, and eventually I could see light. I kicked my fins and exited another open-mouthed cave like the one where I had watched the sharks. Back into open water, I was ready to do it again, but time was up, our tanks low on air, and we surfaced, humans dependent on being above the water once again.

SOUND FLOUNDERING

I had fifteen hundred dollars in the bank. Summer had started, and gold was rising on the prophecy of the dollar's collapse among the doomsday forecasters who made more money on scaring people than on investment results. I mulled tying up my savings in ten ounces of gold with the promise of future profits. It would have been a smart and mature use of my hard-earned money. But a Hobie sixteen foot catamaran with a Tequila Sunrise color scheme of banana yellow hulls and rainbow-paneled sail called to me from the roadside in front of Marsh's Surf and Sea on the Atlantic Beach Causeway. The boat sparked fantasies of girls in bikinis, surfing waves, and skipping across the ocean on a broad reach to Cape Lookout.

I wanted the Hobie Cat, but only had enough money for half of the purchase price. What to do? Through a series of twisted and forgotten machinations, I concocted a plan, if you can call any sort of madness a plan.

"Father, let's buy a Hobie Cat. We can sail it off the beach or out on the sound. Besides, I already have half of the cost," I proposed with the confidence of the used car salesman.

"How much?" he asked.

I could see this was going well and added "And that includes a trailer".

"OK," he concluded. No fuss, no muss, just a positive decision made at near light speed.

Inside, my brain shook, and reason collapsed around me. No way should it have been that easy. No persuasion, no searing interrogation. I wanted clarification, a definitive agreement. I wanted him to confirm that he had both understood and agreed to front half the cost. Instead, I just smiled, giggled to myself and declared aloud, "Great!!"

In retrospect, I should have insisted that he discuss his end of the commitment with his wife, my mother. It never crossed my mind at the time. I was too excited to think straight. Scottish by blood if not geography, Mother managed the family finances prudently, balancing the bank account every month and doling out weekly cash for my father's soft drink habit (when cash starved, he ran a tab at the local Seven Eleven convenience store). When Father told his wife, she was not amused or pleased. She thought he was being childish and irresponsible like me. He pretended he was putting up the money to buy a share for my little sister who was too young to want or sail a boat. She knew nothing about it, but I did not care; I was getting what I wanted.

Marsh's promised to have the Hobie rigged and ready before the end of the week. Mother drove us the fifteen miles from their cottage in Emerald Isle to Marsh's and left us there. I suspected she was hoping that the boat would not be ready and we would be stuck there; in her mind, it would serve us right, a small bit of retribution for our misbehaving.

One of the staff led us back behind the store to a narrow, still, and smelly canal where the Hobie Cat floated fully rigged waiting for us. My heart pounded as we stepped onto the trampoline, the hulls rising and falling in rhythm to our unsteady steps. Father sat on one side of the trampoline.

"You sure you know what you are doing?" he inquired. Frankly, it was a little late for him to wonder. The boat was ready even if we were not. Too late, I realized how nice it would have been to have an owners' manual or a new owner briefing.

I jauntily replied, "Of course!'', being cocky enough to convince him what I was not so sure I believed. Admittedly, I had learned to sail a Sunfish at Camp Morehead when I was ten. In fact, I learned on the same waters that we would sail back to Emerald Isle. I had also crewed a 35 foot Dickinson ketch to Jamaica a few years earlier, but that was very different from sailing a small fast catamaran.

We began to drift toward the sound in a very light morning breeze that was vapid at best. My excitement about being on my own sailboat became anxiety as I realized that the Marsh crew, when we were almost out of hearing, were yelling something about locking down the rudders, gesturing wildly as if that would explain everything, but the rudder blades looked fine to me and would turn to both port and starboard. I could not understand, so I shrugged it off. I had no idea what they meant.

I had assumed we would slip out of the canal with a favorable wind, then scoot down the sound fifteen miles back to Emerald Isle near my parents' beach house. The water tower behind the cottage was the only navigation landmark to identify our destination. We did not bother with a navigation chart. I never really thought about how long it might take us to get there, especially in the absence of wind.

Eventually we floated out of the canal and entered the open water of Bogue Sound, turning the rudders to angle us west to sail down to Emerald Isle, anxiety point number two as it dawned on me how far it was (at least fifteen miles by sea) and how long it might take (forever with no wind, no engine, no paddle), and we had brought neither food nor water.

The water was dark and mirror slick reflecting only the dull overcast sky. The hint of a faint, ephemeral mid-morning breeze whispered past us. How would we move the sailboat with no motor and no paddle and no wind?

As the light breeze teased us, rattling the sail from one side then the other, I began to think of all the preparations I had omitted. Sunscreen? No, it was cloudy. Lifejackets? No, we could both swim. Water? Nope, did not plan to be out that long. Radio? Nope. (Remember the days before cell phones; neither did we carry a radio or any other way to call for help aside from waving our arms in the air. At that time, the only person I knew who had a radio on a small boat was Ranger Ricks in the TV series *Flipper*.) Backup plan? Nope. I wore only a swimsuit and my father wore a t-shirt and shorts. The humidity was already suffocating.

The wind puffed and sighed, playing with us. I suppressed a small welling fear that rose in my belly like seasickness and mentioned nothing to Father about my oversights or misgivings. Instead, I acted like the captain I was not and, with artificial calm, said, "I sure hope the wind picks up. I would hate for this to take all day since we did not bring anything to eat or drink." This was my subtle way of putting him on notice that our voyage might be uncomfortable, as if all the responsibility lay with the gods of wind and sea.

As we drifted in the sound, I could see for the first time the immensity and scope of what I, on behalf of we, had tackled. Without charts or communications or even a "not later than" schedule deadline, I had led us into the open waters of a sound three miles wide and thirty miles long though only an average of four feet deep. Both of us had seen summer squalls with thirty miles per hour winds and the steep short period whitecapped waves that thunderstorms could kick up. We floated tentatively on a small sailboat with little wind, staring far to the west, our landing beach beyond what we could see. Why had I not suggested dragging the boat to Emerald Isle on its trailer? Oh yeah, we had not yet purchased a trailer hitch.

The morning cloud cover and haze burned away. The slick water rippled nervously in sporadic breezes. I was happy to have some time to become familiar with the few moving parts of the boat, the mainsheet and the rudder. What had the staff at Marsh's been yelling to us about the rudder? It looked fine to me, but I continued to fiddle with it and puzzled over what might be wrong.

After drifting hopelessly for almost two hours and traveling only a couple miles, the wind filled the sails. The stern dropped, and the hulls sliced through the water as we accelerated from a limp float to a screaming racer. A new anxiety gutted me. Could I handle a boat as quick and nimble as the Hobie? I had learned to sail on a Sunfish, a fine small boat with a neo-Polynesian sail rig and a centerboard. Fast enough for fun in a good breeze, but not too fast to handle. Compared to the Sunfish, I suddenly realized that the Hobie was like a sports car, quick off the line and slightly tender at high speed. If the Sunfish was a Ford Mustang, the Hobie Cat was a blitzkrieg Porsche. It would burn rubber on land.

The tiller turned the boat sluggishly. Heavy and resistant in the hand, I slowly recognized that the rudders were not behaving properly. The boat ripped through the water as I fiddled with the tiller. The tiller is a single handle extending from a moveable joint where it connects to the bar running between the twin rudder blades. With some effort, I could pull or push the tiller enough to change the rudder blade angle and steer the Hobie, but it was harder than it should have been. As our speed increased, steering became more difficult and control more critical.

I tugged and twisted and lifted and pushed on the tiller. Then I tried a similar tactic with the bar between the rudder blades. Snap! The cross piece dropped the blades into place. Mystery solved, control regained. What the Marsh's staff had been trying to tell me was that I needed to lock the steering bar in place by lifting the bar, pushing it aft a bit, then setting it down to lock it into position. Like I said, an owner's manual would have been nice. Only blind luck solved the problem. Now I could steer in higher winds and have a chance to avoid burying a pontoon and pitchpoling with a twenty-seven foot mast. An upside down catamaran is a challenge to right.

With a steady wind, we ripped through the water trailing rooster tails from the pontoons mile after mile down the sound. The shallow draft allowed us to sail any course that held the wind. The apparent wind from our speed cooled the heat of midday as the sun burned hotly overhead and reflected brightly off the water. What could have taken all day ended in three and a half hours. We charged an empty soundside sand beach, ran the Hobie ashore, and laughed with joy, relief, and the thrill of having a new boat and our first sail on her.

SAILING *Spotted Moose* SOUTH in WINTER

Nothing's perfect. This is what we are taught when confronted by life's disappointments. I prefer "never are all things perfect" because we find small perfections in our daily lives. Not every day. Not every week or perhaps even every year. But we find them. They are the small exquisite joys that bring us enduring happiness and make life worth living.

My wife, Beth, and I have strived to make a habit of finding the small perfections surrounding us. A bluejay chick falls from its nest onto our deck. A baby rabbit hides in the tall grass of our yard, temporarily separated from its mother so that we can admire it. A screech owl winters in the hollow of a backyard silver maple tree, floating away silently each dusk. Our children speak a first word or reasonable facsimile. We toast small achievements as and when they occur; Beth has made sure that we do. We do not postpone the importance of small things nor allow the moment to be diluted with the crush of tasks and chores and everyday happenings.

Beth and I had dreamed of one day having a place on the coast. We did not expect we could afford a large waterfront home, but thought that living on an old wooden boat would be fascinating, surrounded by water and fresh air, dolphins, otters, seagulls and pelicans. Similarly, a decade ago, we decided it was time to move back to North Carolina. We had lived in Atlanta for ten years and enjoyed its culture, excellent restaurants, and proximity to the mountains. Both of our children had been born there. But it was always a long way from our original homes, the towns in North Carolina where our families still lived.

After exploring locations across the state and even across the border into southern Virginia (my mother's home state), we decided to move to the mountains near Asheville. In an episode of delightful madness, I convinced Beth that a small 19th century log cabin with a tiny bedroom and a loft was plenty large enough for four of us despite having only one, also tiny, bathroom and no laundry room. The pastures and outbuildings would make up for the lack of cabin space. A work shed would be the school, and the old spring house would protect the washer and dryer from some of the elements. Cars parked in a tractor barn and maybe one day a studio in the log barn at the head of the upper pasture. The creek flowing past was our night music when the wind did not rush down the ridge and rumble through the woods.

Beth was, as she has always been, a good sport, indulging me in the fantasy that we would build our dream home in the woods above the cabin "one day." After six years and the unfulfilled design of a simple house in the woods, we recognized that time was fleeting, that our daughter was a teenager and that both our children needed the experience of having their own space before they left home. And Beth still wanted a real laundry room; nothing fancy, just a place inside a heated house where she could wash clothes without having to first unfreeze the water hose. We bought a house a few miles from the cabin.

I was developing a mixed-use building in downtown Asheville, eight stories of residential condominiums with street level commercial space. My partner and I had reclaimed a crime-plagued vacant parking lot adjacent to the Thomas Wolfe Memorial and his mother's boarding house, Old Kentucky Home, and adjacent to the old Asheville-Biltmore Hotel, long since converted to public housing for seniors. The project had been well-received, presales were strong, and we had a sound financial partner. Construction began the summer of 2007.

By summer of 2008, the secondary mortgage market had collapsed along with FNMA and FHLMC due in large part to idiotically loose underwriting standards (a classic example being a pizza delivery guy in Florida who bought three $300,000 condos in South Florida despite barely being able to pay his own rent). Lending standards tightened (returning to where they should have been), and several of our buyers could no longer qualify for financing when it was time for them to close on the purchase of their homes in spring of 2009. We lost nearly $5 million in sales. Then the derivatives markets began to spiral downward with the imminent failure of AIG, Lehman Brothers and Bear Stearns. The economy sank into the worst economic recession since the Great Depression. At the heart of the devastation was the collapse of the housing market.

My partner and I lost our interest in the building to our equity partner. After four years of work, we had completed an exceptional building and paid off our construction loan, but there would be no profit for the two of us. More importantly for me, the financial carnage meant that I would not be able to develop another project for many years, and given my age, if ever. What would we do until then?

Beth and I took a quick retreat over Hickory Nut Gap to The Esmeralda Inn in Bat Cave, an historic inn once visited by northeastern notables including F. Scott Fitzgerald and his wife, Zelda, as well as Hollywood stars seeking seclusion, notably Mary Pickford and Douglas Fairbanks, among others. Lew Wallace finished the *Ben Hur* script in Room Nine. I hoped for inspiration as we sat in our small room at the historical inn discussing options for our future. My real estate skills were mothballed until the country resurrected a normal economy. The depth of the housing crisis was so severe that I doubted a full recovery for a decade, perhaps even longer. Should we stay in the mountains and fight to make something happen while the economy drowned? Should we start another business and, if so, what?

We had no answers. We knew we did not want to wallow in disappointment and frustration. We wanted to retain control of our lives, our futures, in some fashion. We had neither income nor prospects for any, and jobs were evaporating like rain puddles on asphalt in summer. We had some savings. Maybe we should take a sabbatical from the world of business and bank loans and profit and loss. Maybe we should make a decision as surprising as buying an old log cabin in the mountains. Maybe we should buy a sailboat.

The idea stuck like a deep keeled boat on a mud bank. Even though I loved the idea and the potential, it scared Beth. Obviously, she is the sane parent in the family. We would investigate further, but it could be a positive way to spend a couple of unsettled years while the nation and the economy worked through the turbulence of a recession. We would see the world from a new perspective.

We had dreamed of one day exploring the nooks and crannies of coastal North Carolina as well as venturing to the Gulf of Mexico or the Bahamas or wherever. We had hoped we might be able to do that when I retired. But here was a terrible economy, and maybe the time was now. Put behind us all the worries of a business, sell everything (almost) and move onto a sailboat. Go cruising for a couple of years or so while the economy sorted itself out. We might just find opportunity during our travels.

We bought a 28 year old Bristol 45.5 center cockpit sloop and took possession of the frozen boat in Annapolis in February 2010 on the heels of two storms that had dumped over 30 inches in two weeks. When Cameron and I arrived at Port Annapolis Marina, the boat had been in the water for about six hours. The cockpit was half full of snow and frozen slush. The bilge was full of water above the lower part of the engine block (no one had bothered to turn on the bilge pump much less check for a possible leak). It was cold and gray, nearing nightfall. We were tired from a gloomy eight hour drive up, and we were glad to get on board despite knowing that we had a lot of work to complete in the next four days to prepare the boat for a trip back to our North Carolina home waters in winter. The previous owners had named the boat *Spotted Moose*, apparently after their cat. I would learn later that Canadians have a certain reputation in the cruising community, one that I have not experienced.

Over the following days, we cleaned (sort of), reorganized gear (enough to know some of what we had on board and to create some space for everyone to sleep on the way south) and bought enough food to get us to Oriental. Cameron more than carried his load. We had good times running around together, even when it took almost two hours to provision our groceries, a long and boring period of time to wander each and every aisle of a grocery store.

Every morning we were hungry from our previous day's efforts. So, Eggs Benedict at The Main Ingredient, lunch at Grumpy's, and dinner at Jack's Fortune, at the time one of the best Chinese restaurants in Annapolis, though we chose it solely because it was close to our marina. Every evening we were exhausted. I was in pain from moving so much gear and banging my head (as well as other body parts) into every part of the boat imaginable, but especially anything near head height. It would take a while to accustom myself to moving around on a moving boat without injury. Cameron predicted all of us would have concussions.

"It will be the Concussion Club for our entire family," he mused. I jokingly suggested wearing helmets but found that the helmets increased the incidence of head banging due to the additional height.

My good friends Paul and Chuck arrived on Thursday to help bring the boat south. We were promptly delayed a day by a nor'easter that rocked and rolled us all night. Paul introduced us to blue crabs at Cantler's, a way-off-the-beaten-path kind of crab shack where the steamed crabs are poured over the table on brown paper. Au naturel.

I learned to sail when I was ten years old. Spending a month at Camp Morehead-by-the-Sea on Bogue Sound in North Carolina, lots of kids learned to sail during summer sessions filled with swimming, shooting, archery, and oyster roasts as well as long days on the water. Captain Purcell, owner of the camp, was full of mischief, racing his golf cart around the open lawn before the mess hall dinner, nearly turning over to his delight. Local legend Headless Hattie haunted the camp at least once each session from her watery grave near channel Marker 13, shouting distance from the camp.

That summer, I earned both my red (fair) weather mark and my blue (rough) weather mark. Red weather was easy sailing in light wind in a Sunfish. Blue weather sailing required a solo sail in white caps (winds over ten knots). My knuckles literally turned white and cramped with the effort of maintaining control over the taut, wet main sheet that threatened to slip from my grip. It was the most exciting challenge I had ever had.

On a more relaxed day, we made a group trip across the sound in Lightnings, a 16 foot open centerboard dinghy with a sloop rig. It was hot and clear with just enough wind to pull the wooden Lightnings into a gentle heel. We landed near Salter Path along an empty stretch of marsh. Being the tallest of the crew, the counselor at the helm designated me to pull the boat the last 30 shallow yards to shore. As we splashed into the marsh, our happy feet scattered fiddler crabs by the dozens into the grass and myrtle thickets. We swatted at flies and mosquitoes while we trekked without complaint across hot sand to the ocean on the other side of the island.

When we woke at Port Annapolis Marina on Saturday morning to leave Back Bay for North Carolina, there was again snow on the deck and the dock, but sun in the sky. Cold, but not too much wind. We motored over to Annapolis City Marina, fueled up and set off.

At that time, you could put what I knew about handling our new boat in a very small thimble. I literally had barely learned how to turn on the engine. I had NEVER steered the boat; I had ridden on it when we did the sea trials, but a paid captain was at the helm. I could light the propane stove, but we had no running water and one of the heads (i.e. toilet) died on us before we even left dock. The electrical panel that controlled virtually all the systems presented a confusion of toggle switches in four columns. Somehow the labels failed to correlate to the function of each toggle, or so I thought. Nevertheless, I knew that Paul's experience and Chuck's mechanical aptitude would get us where we needed to go. Of course, neither of them could have known what types of operator errors (me) they would be confront.

Being behind schedule (Note: Never have a schedule when cruising; it only leads to trouble.) a full day, we motored south down the quiet off-season Chesapeake Bay. Cameron and Chuck tried to get the chartplotter and radar working since we decided to gain some lost time by continuing underway through the night, bypassing the challenges of anchoring in unfamiliar waters. We had charts in addition to the chartplotter, but we expected the chartplotter to comfort us by illuminating distant freighters as smeared green radar targets (not the pinging blips shown in movies) long before they passed us as looming dark shadows with a confusing array of navigation lights -- a red, a green and a few whites scattered about. Several tug boats, barges and freighters approached us in the night. At one point, I forgot momentarily how to read the oncoming and retreating light patterns. One freighter passed within a few hundred yards, and I watched it recede into the black emptiness north. Turning around a while later, I was surprised to see what I assumed was the same freighter, which should have long since passed beyond what I could see; then I realized that I was seeing a new freighter, this one bearing down on a course that could intersect with ours. The incident completed my refresher course in nautical lighting. I paid closer attention to both the radar and everything visible around me. Fortunately, the night passage was mostly uneventful, star-filled and cold.

Night is a magical time to be on the water. Without depending on your sense of sight as much as during daylight, you smell and hear what might otherwise become background. And your sight can be challenged by mysterious silhouettes like the sunken warship that turned out to be an unlighted hazard to navigation used by the Navy for target practice.

Sun rose on a gray dawn as we approached Norfolk and the primary channel into and out of the Chesapeake. Everyone was ready to get ashore as we motored into Hampton Roads, crossing over the Hampton Roads Bridge Tunnel, passing old Fort Henry. Our first adventure came mid-morning. Norfolk/Hampton Roads is a busy port. Pleasure boats mix with freighters and Navy warships leaving for sea and returning to dock. Fortunately, we had timed it perfectly and arrived in the main channel on Sunday morning when activity was trivial. Plenty of time to find the marina where we planned to let Chuck off and then continue to an anchorage just past Norfolk so we could have an early start (and miss the bridge that does not open on weekdays during rush hour).

Suddenly… silence. The engine just stopped. In the middle of the Norfolk Channel with the wind blowing just enough to push us toward the docked Navy ships.

Paul asked expectantly, "Do you have Towboat US?"

His shoulders relaxed when I said, "Yep."

"Better call them."

Which I did. On my cell phone. I did not even have the VHF radio turned on and had not the entire way down the Bay. Dumb. The Towboat captain said he would join us in about an hour. I reminded him that we were adrift in the main shipping channel. He told me he understood, and that he would call me on Channel 16 when he was in sight.

(Past) time to turn on a radio. So I picked one of the antique handheld VHFs (even though we have a cockpit remote VHF that connects to the fixed radio mounted at the navigation station), one that I later learned would not permit me to change to any channel I wanted, a problem when trying to coordinate channels with a towboat or any other vessel wanting to communicate with you.

We drifted for a few minutes before deciding that we really needed to raise a sail. Paul was organizing the crew (Cameron) to set the genoa when I realized that someone was trying to hail me on the radio.

"Blue hull sailing vessel in Norfolk Channel near marker 9, do you read?"

Geez, I was going to have to talk to this voice and act like I knew what I was doing. As with many things I was going to have to learn about the boat, I had hoped that I would be able to arrive in the safe waters of coastal Carolina before I had to know everything. The radio was on that list. In my prior boating experience, we never even carried a radio. I knew I should know something about the protocols (other than "copy that" and other phrases I picked up in movies, none of which applies to nautical radio practice), but I did not.

I replied, "This is *Spotted Moose*, I read you." I could hear the smile on the other end when I announced our boat's name.

"This is the container ship to your north. We are under tow and headed for the dock that you are currently in front of. Our course will take us to your location. We need for you to move."

I had not even seen the massive ship approaching. It would have taken the ship a mile or more to stop its forward motion. We were so focused on trying to get the genoa set that I had only looked for obstacles in the path of our drift. We had been getting close to the docks on the north side of the channel, but I did not worry because there was no visible activity. Suddenly there was a very large container ship being moved by two very large tug boats in our direction.

"We have no engine power and are attempting to raise our sail. Understand your course."

"Thank you *Spotted Moose*."

Easy for them to sound calm. We would barely scratch their paint if they hit us. We, on the other hand, would likely be dismasted AND sink if they hit us.

Meanwhile, Paul, Cameron, and Chuck were all working to get the genoa launched from the roller furling on the bow. Paul had earlier cautioned Chuck to be careful about the winch handles as they can easily slip out of your hands and drop over the side, an expensive piece of jetsam. Now, Paul in his haste (and we needed all the hastening we could muster) did not fully lock the winch handle into the genoa winch. Over the side it went with a quick splash followed by the brisk alert from Paul, "Shit!"

Silently, I agreed. Sure do not like losing those suckers over the side, especially when trying to get a sail up with no engine power in the middle of what was becoming a busy channel. Yes, but we had another, and Cameron had it in Paul's hands before I could echo with a "Shit!" of my own. The wind filled the sail, and we slowly gathered seaway. The container ship was still bearing down, but we were moving out of its path, slowly.

"Blue hull sailing vessel in Norfolk Channel, this is the container barge ------. We are on a course that may intersect with yours." I looked back toward the container ship and saw a tug pushing a barge of shipping containers sort of in our direction, but still a good ways off. "Roger, we are moving across the channel and should be clear of you." I wanted to add "smart ass" because he was nowhere near intersecting with us.

For a moment, it felt like we regained control. The sun was shining, and we were sailing, albeit tentatively in a light wind.

"Blue hull sailing vessel near Marker 9 in Norfolk Channel, this is the container ship ------- to your starboard. How would you like to approach?"

Damn, not again. It was like every bloody freighter in the harbor suddenly wanted to be right where we were. What this pilot was really saying was that we are supposed to pass port to port (left to left, like cars on a highway), but I was starboard of him. I suspect he was concerned that we would suddenly dart out in front of him to be on his port side. Right (sarcasm). At our speed, sailing in a light breeze, we would be lucky to put ourselves in front of his bow in the next thirty minutes.

With artificial confidence and my best captain-like voice, I replied, "Roger. We have no engine power and will remain on this course."

"Thank you. We will pass to starboard." Very polite and professional.

As far as I was concerned, that was enough of that mess. Where was our Towboat?

Shortly, he did arrive and performed efficiently, taking us under tow by the bow and asking that I steer to remain behind him as his was a smaller boat than ours. I could not help but wonder what would happen if I steered our 35,000 pounds away from his 22 foot runabout. Crisis passed; humor returned.

He delivered us to the very marina where we had planned to stop anyway. Famished because Chuck, understandably, did not bother to fix breakfast while all the other chaos afflicted us, we ate at the marina about 1400 (2 PM). It was an average meal that tasted sumptuous given the circumstances.

Chuck had a plane to catch, so we bid him farewell, and he climbed into a taxi leaving the excitement behind.

Soon after sunrise the next day, before I had my tea, I hurried to the on-site repair shop as soon as it opened to request a mechanic to look at our engine, diagnose the problem, and hopefully, get it running again so we could continue south. A young man in shorts followed me back to the boat (fortunately we did not have to get on a long list of other boats needing repair). He stuck his head in the engine room (an exaggerated name for the minimal area under the cockpit that houses the diesel engine, hot water heater, batteries, inverter, bilge pumps, etc.), tried to start it, checked the filters and some other things I could not identify, then lifted a hatch in the cabin sole and unscrewed a round port covering one of the diesel tanks.

"Captain, you're out of fuel."

An empty fuel tank is easily remedied but baffling as we had topped off the 150 gallon tanks before departing Annapolis. Burning no more than a gallon per hour, we should have been down about twenty gallons with 130 still available. I looked at the mechanic after explaining my confusion, "So how could we be empty?"

He politely, with neither condescension nor any belittling sarcasm, gave me another lesson in the workings of diesel engines. No doubt he was thinking to himself, "This dumbass has a boat that he doesn't even understand how to run. What a loser." But he competently described how I had failed to turn one of the valves that controls the flow of the fuel. One valve opens to the engine itself. The engine only burns about a third of the fuel it receives, so the balance is returned to the fuel tank. But it is only returned to the fuel tank if you turn the valve that directs it that way. I had not. Operator error.

By the following morning, Paul's personal weatherman (one of his old sailing friends) had alerted him to a serious nor'easter that was going to hit in a couple of days. We could keep going until then, but we would likely be stuck in the tiny burg of Coinjock, North Carolina for a while once it hit. The remaining three of us agreed that it would be more fun to wait it out in Portsmouth. So we did.

We toured the *USS Wisconsin* as well as a fine exhibit of the pirate loot recovered from the slave ship-turned-pirate ship, *Whydah,* by Barry Clifford, reportedly the only pirate treasure ever salvaged in modern times.

The night the nor'easter hit, Paul, Cameron and I were eating at a nice seafood restaurant in Old Town Portsmouth. When we left to return to the boat, it was a blowing wet blizzard. Once again, snow on the boat. The next morning, the snow melted quickly, and we continued south. At last. A beautiful clear winter day with the sun bright if not warm in the sky. We navigated a couple of drawbridges and then arrived at the Great Bridge Lock.

Ahead of us all morning had been a big catamaran. *Surprise.* To me, naming a sailboat *Surprise* is almost the same as calling it the *SS Minnow* or *Titanic*; you are asking for more trouble than you will find as a matter of course. While waiting for the water to rise in the lock, the owner came back to talk to us. He and his wife were on their way to the Bahamas to take a few charters – "the economy," he said. He asked our mast height. 62. His was 64.5 feet. The fixed bridges on the Intracoastal Waterway are generally 65 feet clearance. He was a bit nervous, so he asked if we would go first under the next bridge.

We agreed, though we were also a bit nervous since three feet is not a lot of clearance, and water levels can vary a lot, depending where you are. Some bridges have gauges that indicate the height of the bridge above water level but not all. None of us were familiar with the water in that stretch of the ICW, whether wind or water tides affected the level, for instance. We continued motoring merrily down the channel, passed through a swing bridge, then saw the high bridge ahead a mile or so. We passed *Surprise* to take the lead.

A few hundred yards later, silence. No diesel rattling down below. All power lost. Not again. But yes, again. I scrambled forward to drop the anchor as Paul radioed *Surprise* about our situation. Normally dropping anchor would involve lowering our 55 pound plow with an electric windlass, but without power, this was a manual effort. I seized the anchor chain from the windlass gypsy and let it fly. The anchor clattered happily off the bow and set quickly in the mud bottom, stopping our forward momentum and turning the bow upstream. *Surprise* pressed on.

I began to think maybe the new name of our boat should be *Surprise*. Completely mystified as to the cause of the problem, we cranked up the small generator that Chuck had loaned me just for this kind of unexpected problem. It worked and charged the batteries, though I knew not why. I suspected operator (me) error. This was to prove correct once more.

I had failed to understand the mathematics of using an inverter to provide power from a DC battery bank to an AC electric heater (lots of amps consumed). It was a chilly morning following the nor'easter, so I had left the heater running in the saloon. Because we were motoring, I assumed the engine would keep the batteries charged. Once again, partial and incomplete comprehension. Due to the loss of power from the inverter conversion of DC to AC power (approximately 30%), the heaters consumed more battery power than the engine could recharge simultaneously. With the engine running, the space heater killed the batteries. It was hard to wrap my head around that concept, but there it was. I would have plenty of time later to second guess the electrical engineers.

Back underway, meandering through vast swamp land, we continued to Coinjock without further excitement. We spotted a bald eagle perched in a bare tree alongside the channel. And we saw an osprey as well. But mostly it was quiet and still except for the clatter of our diesel. A solitary tug overtook us in a series of looping turns of the channel, passing us easily while throwing up a four foot wake. Rock and roll. Bright sun and cool wind and lazy motoring down a black water canal.

As we approached Coinjock, we had a serious decision to make. East side or west side. Both sides have a marina. And both sides have a restaurant. Unless you have a dinghy – which we did not – you are stuck on whichever side you choose as it would be a hike of a few miles to cross at the downstream bridge.

We chose the east side. Turns out we chose wisely. Cheap fuel and good food. Wednesday night all-you-can-eat oysters, fried or steamed. And in the bar next door, Karaoke Night. Paul and I looked at the petite filet with shrimp and decided we had had enough seafood for a while. Steak it was. We passed on the $300 bottle of cabernet featured on the limited but rich wine list, especially considering how remoter Coinjock is. Cameron, on the other hand, was eating seafood like he never had before and as if he might never have the chance again (living on a sailboat). He ordered the oyster special. None of us joined the Karaoke Night in Coinjock, but I am sure it would have been a hoot.

We slept well, rose early and fueled up. Our next leg took us across Albemarle Sound and positioned us for an overnight run across Pamlico Sound to the Neuse River and Oriental. It was sunny and windy out of the north. Paul and Cameron set the genoa so we could motorsail. Cameron wanted to put up the main as well (and turn off the engine), but we were about four days behind our schedule. Thank goodness Paul is retired and able to be flexible with his time. Still, we did not need to further extend the journey any longer than necessary. It was still winter, and weather could get bad. So we motorsailed.

The swells on Albemarle Sound were running three to four feet, steep and rolling. With the wind, we were making seven knots. The waves were on our stern, but they also created some wicked periodic yaw and roll. Making ramen for lunch (and managing to keep it in the pot even with a gimbaled stove) was an adventure. It was a fine day with long range views of the Wright Brothers Memorial and Jockey's Ridge on the Outer Banks at Kitty Hawk. We slipped around Roanoke Island and east past the Lost Colony and Andy Griffith's compound, then Manteo and Pirate's Cove Marina and under a tall bridge that did not even exist when I lived in Duck while working at the North Carolina Maritime Museum (a small aquarium at the time).

Our course along the narrow channel took us past Wanchese Harbor where the fishing trawlers congregate on Roanoke Island. Then we intersected with the channel from Oregon Inlet Fishing Center, access to and from Oregon Inlet and the deep sea fishing off the continental shelf. What a twisting route. Some of the time, we were heading straight for a conspicuous sandbar, only turning at a channel marker when we seemed to be within jumping distance of the sand.

As the sun began to set, we left the channel markers behind and entered the wide open waters of Pamlico Sound, the second largest body of inland coastal water after the Chesapeake Bay. Several miles to port stretched Hatteras Island. Pea Island Wildlife Refuge, legendary lifesaving stations Little Kinnakeet and Chicamicamico, Avon, Salvo, Waves, and Frisco. To starboard, Stumpy Point, Englehard, Swan Quarter, Lake Mattamuskeet a few miles inland and the inner banks of North Carolina, country that I love and about which Bland Simpson has written so eloquently.

Soon after sunset, the flash of the Cape Hatteras lighthouse appeared due south. For a while, we seemed to be heading straight for it. But as night settled in, we left it to port like the rest of Hatteras Island and began to feel our way through the darkness with the chartplotter. No other boats crossed the sound with us. The autopilot set and winds still astern, we rolled through the night, a lone and lonely ship on a small sea. The closest land? About 15-20 feet below our keel. The markers? Forty-five foot tall flashing shoal markers that we used to set and confirm our course.

It was cold that night, colder than I can ever remember being (even when camping in Slickrock Wilderness during the Blizzard of 1993). Paul and I took short watches because we were both tired. We passed Ocracoke in the wee dark hours, heading for the light at Brant Island Shoal, the last course change before we entered the mouth of the Neuse River, the widest river in the country. It was tempting to detour to Ocracoke, but I knew there would be plenty of time to sail there in the future.

When I woke about 0515, Paul was freezing and needing sleep. At nearby Swan Quarter, NOAA reported a temperature of 39. With the 10+ knots of wind in the damp air, the wind chill was well below freezing. And it felt like it. I took the helm from Paul, and he suggested that we not try to enter Oriental harbor in the dark, so I set a course upriver until sunrise, then turned back to Oriental. Paul later told me that he had gotten so cold that he had come into the saloon, lit the stove and stood with his head sticking up into the cockpit to keep watch. Unfortunately, it did not help to warm him much.

About 0800, we made the outer marker for the Oriental channel. It was a clear, crisp, quiet Saturday morning. A perfect day to arrive safely at our new home port, break a 55 pound anchor on a dock piling (another operator error), walk to breakfast at Brantley's diner, and then sleep past noon, in that order. All in all, it had been a good and successful voyage home.

A week and half later, we had moved out of our house in the mountains, moved Taylor, our daughter, into an apartment in Asheville (so she could continue college) and arranged to sell most everything we owned. We moved onto our boat full time. On the boat, we had much to learn and much to prepare. For the next few months, we needed to practice sailing her, needed to work on boat systems, haul and paint and purchase and stow provisions. We met and learned from other cruisers. We re-christened the boat *Wild Haggis*, a whimsical reference to our Scottish heritage, following the proper traditions for appeasing the gods of sea and wind with recitations and libations. And we made Oriental our new home, a place to which we would return between voyages. It was a dramatic, exciting, but also demanding change in lifestyle. Many of our friends thought we were nuts. All of our friends thought it sounded like a grand escapade.

SCRABSTER to STROMNESS, ORKNEY
Scary Ferry #1

An Unsent Letter to Redmond O'Hanlon, British Adventurer, Writer, Scholar.

Dear Mr O'Hanlon:

I just read *Trawler* about your adventure on the North Sea. A big fan of your earlier works about your travels in Borneo and the Amazon, I was eager to read your new book.

Aside from the terror and marginal insanity of the trawling experience, it was the opening of the book that reminded me of a journey my wife and I took to Scotland several years ago.

It was late in winter, when tourists are still in hibernation and the locals are grateful -- cold and windy, the sky spitting drops of rain, snow, freezing rain, and sleet in no consistent order. We had taken the train to Thurso on the north coast where the end of the land looms over Pentland Firth on our way to the Orkneys. After a warm night beside a coal fire at Mrs Michaeljohn's B&B, the next morning we hiked around and around about the town, enjoying the many rainbows spawned by frequent rain showers. The second day, we walked down to the same docks in the protected harbor at Scrabster from which you departed. We planned a short dash to the Orkney Mainland, hoping to land in Stromness and catch a taxi to Maes Howe, past the Stones of Stenness, the Ring of Brodgar, and on to Skara Brae, then return on the late afternoon ferry.

As we strolled toward the harbor, we scanned Pentland Firth, watching the cliffs of the island of Hoy appear and disappear through curtains of passing rain. We also noticed a fishing trawler crossing from east to west. Its motion was more up and down than horizontal. A leviathan swell was running.

A ship's horn blasted, and we realized were about to miss the ferry. The bow, which had been lifted to permit vehicles to drive aboard, began to lower into position for setting to sea. My wife, pregnant at the time, agreed we should walk as fast as her feet would carry her to catch the ferry. Which we did. Perhaps we should not have.

On clearing the harbor entrance and its protective seawall, the ferry was tossed by wind and sea. I told my wife "no worries" because the ferries are equipped with stabilizers. After watching the rise and fall and rise and fall of the ship for a quarter hour or so, she decided she should retreat to the salon for the rest of the crossing. I could not. I needed the fresh air, the invigorating wind, the occasional sunlight, and an open field of view from which to keep as focused as possible on the horizon in attempt to pre-empt seasickness.

The ship lurched and dropped and rolled, and I wondered when the stabilizers would make it all better, when they would in fact stabilize the ship. Then a shudder, a slow roll to starboard, the bow beginning to rise, slowly rising up and up until, perched above the abyss of another trough, the bow pitched headlong into where the sea had been and from where it seemed to have vanished, diving as if with no bottom in sight. Again and again, the tortuous rhythm numbing time.

As the ferry reached the mid-point of the crossing, more and more of the passengers joined me topside. Charging from the door across the heaving deck, they (men, women, children, old and young) lurched to the railing and leaned over as if having lost something, themselves heaving. I gave all a wide berth to avoid catching what they were losing. Soon my wife also joined me. The sun was bright, the air crisp, the wind whipping, and she was ready to chum the North Sea. Which she did, with me supporting her from behind and slightly upwind. She laughed lightly when she realized that I was standing far enough behind her to dodge "her cookies".

A friendly chap from southern England had been standing near the aft railing much of the time I was topside. We had exchanged brief salutations, but no real conversation. Upon witnessing my wife's situation, pregnant and vomiting, he asked if there was anything he could do. We began to talk. He was a retired train engineer who made the trip to Stromness each year about the same time. He asked how long we planned to stay. I replied that we were just heading over for the day and intended to return to Thurso that afternoon.

"By plane?" he asked.

My heart sank as a puzzled look crossed his face. "No, we plan to take the late afternoon ferry."

"I've made this trip seven times, and I am not aware of another ferry until morning."

Unfortunately, my wife heard this also.

The Englishman and I began to discuss the Orkneys and traveling by ferry in stormy weather, and he recounted some recent experiences of ferries on this same route; for instance, one ship could not enter the channel between Hoy and the Mainland due to heavy seas. He described how the ferry circled for six hours waiting, due to breaking waves in the channel, for the tide to rise and the waves to fall. Ultimately, the captain had to return south and east and enter from the other side via Scapa Flow. The passengers endured over ten hours of heavy seas for a crossing that should have taken about two hours.

We passed the Old Man of Hoy, a natural stone monolith rising close to the cliffs, still rolling heavily in the heaving seas. My wife retreated to the salon again, hoping for a bit of peace with her eyes closed. I dared not leave the afterdeck for fear I would succumb to the same seasickness as all the others.

When we turned into the channel, the waves were big and peaking as if they might break, the swell rushing landward, but none crested. As the ship's stern lined up perpendicular to the oncoming waves, we felt the closest thing to calm seas that we had felt since leaving the Scrabster. Modest order was restored. A half hour later, we walked off the ferry and onto the Stromness dock. Solid, still, unmoving land.

My wife's relief from nausea was immediate as was her relief that we could not return to Thurso that night. Through the generosity of a taxi dispatcher who coordinated various taxis delivering us from one place to another (between picking up and dropping off school children), we managed to visit the prehistoric sites we sought, crawling down the tunnel into the chamber of Maes Howe with its Viking graffiti and hiking along the seashore through a darkening dusk to the Stone Age settlement of Skara Brae, its ruins beautifully preserved under the sand dunes by the North Sea.

One of our several patient taxi drivers parked in the parking lot and pointed across an adjacent field.

"See the flagpole?"

I replied that I could even though I assumed I was imagining the small stick in the distance.

"It's about half a mile. Cut through the sheep pasture."

Huddled against the sharp northeasterly wind, we trekked across the trackless field until we spotted a bundled figure approaching us. The keeper of the site was heading home a few minutes early because I am sure she expected no one would be touring so late in a winter gale. Generously and without complaint, she turned around, unlocked the museum, and gave us a quick overview of the site. Ever curious, I opened a wooden hatch that revealed part of the drainage system built by the original inhabitants, in effect a Stone Age sewer. As we stood among the stone walls viewing the stone beds and dressers constructed by people living on this harsh remote island 5,000 years earlier, we had to marvel at the tangible evidence of human history.

Later, we checked into the Stromness Hotel. The front desk clerk, long black hair and pierced ears like a pirate, remarked, "Nasty weather we're having, heh?"

"What's it usually like?" I queried.

"Like this," he grinned mischievously.

Back out into the night, the island pelted by wind and sleet, we found a cozy pub for me to savor a pint of ale. Then we called Mrs Michaeljohn to apologize that we would not be returning to Thurso until the next day. She wished us well and calm waters.

During dinner at the hotel, we heard tapping at the large windows of the dining room. I pulled aside the heavy draperies and watched as sleet and snow swirled above the courtyard covered in ice. We slept well even though the hotel, just like the B&Bs, turned off the heat at night. A duvet kept us warm inside while the winds wailed outside.

I had planned to have a breakfast of smoked haddock with eggs or porridge with a wee dram of whisky, but caution steered me to lighter fare. The wind had clocked around to the north, but the seas still ran high, so I did not want to challenge my stomach's ability to retain what I fed it. Once back on the ferry, the swells ran with us, easing the ship's motion. Hoy was shrouded in rain and mostly invisible. I sat quietly in my seat and tried to relax.

We returned to Mrs. Michaeljohn's. She had been concerned about our adventure, especially with Beth being pregnant. But we assured her all was good, Beth feeling fit, but then we had to pack and hurry to catch a train south back through the Highlands with its snow-capped hills and heather-covered moors, sheep, stags and wild hares in abundance along the railway watching as we rambled past.

MAIDEN VOYAGE of *WILD HAGGIS*

Our initial cruising destination had been decided months before we even bought our boat when Beth's nephew announced his plan to wed in Charleston, South Carolina in June. Not the most desirable season to visit Charleston, but a good destination for the boat nonetheless. Four hundred plus miles of shakedown for captain and crew. Several days down and several days back with a couple of weeks to enjoy Charleston in between.

We had planned to depart Oriental on June 1. A number of boat projects delayed us (mostly due to the incompetence of the boatyard), but we were determined not to leave later than the end of that first week of June. Although we could see that we would be ready by Thursday, Beth vetoed a Friday departure because of the sailor's superstition that it is bad luck to begin a voyage on Friday. So it was that we cast off our dock lines and motored out of Oriental Harbor Marina just before noon on Saturday, June 5, to start our cruising life.

We motored several miles across the Neuse River and a couple of miles up South River, a wide and remote anchorage off the Neuse. Beth and Cameron set anchor for the first time. Thankfully, it went well. So we sat back to relax the rest of the afternoon and enjoy the true start of the cruising part of our cruising life. We celebrated with champagne and fresh vegetables from the Oriental Farmers' Market.

After dark, we took bucket baths on deck in the privacy of the open water that surrounded us. The cool salty water flowed heavily over each of our bodies in turn as we cleansed ourselves of our landlubbers' lives and baptized ourselves, symbolically, as sea gypsies. Our entire lives were floating at anchor that night.

We had met new friends in Oriental as well as cruisers passing through on their way north from the Caribbean. Although we had left behind some new and fast friendships, we knew we would see and stay in touch with all of our boating and cruising friends from Oriental and beyond in the same way that we expected our Atlanta and Asheville friendships would survive us moving onto a sailboat. All of those friends nurtured and supported us as we pursued our dream. And that meant of course that no matter where we traveled, anchored or docked, we were not alone. As with much of our new life, we had mistaken notions of what the future would be.

That night, we dreamed of adventures ahead, tropical islands, sunny seas, fair winds. Despite the opportunity to have new adventures, we did not view cruising as a vacation so much as a change of lifestyle. We lived on a boat, not in a house on land. And that made all the difference in the world.

After our first night sleeping on the hook – and not dragging—we pulled out of South River to head back up river past Oriental to Adams Creek and on to Morehead City. Adams Creek, part of the Intracoastal Waterway (ICW), is mostly a canal passage from the Pamlico Sound via the brackish lower Neuse River to Newport River and the salt waters of Bogue Sound.

It was Beth's first opportunity to see how close our mast clears the fixed bridges we would pass beneath on the ICW. Our mast height is 62 feet. The fixed bridges on the ICW are 65 feet, supposedly at high water, though we have discovered more than one that has less (and as little as 62 feet) clearance than they are supposed to have. As we approached the bridge over Adams Creek (where the name has changed to Core Creek for no reason known to me) near a small bend-in-the-road called Harlowe, Beth looked up to watch our progress as we neared the bridge and the mast seemed to stand taller and taller, reaching higher and higher toward the bridge.

"Oh no. Oh no. OH NO," Beth cried out.

Fishermen floating in two johnboats alongside the channel under the bridge stopped fishing to look up where she was looking. They seemed to duck when they thought we might hit, but then began to laugh once they saw that we would in fact clear the bridge with plenty of space to spare.

As we emerged from the creek into the open waters of the Newport River, we faced, literally, our first big headwinds and adverse currents, fighting and slowing us all the way to the port at Morehead City.

We slipped under the fixed bridge at the port, conveniently marked with a gauge indicating the clearance) through the open rail bridge, then past the Morehead City Port docks in the chaotic collision of currents, wakes and waves of ocean, sound, river, and boat traffic to the quiet water behind Sugarloaf Island. The current was not quiet. A strong ebb tide forced boats rounding the island to skid as if hitting sand on a curve in the highway.

We tied up at the dock of The Sanitary Fish Market & Restaurant— Tony's, for my generation. When I was young, many years ago, I had worked at the restaurant for a summer, up to my elbows in leftover cole slaw, and I always envied the people who docked at Tony's when we ate our big seafood dinners with homemade chunky cocktail sauce (that they do not serve anymore). Once or twice our family pulled up to the dock in our 16 foot runabout. Now, Cameron, Beth, and I tied to the historic dock. Yep, we ate there too.

Monday morning was a clear sunny day in mid-June. Beth bought some inexpensive seafood and ice at the market. Scout enjoyed being able to "go" on land. Then we set out southbound, to the west. (Look at a map of the central North Carolina coast; mostly it runs east and west from Cape Lookout to New River.) It was warm, but not yet hot when we cast off from the dock. The current behind Sugarloaf Island pulled us swiftly toward the Port wharf and turn-around basin. Clear green waters lapped at the bow of *Wild Haggis* as we motored back to the Intracoastal Waterway and turned starboard toward Charleston.

A couple of hours later, we sailed past my parents' house on Bogue Sound. We called them when we cleared Atlantic Beach Bridge (at low tide, luckily, since it is only 62 feet at high tide, when it is supposed to be 65 feet). We called them again when we were at the channel marker nearest them to the east. Mother waved from the end of their dock; Father waded out onto the sandbar as close to the ICW as he could get without drowning. From the water, Father was a tiny speck, only recognizable because we knew he was wearing a white shirt (and who else would be trekking so far out into the sound with a camera?). Lots of waving to and fro, lots of futile yells of farewell, our voices swallowed by the distance, a few blasts on our horn, and then we were beyond where we could even see them waving.

We continued west, passing Bogue Inlet junction where it pours through the shoals between Emerald Isle and Bear Island, both old haunts for me in my teens and early 20s, until I began a real career. Surprise currents and shoaling in the channel.

We hailed Dudley's Marina to take on diesel. JW (Dudley) brought the whole crew out to help us dock in the channel to their tramway where they haul boats the old fashioned way, in a cradle on a rail winched ashore (rather than a tall, skeletal Travelift). Fuel, water, cold drinks and some ice.

Then back onto the ICW, dodging shoals in the twisting channel near Swansboro, past Hammock's Beach landing where Beth and I had launched our canoe with all three of our Labradors back in 1990. It was a beautiful paddling and camping trip to Bear Island where we hiked the dunes from sound to ocean, where we saw a herd of small island deer and reveled in the soft, cool sand by an open fire. And swam in swells of the ocean off a deserted beach. There was no more special place for many, many years.

The landing passed quickly as Beth and I remarked on the kayak trail laid out by the park service, the winding channels of which we created for ourselves when I convinced Beth (on the original paddle trip) that we could find a shorter way back through the marsh. Good memories on top of new beginnings.

Soon after leaving Swansboro astern, we entered Camp Lejeune Marine Base. A large billboard with big flashing lights (not on at the time) and a guard tower marked a part of the ICW where the US Marine Corps sometimes engages in live fire maneuvers. You could die if they let you pass, so they don't.

On and on down the narrow channel. Coastal marsh on either side. A few dolphins near Bear Inlet, the "whoosh" of their breathing surprisingly close to the side of the boat. Scout was immediately interested and kept watching for them to re-surface, in the same place.

After a while, we approached Onslow Beach Swing Bridge. Try saying that three times fast, which is what I am supposed to do when hailing the bridge tender on VHF to open the bridge.

I hailed the bridge tender a bit early. The swing bridge only opens on the hour and half hour, and we were close enough that I thought I could make the

4:00 PM opening. We couldn't, but I could not accept that until I throttled up. We had been cruising at about 5.5 knots, and I was sure we could bump that to 6.5 or so with a few more RPMs.

I throttled up. Nothing happened. Throttled down. Little response. Back up. No response. All bad responses. I asked Cameron to check the engine temperature.

He called up, "There's smoke!" Beth went below, opened the engine room door and reported lots of smoke. I could not believe we were on fire!

Beth pulled two fire extinguishers from under the navigation table.

"I don't see any fire, just smoke," she reported.

I was circling trying to keep the boat to the side of the channel in case we lost all power. I called the bridge tender and told him we would not be requesting an opening, then turned back into the current and told Beth and Cameron to prepare to drop anchor. We edged the boat toward the shallow water near the edge of the channel and dropped the anchor. It held, and we held alongside the channel, out of traffic. I knew that would change, and we would spin into the traffic on the changing tide, so I kedged an anchor off our stern. As with many imperfect situations, it was a decent idea with an imperfect result.

Beth's phone rang. I was down in the cabin—closest—so I answered. It was an Asheville friend and neighbor calling to tell us that a dear friend had died within the previous hour. Although he had been a candidate for a lung transplant, we were totally and completely shocked because mostly his treatment had been progressing well. All three of us cried. The irrationality and unfairness of him being taken from his family and friends. He was in his early 60s. Suddenly, nothing else mattered. Beth needed to get back to Asheville to comfort his wife, one of Beth's closest and dearest friends.

Decisions are curious events. They cannot be wholly objective. And even the subjective elements are only flimsy pieces of the ultimate decision. I chose to call Towboat US, and it was the right decision. But for reasons beyond what I thought at the time as well as for reasons I may never fully grasp. We were not on vacation. We were simply living on a boat and travelling south. Life goes on, and life includes death. Our friend's death was a shock, and we knew that being there for his family would be a priority, notwithstanding our cruising plans.

Towboat towed us at fair speed back to Swansboro, occasionally wandering off course as the captain swatted a vicious attack of biting green head flies, and literally dropped the towline at Dudley's Marina where we had fuelled earlier in the day. Next morning, Dudley's referred me to Earl (and his brother Al) for my engine troubles. Earl and Al showed up within thirty minutes. They logically dissected and identified each of three separate problems that contributed to our smoke on the waterway, only one of which I *might* have figured out. Earl and Al were great. The boat was fixed before noon, but we chose to spend another night at the quaint marina with its wooden docks.

It was another clear, warm morning with a fair tide when we pulled away from Dudley's dock for the second time in two days. Still shocked about our friend's death, we hoped that the day would not be as interesting or disruptive as two days earlier when we floated this same stretch of water. We pulled into the ICW and rode an easy current westward, retracing miles we had already covered. Hammock's Beach landing, the Marine shooting range, Onslow Beach Swing Bridge. We passed them all and slipped through the empty coastal marsh toward Surf City, where we stopped at Beachhouse Marina as late afternoon winds built to 15-20 knots with gusts to 25 and thunderstorms expected.

Beachhouse Marina is only a block or so from the ocean. Cameron was eager to swim in the ocean, so we walked over. Beth and I sat in a beachside bar sipping Coronas with lime. Cameron was people watching while enjoying the waves.

The wind held high all evening into the night, so we were glad to be tied in a slip as there were no good anchorages in the area. It would be our last marina slip until Charleston.

Motoring or motorsailing, the ICW is okay even though it can be hot, buggy and, in places, monotonous. Nevertheless, it was a good shakedown for our crew. Little stress, new sights and fewer bugs than I expected. We anchored and weighed anchor in various conditions, currents and bottom types. We rode out a good squall in Carolina Beach that spun the boat 180 degrees to test our anchoring skills. Calabash Creek, just off Little River Inlet, surged with current on the ebb tide, then turned and surged from the opposite direction on the flood.

Our anchor always held. We navigated the winding narrow channels of the Waterway, crossing the shoaling areas at higher tides.

Even boat traffic was light. We had passed only one barge (back in Adams Creek). Even on the weekend as we cruised through Myrtle Beach, there were few boats out. We assumed it was evidence of the ongoing economic malaise.

Leaving behind Myrtle Beach and the unforgiving channel known as the Rock Pile (the channel had been blasted from bedrock, not scooped from sand), we eased into one of the prettiest places we travelled, the cypress swamp of the Waccamaw River basin. Winding along in deep channels with dark and impenetrable forest surrounding us, we left salt water and brackish water and found ourselves floating in fresh water for the first time.

In the Waccamaw, we knew where we were going to anchor because had planned a rendezvous with S/V *Southern Cross*—our friends Darcy and Kyle—at Bull Creek. Darcy and Kyle are two gutsy people (I call them "the Kids") in their early 20s who decided to go cruising. We admire their tenacity and commitment to making their voyage their way and not measuring it by what other people think. They were making it happen without postponing until the stars align, the bank full of lots of money, or they retired from their third career. Too many people postpone their dreams until the dreams are no longer attainable or the dreamer no longer able. Darcy and Kyle met as engineering students on a work program in New Bern. Kyle has a 34 foot full-keeled sloop; Darcy had not sailed before. Like us, they took some time in Oriental to provision and prepare their boat. Their ultimate goal was Rio Dulce, Guatemala.

Kyle and Darcy left Oriental a month or so before we did and cruised down the ICW to St Augustine, then realized their weather window to safely cross the Caribbean had pretty well closed as a major tropical storm ripped into Guatemala killing dozens. Although they could have pushed their progress, they wisely did not. Their voyage was not about schedules and speed, it was about experiencing the special places along the way.

We had just rounded yet another bend in the river when we spied *Southern Cross* at anchor, and the radio came to life with "*Wild Haggis, Wild Haggis*, this is *Southern Cross*." With that, we for the first time re-connected with cruisers we had met in Oriental.

We dropped anchor in 20 feet of water with a stiff current and lowered the dinghy off the stern. Cameron and I floated down to *Southern Cross* for a brief chat before running a couple of miles downstream to Wacca Wache Marina, a surprising middle-of-nowhere place with a lively bar and a patio of shaded tables alongside the river. We bought some ice, a couple of cold drinks and let Scout "go" on land.

At anchor, the only practical way to get Scout on and off the boat is to raise and lower him in the dinghy. He is a patient soul despite the unavoidable pitching of the dinghy on its davit rings. On Bull Creek, when we returned from Wacca Wache, Cameron and I had hoisted the dinghy up, but had not secured it against the railing when Scout decided he was ready to jump aboard the boat. The dinghy rocked sideways, Scout missed the boat and splashed spastically into the creek. We dropped the dinghy fast, and I called Scout to encourage him to swim harder against the current and back up to the dinghy where I could grab him. I knew I could pull him into the dinghy, but did not know what I would do if I had to swim for him.

Anyway, I got soaked pulling him in and realized how refreshing the water was. As soon as we got Scout back aboard the boat, Cameron and I jumped overboard at the bow so we could hang onto the anchor chain. The water was just cool enough. If we dodged the tree trunks sweeping along in the current from upstream flooding, hanging off the chain was quite relaxing. And it washed off layers of the days' sweat from our long hot ride down the ICW.

Darcy and Kyle rowed upstream to join us for dinner. It was great to catch up and hear their tales. Next morning, we continued south and they north.

We rode the Waccamaw River current out of the swamp, and the river opened up with abandoned rice fields beyond the tree-lined waterway. All was still except for the shrill of ospreys keeping watch over their massive stick nests and hatchlings. Nests in big trees, dead trees, channel markers. We saw more ospreys than people along that stretch of the ICW.

The Waccamaw and Pee Dee rivers merge in Winyah Bay near Georgetown, South Carolina. We caught another favorable current as we left the Bay and entered the Minim Creek canal, as homely as its name. Narrow, hot, still, and with little natural beauty until it pushed us into a vast salt marsh where we anchored for the night in Minim Creek proper, just off the canal.

Green-headed biting flies had accompanied us off and on since Swansboro. They thrived along Minim Creek and the surrounding marsh, swarming around our ankles in the bottom of the cockpit. We made a game of killing them with hands or feet or whatever was handy. They were somewhat slow and dopey, but their bites were smart. Scout snapped his jaws on his share of the little bastards.

As usual, we retired early, in part because of the mosquitoes that had joined ranks with the biting flies. Hatches open to the breeze, we crawled into our berths to read before falling asleep. I fell asleep without reading, but Beth and Cameron woke me an hour later as a big storm illuminated the sky. I lifted Scout from the cockpit down into the saloon and closed the companionway hatches as heavy drops of rain plopped loudly onto the deck and a magnificent electrical storm flashed through the clouds all around us. Truly spectacular.

In the morning, the storm had passed, and the air was still, the water slick and gray. We departed Minim Creek and crossed the North and South Santee Rivers. More open marsh land as we approached Cape Romain National Wildlife Refuge. It was not yet 9:00AM when we spotted the first alligator sliding along the bank of the marsh. Two knobby eyes protruding like knots on a piece of wood floating at the edge of the water. By 10:00AM, we had seen almost a dozen alligators, mostly 6-8 feet long. We cautioned Scout not to fall overboard.

The marshes around Cape Romain NWR stretch east to the horizon and beyond. On the mainland side of the ICW, there are occasional clusters of houses with boat docks to remind us that the rest of the world did still exist, easy to forget in the broad and vacant marshland. Narrow water, shallow water, rarely a boat. Marsh grass and shell-piled shorelines. Sometimes a dolphin or two, especially near the creeks that wind serpentine through the marsh to rejoin the ocean.

Our destination anchorage was Dewees Creek, just such a link to the ocean. When we reached the junction of the creek and the ICW, a few dolphins surfaced. We could see ocean breakers beyond the distant inlet. We turned west and the depth of water under our keel jumped from 10 feet to between 60 and 70 feet, a huge hole for inside coastal waters. We knew upstream in less depth would be a pretty place to anchor.

However, it was early afternoon, not yet 2:00PM, and we could see across the marsh in the distance the suspension towers of the Cooper River Bridge in Charleston. Could we make it the remaining 15 miles to our slip? I looked at the charts, tides, and currents as well as the bridge schedule. We needed to pass Ben Sawyer Swing Bridge before it closed (for rush hour) from 4 until 6, and we needed to arrive in Charleston on a slack tide to avoid the nasty swift currents that I had heard can make grown sailors cry.

The timing looked good, so I spun the wheel around, and we continued past Dewees Island, Isle of Palms and Sullivan's Island. Soon we emerged in the broad waters of Charleston Harbor, straining to identify our channel markers among the many that lead in different directions to continue the ICW, up the Ashley River or out to sea (okay, the route out to sea was not hard to discern). Our markers needed to show us the shipping avenue up the Cooper River. Of course, we could *see* the impressionistic "sails" of the Cooper River Bridge, Charleston's spectacular modern suspension bridge. And we could *see* the aircraft carrier USS *Yorktown* at Patriot's Point. But we needed to *find* Charleston Maritime Center, the marina where we would stay the next two weeks.

We found it, and the slack tide was not quite slack (I should have relied on my own information and not on the young, enthusiastic marina staff). Thus, trying to pull alongside a floating dock in the marina was challenging as the current wanted to push us all the way to shore. Still, we arrived, safely and happily at the end of our first cruising voyage. We had plenty of work on the boat to do while there, but we planned to have some fun as well.

Our first night, we splurged on a taxi to eat at one of our oldest haunts, The Variety Store at City Marina on the opposite side of town. As non-descript as the name is, the food is a blend of contemporary and down home cooking. Celebrating the completion of our maiden voyage, we felt we had earned a certain indulgence.

After a good night's slumber, our first outing was a short walk to a nearby deli for breakfast. We arrived saturated by the humidity, but we thrilled to the chill of the deli's air conditioning, dry air so cold it took our breath away and let us dream of a hot cup of coffee, something we never enjoyed during our sweltering travels down to Charleston. The waiter smiled when he saw that we were literally dripping onto the floor. He served us ice water and plenty of it. We ordered Eggs Benedict and more coffee.

We tied *Wild Haggis* to a floating dock adjacent to a fine wooden tall ship, *Spirit of South Carolina*, a teaching platform for high school age students. Upstream of us stretched the exquisite Cooper River Bridge, its suspension cables forming abstract silver sails. Huge freighters slipped unnoticed below the span. Water taxis shuttled across the river from the Aquarium to Patriot's Point and the aircraft carrier USS *Yorktown*. Tour boats honked, whistled and scurried around the harbor to chase dolphins, sunsets, and ghosts.

The heat of each still and wilting day wrenched unending buckets of perspiration from our bodies. Dawn came early, already warm, and the unmoving air smothered us in stifling, thick humidity. Every day we drank several liters of ice water, thankful that the icemaker was one piece of boat equipment that had performed faithfully. As the heat index hovered between 105 and 115, it was nearly impossible to do any work on the boat after ten in the morning. In less than five minutes of effort (which includes just standing), a greasy, slippery, puddle of sweat pooled under my feet.

By late afternoon, the clouds stacked heavily skyward, cumbersome and laden to the point of breaking. We prayed they would collide and release their moisture with a cooling breeze advancing before a storm. The storms were never much respite but better than nothing. For a half hour or so, the clouds would darken in front of the sun. Shadow was followed by breeze, sometimes whipping violently from the dark sky. We delayed closing the hatches until rain actually pelted the deck. We huddled under the dodger in the cockpit worshipping the fresh air. The tangerine and plum skies vanished with the return of the sun, and the wet surfaces evaporated in steam.

The mantra for meals was less is best. Nothing cooked. Lots of cold pinot grigio that was instantly metabolized. Early to bed with no cover, not even a thin sheet. Sweating all night long. I did not know that I could sweat all night. I did not know I could sweat in my sleep. I did not know that the wee hours just before dawn could still be so warm that I could sleep naked and unprotected against the night air.

We enjoyed a long visit from dear friends from the mountains, the first of Cameron's peers that he had seen in a couple of months. We rented a car and returned to Asheville for our friend's wake, a time of sadness as all of us struggled to find reason in the midst of grief.

One of our tasks while in Charleston was recertification of our life raft. Air Sea is an approved servicer, and they came to the dock to collect the 115 pound raft in its hard canister. Cameron, Beth, and I wanted to see what the raft looked and felt like, what supplies were packed with the raft, how it inflated, so we visited Air Sea on the morning they were planning to open the canister and begin reviewing the condition of the raft. Cameron videoed the moment when I pulled the valve to deploy and inflate the 25 year old raft. As old as it was, the staff had told us it might not inflate and, if it did inflate, it might immediately deflate or it could explode. They had seen many catastrophes in their years of servicing old rafts. When I pulled the valve, a bottle of pressurized CO_2 rapidly filled the rubber tubes with a loud rush of gas. The canopy lifted and the float tubes inflated. But the noise of the gas continued. I was certain there was a leak, but the staff assured us that the pressurized bottle was intended to overfill the tubes in order to fill the raft as swiftly as possible in an emergency. A worthwhile lesson. Based on the sound or the air escaping from the relief valve, if we had been abandoning ship, I would have chosen not to let anyone aboard what seemed to be a leaking raft. The staff walked us through the supplies, including the tiny aluminum paddles they referred to as "shark beaters". While better than nothing as paddles, they probably would have been more effective dissuading sharks.

After two weeks, Air Sea returned our newly recertified life raft. Cameron's friend, Juliano, joined our crew for the passage to Myrtle Beach. It was time to head north. We untied from our floating dock at 5:30 AM and eased out of the marina into a slack tide. We needed to cross the dark harbor and reach the Ben Sawyer Swing Bridge before 7:30 when it would close for a two hour rush hour. From Isle of Palms, we retraced our route north, seeing a couple more alligators and re-visiting our Minim Creek anchorage. As we headed toward Georgetown, rain fell from overcast skies. A cold front was approaching.

Back in Bull Creek, Cameron and Juliano swam in the fresh water for a couple of hours. Despite being deep in a southern swamp, I dismissed the risk of alligators due to the current and deep fresh water. The cold front brought refreshingly cool air and clear blue skies. We slept under a sheet for the first time in weeks. Next morning, as we motored the dark deep channels through the swamp, Beth spied a ten foot alligator stretched along the shore. I should have been worried about the boys hanging off the boat as alligator bait. Next time.

A few hours under motor brought us back to Myrtle Beach. We rejoined Beth's entire family to celebrate her mother's eightieth birthday, then took front row seats at the marina, on our bow and dock, to watch the Fourth of July fireworks across the ICW.

Hoping that the waterway would be quieter the day after the Fourth, we left late to catch the tide north toward Calabash Creek again. It was a quiet and familiar evening at anchor. Cameron rowed Scout to shore in the dinghy, and we went to bed early. We rose just after dawn to catch the outgoing tide through Little River Inlet into the ocean. Leaving the ICW meant avoiding draw bridges and their inflexible schedules. Swells had been forecast at two to four feet with winds five to ten, good conditions for our first time taking *Wild Haggis* to sea. Unfortunately, the wind was light during the morning, leaving us to roll in the swells as we motored almost due east toward the Cape Fear River Inlet. Cameron and Beth were soon seasick. We considered turning back, but everyone had looked forward to being on the ocean, and I promised them that it would settle down as soon as we could fill the sails with the absent wind.

Beth threw up and sat barely conscious on the cabin roof, trying desperately not to think about how sick she felt, trying not to wonder how long it would be before she felt okay again. Cameron dozed, not truly asleep, but enclosed in his own world of denial. After a couple of hours, the wind had arisen sufficiently for me to set the genoa. The rolling of the boat eased noticeably. Cameron began to feel better. Not hungry, but not as badly as he had felt all morning. He helped me set the mainsail and actually enjoyed sailing during the early afternoon as we slipped wet miles under our keel toward the inlet channel.

Our timing was perfect. We reached the channel off Bald Head Island at flood tide, swept swiftly upriver into calm and protected waters. Beth immediately felt better. She had not believed that, once seasick, she could recover without getting off the boat and onto land. She smiled, not feeling great, but appreciating the improvement.

We were heading north up the river channel at seven knots when an ungodly metallic clanking sound rose from the engine room. I had not seen a decline in power, so I prayed the engine was okay. And then it hit me – the engine-driven refrigeration. Sure enough, I stuck my head into the engine room and saw that the refrigeration motor had seized up, frozen as it were, motionless, lifeless. One more thing. Still, I was glad it was not the engine.

At Carolina Beach, the same anchorage as when we had come south, Beth pulled fresh shrimp from the freezer and made Shrimp and Grits. We had hundreds of dollars worth of food in the freezer, and now we had to consume as much as possible before it spoiled. Beth and Cameron, their seasickness a bad memory, relished the meal, as did I. None of us had eaten a real meal all day.

The next day's anchorage was Mile Hammock Bay on Camp Lejeune. It was a long hot day on the waterway. But there were no real options other than marinas, and we had read that Mile Hammock was a good protected spot unless the Marines decided to have maneuvers. They might wake us in the pre-dawn dark and command us to leave. As it happened, the Bay was quiet with no boats at anchor. A small runabout puttered into the Bay near sunset looking for dolphins which obliged by making a playful appearance. The couple in the runabout stopped their motor nearby and chatted with us. They lived back up the New River near Jacksonville but tried to get out to Mile Hammock most evenings to watch the sunsets and the dolphins. They had a small sailboat that they dreamed of taking cruising. Soon after the dolphins eased out of the Bay, the couple followed. We embraced the silence, hearing only the waves breaking on the ocean side of the dunes along the ICW, much closer than we had realized.

As the sky began to brighten a soft gray the next morning, I heard through my sleep the rumbling vibration of a large motor. As my brain slowly engaged, my caution as a boat captain kicked it. "A barge is coming toward us," I thought, sitting upright immediately. Then I remembered that the draw bridge was closed until 7:00 AM, another hour and a half. So what was it? I peered out a porthole. A large camouflaged landing craft flying the Belgian flag was easing past us. In its wake, a train of landing craft coming up the ICW and turning into Mile Hammock Bay. They were dark and ominous in the dull morning light.

I woke Beth and Cameron, and all of us watched as the landing craft proceeded to the end of the bay and disgorged Hummers and trucks onto the concrete ramp. No one said anything to us much less chased us away, so we made tea, ate breakfast and prepared for another day crawling up the ICW.

We hovered in the channel, circling as the clock ticked off slow minutes while we waited for the bridge to open. Relieved that the ICW was not closed for live-fire exercises, we pushed past the open bridge and began the long slog through Camp Lejeune toward Swansboro and onward to Morehead City. The closer we were to Oriental and the end of this voyage, the closer we were to the reality for which we were not prepared. We tried not to think about the future beyond our boat, but it was quickly overtaking us.

Once we rounded Sugarloaf Island at Morehead City, we surged toward The Sanitary on a flood tide. I turned the boat into the current and eased her alongside the dock. We ducked into the Ruddy Duck, a nice pub (formerly DeeGee's) just down from The Sanitary, and a gracious waitress kept our iced teas refilled to the tune of a half dozen each. A half hour later, people were gathering beside *Wild Haggis* to watch a young man and his father fight a large sea creature in the channel. The fishermen were patient as they traded the rod back and forth, gained line and lost it for nearly an hour. We yelled across to ask what they thought they had hooked. Probably a large ray, the father replied. Both inside and outside the restaurant, people stopped to watch and silently cheer the effort of the man and his son, rooting for them to land whatever it was they had hooked even if only to satisfy our collective curiosity. They worked the rod and reel deliverately, trying to hold any advantage they gained without releasing the fish. Passing boats approached from up and down the channel and grasped that there was a great struggle between the fishing boat and the creature below. They would hover near, but not so close as to interfere with the fishermen. All eyes watched the father, the son, and the line where it penetrated the sea.

Snap! The sound of the line breaking and the backward stumble of the young man said it all. The fish or ray or whatever had won. The long battle ended. Everyone who had been watching applauded and cheered out loud. The young man fought the tears of disappointment, not truly comprehending how all of us had pinned our hopes to his determination and grit and how much he had given us by persevering, by neither rushing nor quitting. It was an heroic moment, one I knew his father would help him appreciate later.

Restaurant patrons tended to walk the dock before and or after dinner. That night, there was a fine sloop with navy blue hull tied to the aged, creased, and rickety dock that had seen so many boats before. Two couples stopped and asked Beth where we were headed. She answered their questions and talked about living aboard.

One man declared, "I would love to do this, buy a boat and go cruising."

His wife, standing beside him, looked into his eyes, smiled and said, "Then do it. What's holding you back? I would be fine with moving onto a boat."

He shuffled his feet nervously, muttered some reasons that were clearly excuses. His wife grinned and repeated her suggestion. Eventually he laughed it off, and they said good night.

The next morning, we caught another favorable tide and motored across the Newport River into Core and Adams Creeks. It was another still and humid morning. We were nearly back to Oriental. I called the marina and told Mack that we needed a slip, possibly for as long as several months. He had one left. Anxious as we were about what might happen in the following week, for the moment we had nearly completed our own full first voyage out from and back to our adopted home port. When we emerged from Adams Creek into the Neuse River, we set the sails and "raced" a couple of large catamarans across the river.

After a few months of outdoor living aboard the boat, our hands and feet had toughened, our muscles had slimmed, and our hair had brightened. It had been a happy and active life focused on the boat and living in a floating home. We had prepared to cruise and learned much that we did not know we needed to learn. It had been a full and satisfying lifestyle despite feeling like something always needed attention on the boat. And it was just life-style. Living, but living differently than we had on land. We had inhaled the fresh air, open sky and water surrounding us. It had been easy to swell with optimism and dreams for what lay in our future.

Beth and Cameron had become proficient at navigating the Waterway with its sometimes confusing channel markers. They also became proficient at setting and weighing anchor. We found quiet and remote anchorages off the Waterway where we had rested through the heat of the afternoons and slept through the quiet nights. We watched ospreys nesting on trees and channel markers. Saw storks sweeping over the marsh and dolphins playing alongside the boat. We saw alligators ease eerily along the shore in still, brackish water and witnessed brilliant electrical storms lighting the sky at night.

HURRICANES

Hurricanes exhaust you with a cornucopia of feelings from anxiety and fear to fatigue and boredom. From the first yellow mark on the National Hurricane Center (NHC) tracking map, a disturbance coming off the coast of northern Africa, from the Sahara, or spawning near the Cape Verde islands, we have at least a week to watch the storm evolve, grow, shrink and grow again. All storms are different, and all are unpredictable despite modern computer modeling. We use at least five sources of information. To have a feel for how much more data is available, take a gander at www.spaghettimodels.com (aka Mike's Weather Page). The web site has nothing to do with Italian food, but it will give you a taste of the bewildering volume of types of weather data relevant to tropical storms and hurricanes that are used in the models (approximately 16 different ones that, when laid over a map in different colors and with a variety of tracks, can remind you of spaghetti). In addition to fearing for your life if one of the big storms draws a bead on your location, the array of data can give anyone a migraine.

Living in Pamlico County for ten years, we have experienced several tropical storms as well as several hurricanes: Earl (2010), Irene (2011), Sandy (2012), Arthur (2014), Matthew (2016), Maria (2017), Florence (2018), Dorian (2019), Isaias (2020). We rode out Sandy and Arthur aboard our sailboat, *Wild Haggis,* at dock in Whittaker Pointe Marina. Each experience was different in intensity, duration, and damage, but all had a similar preamble: preparation.

Hurricane Earl

For Hurricane Earl, only seven months after we had bought *Wild Haggis*, I drove down from Greensboro and prepped the boat at dock in Oriental Harbor Marina with help from a couple of friends and our steadfast dockmaster, Ross, a bandy-legged (before he replaced his knees) old salt who revealed something new to me every time we talked. A philosopher as well as a sailor, he proffered gentle lessons in how to correctly tie a bowline or a proper cleat hitch or set the appropriate length of anchor rode for day, night, or storm. Interspersed were uncritical observations about people fueled by his long life. After stripping the boat of exterior canvas and double-tying the dock lines (16 when I was done), I had reached my breaking point and did not know how I would complete the prep. With hunger pangs and dehydrated, I could only admit to myself that I had failed to care for my body as I should have. The afternoon before landfall, as I wrestled with a tangle of sail and struggled to push the genoa down the hatch into the forward cabin, the winds gusted to 35 mph. Having never experienced a hurricane before, I feared that the winds would continue to increase making my task nearly impossible. I completed preparations just before dark.

As luck would have it, those afternoon winds were higher than the winds when Earl arrived the next day. Yes, I was content to have prepped for the storm, but the effort was for naught. Much ado about nothing. Only in my dreams would it always be so easy.

There was plenty to learn about hurricanes as you can read below. With each one being distinct, each offered new lessons. For Earl, I was a novice. By the time we stayed through Florence, I had evolved into a realist with a harsh understanding of how destructive these storms can be.

Hurricane Irene

A year after Earl, Hurricane Irene left The Bahamas as a Cat 3 and approached the east coast as a Cat 2 that was forecast to landfall at Cape Lookout, less than thirty miles southeast as the old crow flies, as a Cat 3 or 4. Yes, the intensity was up, then down, up, then down, then up and up. It would be a fierce hurricane. As soon as our slip mates woke us to alert us to the danger, we called a local boatyard to get on the list for being hauled out. They had no capacity, so we decided to take the boat down river to a protected, man-made harbor at River Dunes where the floating docks allowed us to secure *Wild Haggis* without riding out the storm itself (riding a Cat 4 would be stupid) because we would not need to adjust the docklines as the storm surge lifted the boat. Anxious to secure our slip as so many were doing the same, we immediately cast off for River Dunes.

On Monday, NHC predicted that Tropical Storm Irene would become the season's first Atlantic hurricane. It did. As it tracked west past the Dominican Republic (drowning the mountains of Haiti in the process), it pushed through the Turks and Caicos into southeastern Bahamas. From there, the various models used by NHC began to diverge. NHC prediction accuracy diminishes rapidly beyond 48 hours. On one extreme, models showed Irene becoming a Major Hurricane (Cat 3 or stronger) over the central Bahamas before landfall in southern Florida where it would recoil as a Tropical Storm travelling up the west coast of Florida. On the other extreme, Irene would stay just east of Florida as a Major Hurricane drawing energy from the hot Gulf Stream waters with landfall somewhere between Georgia and North Carolina (a common option for western Atlantic hurricanes). A cold front over the southeast together with the influence of the Gulf Stream might have pushed Irene to sea before she rounded Cape Hatteras. Two days later, Irene was forecast to reach us in North Carolina, in whatever form, on or about Saturday.

Another day, and the models aligned for a better consensus. Irene would become a Cat 3 hurricane. Her forecast path showed landfall around Myrtle Beach, South Carolina, passing us over land to the west. While that sounded promising, it put us in the most dangerous quadrant for wind.

A stiff wind out of the northeast slowed our speed, but the sun shined brightly, and the skies were blue, so we relaxed and motored down the river into a moderate swell. As we neared Broad Creek, the entrance to the harbor, a flicker landed in our cockpit under the dodger and peered longingly into the companionway as if it wanted to go below into the saloon. It flew away, swept upstream in the wind in spite of beating its wings desperately in an effort to cross the river against the wind. Soon a seagull also landed on the boat, at first perching on a lifeline, but this bird settled down for a ride and stayed on the cabin roof for several minutes. We commented how odd it was to have a bird so comfortable on a moving boat, and then the phone rang. My sister called to ask if we had felt the earthquake. Earthquake? I told her we were on the river and had noticed nothing. Her hospital, a six-story building fifty miles away, had been shaken even though the earthquake epicenter was closer to northern Virginia. Odd. When we reached the harbor and tied up the boat, Taylor, who had been waiting for us in her car, told us how she had been listening to music, wondering why we were delayed, and she felt the car rock and bounce as if Scout was in the back shaking (he was on the boat with us) or as if someone jumped on the bumper. Earthquake. An omen?

All four of us set to work tying multiple docklines and offloading some clothes and valuables. Based on the forecast of Irene possibly reaching Cat 4 strength, we discussed the need to be prepared that we might return to a sunken boat. Cameron took the warning to heart. I noticed that he was removing more of his belongings from the boat than he needed for a few days ashore. When I asked what he was doing, he said, "I'm taking *all* of my stuff. I don't want to lose any of it if the boat sinks." Point made, point taken.

All day, Beth, Taylor, Cameron, and I prepared the boat for 100+ mph winds and an undefined storm surge. All canvas off. Genoa stowed. Mainsail secured. Dorade boxes taped. Wind generator and grill down. Double lines and chafing protection. Dinghy deflated, bagged and stowed in the saloon. Cameron and I finished about 1730, tired, sweaty and famished. The girls had already left, but they were in a similar condition as they drove west.

Our challenge is that all the known factors as well as the forecast factors can change daily if not with each Public Advisory. As I learned with Hurricane Earl the year before, a good strategy at 10AM may be a bad strategy at 11AM when the advisory is published. (And it may be good again when the next advisory comes out.)

Always, we watch, wait, and plan without knowing the actual timing or how powerful the storm will be when we begin to feel the leading edge winds or how high the storm surge will be when it passes (high water or low?). Timing matters in multiple dimensions.

A day later, there was less doubt about Irene's course and strength than many storms we have followed. Barring another significant factor that would change her path, Irene was poised to strike sometime Saturday with the eye passing early AM Sunday.

The next day, it was virtually certain that Irene would make landfall in North Carolina. The effects of the cold front were not only disregarded, the forecast called for Irene to slip through a break in the low pressure trough.

On the other hand, the NHC models began to show Irene tracking more easterly than previously. If that held, we would not be in the northeast quadrant any longer. Also, the low pressure trough that was forecast to have little effect on Irene was suddenly forecast to push her away from the NC coast. We would still have a brush with tropical storm force winds, but the hurricane winds would be offshore. We could cling to such hopes.

Regardless of track, Irene continued to have favorable conditions for strengthening. The models began to show Irene passing over Cape Hatteras. With hurricane force winds extending 50 miles from the eye, and with Hatteras being 70 miles east-northeast of Oriental, we would be outside the fringe of hurricane winds. And, being west of the eye, we would avoid the worst of the storm, the northeast quadrant. If she would slip just a little further east each day, North Carolina might escape a direct hit. The storm was still huge with significant low pressure, but the strongest winds should remain off shore. (Surprisingly, despite Irene strengthening, her hurricane force winds remained close to the eye even though the storm itself stretched more than 700 miles across.)

In the next report, Irene was forecast to become a Cat 4, an even more deadly storm. It is easy to forget that wind strength is exponential. For example, a minimal Cat 4 with 135 mph winds increases the damage potential by a factor of 110 as compared with the damage from a minimal Cat 1 with 75 mph winds. Thus, even if the worst of the storm was off the coast, we could still experience serious damaging winds. NHC had not yet forecast the storm surge. Anything above eight feet would be problematic for us as the floating docks could rise above their pilings.

But this is a good example of how imperfect our options are. We select the "solution" that we feel best about with full knowledge that no "solution", no decision, is right per se. You simply must choose.

Friends in two boats decided to anchor in South River across the Neuse from Oriental, a decent anchorage that offers some protection from wave action, has a good holding bottom, and allows plenty of room to swing at anchor. It would be a scary and nerve-wracking day and night as the outer bands of the tropical force winds crossed them in advance of the eye of the hurricane. We worried about their safety.

Overnight, the forecast track was revised to the west. Unless there was another shift, which was possible, that would put Irene arriving Saturday night with a direct hit on the Outer Banks. That meant hurricane force winds along the Neuse River.

Storm surge models had not been officially issued, but early guidance (which is normally cautious) was forecasting major impact in southern Pamlico Sound as well as Neuse and Pamlico Rivers. Again, this very much included *Wild Haggis*. Preliminary surge forecast was for 4-8 feet and possibly closer to 5-10 feet. Anything above 8 feet could be problematic for the floating docks at River Dunes where the pilings were only eleven feet tall. Add the motion of large boats and the choppy waves, and conditions could sweep a dock over the top of a piling. Disaster would follow.

Ironically, our weather leading up to the event was excellent. Sunny skies and moderate winds. By Friday afternoon, early bands from Irene began to arrive along with stronger winds. By Saturday AM, rain and thunderstorms increased. Saturday night, as Irene closed in, torrential rains accompanied the hurricane force winds. Unusually high tides amplified the effects of storm surge. Being to the west of Irene, her winds would blow from out of the northern/northwestern quadrant which would push more water up the Neuse, yet another enhancement to the storm surge.

Timing is everything. If Irene landed during low tide, we would get less water. If she accelerated in forward motion, we would get less water. If the Great

Lakes trough pushed her just a little bit east, we would get less of everything. Or the opposite could occur since even the NHC forecast track is a blend of models and best guesses based on anticipated conditions.

Friday morning was an "Oh Shit" morning. I had hoped that the later advisories would modify, if not refute, what I read at 6 AM. It did not happen. Cameron and I returned to *Wild Haggis* to re-check everything. Irene had strengthened. Hurricane force winds extended 80 miles from the eye. If the eye crossed Cape Hatteras, 70 miles away, hurricane force winds would reach the marina. Tropical storm force winds extended 280+ miles from the eye. Even worse, the updated projected path passed over my parents' home on Bogue Sound, over Oriental, and over River Dunes Marina where our boat, our home, floated in a slip. A direct hit.

None of this was good. After confirming we had done all we could to prepare *Wild Haggis*, Cameron and I drove to my sister's house in Kinston where Beth, Taylor, and Scout had spent the night. Beth and Cameron then drove to Greensboro where tropical storm force winds would reach Saturday. Taylor, Scout, and I stayed in Kinston along with my mother knowing we would feel the impact of hurricane force winds, but I wanted to be close to the boat when the hurricane passed on Sunday.

Updated forecasts mentioned the possibility of further strengthening. The storm surge models never became more specific than 6-10 feet.

Waiting was a wild ride.

Ups and downs. Saturday morning, mostly up. Irene weakened overnight (though she could re-intensify), and her forecast track shifted east, taking my parents' house, Oriental and *Wild Haggis* out of the crosshairs. All would still be close enough to the center to get a severe beating with maximum winds above 115 mph, but at least all would be away from the northeast quadrant. Even better, our friends at anchor in South River would be away from the northeast quadrant.

Continued good news. As Irene approached the coast, she weakened further with maximum winds diminishing to 100 mph. More promising was the fact that the pressure rose a bit, finally signaling an end to dropping pressure (a good measure of the core strength of the storm). The forecast track did not change from the morning, but Irene was no longer predicted to re-strengthen before hitting the NC coast. Landfall of the eye was projected for 0800 which meant that tropical storm force winds had already reached the coast. The storm was moving a bit faster so its damaging winds would move out more quickly.

Of course, Irene was still a huge and powerful hurricane. Winds of 100 mph with higher gusts could cause plenty of serious damage. *Wild Haggis* was secured as well as we could secure her, so the rest was in the hands of fate.

Elsewhere, Tropical Depression #10 was hovering in the eastern Atlantic as if watching how Irene faired before launching itself in our direction. Our concern for the threat of that system could wait.

Irene endured longer than many hurricanes. We watched the updates on TV as long as we had power. It mattered not. Before the hurricane had left the state, before the eye had even reached our latitude, the major news networks began coverage of the pending menace to Long Island and New York City, center of the universe. While trees still fell, rivers flooded, and people died in North Carolina, news coverage ceased in favor of the all-important denizens of the northeast. We lost power an hour or so later, blind in the dark as the storm raged with the roar of gusting winds and the drone of torrential rain. Ancient oaks uprooted, massive limbs snapped, and pine trees broke midway up the trunk. When the sun rose, the wind had switched direction, but the storm continued.

Kinston was a disaster. The storm was HUGE and seemed to last forever. On one level, it was "just" wind and rain. But it left widespread devastation. At one point during the early part of the hurricane, we were sitting in my sister's sunroom when we heard cracking as the massive (6 foot diameter) pin oak beside the house shed a thirty-foot long limb. Without waiting to see where it would land, and worried it might break the windows in the sunroom, my sister and I pulled Taylor and our mother out of the room. The limb fell beside the street.

Taylor and I got cabin fever late in the storm while the wind continued and decided to drive around. No, it was not a good idea. We dodged a falling tree and observed the demolition of several houses from huge oaks or pines falling onto the roof. Power poles snapped low. Debris was scattered everywhere. High winds gusted and breathed and gusted some more. Just when we thought the rain might subside, a torrential downpour surged through.

Storm winds lasted late into the night. When I heard the frogs singing in the pre-dawn darkness, I knew the storm had departed.

In the morning, I began to research access to the coast, damage and roads etc. We could not reach anyone down east by phone, so Taylor and I decided to just head east and see if we could get through. Skies were clear, the breeze fresh and cool.

Towndock.net had published photos from the hurricane and during the passing of the eye (directly over Oriental). Major storm surge, flooding and a sunken boat at our home marina (Oriental Harbor Marina).

Driving east, debris and fallen power lines revealed the strength of the storm as did houses missing shingles and broken by fallen trees. The storm surge had been higher than predicted. I worried what that meant for *Wild Haggis*. I could visualize a pile of yachts in the leeward corner of the harbor, a jumble of expensive plastic stacked together like so much rubble. We wound along the entry road in River Dunes and emerged at the harbor. Tranquil as when we had left it, we saw no evidence of a hurricane having battered the boats for much of a day. I stopped to speak with a couple of sportfishing crews who had ridden the storm on their boats and asked how high the storm surge lifted them. "Oh, the water rose to within less than a foot from the top of the pilings." That was the margin of error or, in our case, the margin of luck. Less than twelve inches prevented all 97 boats from being lifted free of the floating docks and blown into a heap on the downwind shore.

Wild Haggis was fine. She looked as if we had left her 30 minutes earlier. Not a scratch. No chafed lines. We dodged the bullet.

I spoke with another captain and we agreed that, had this been a strong Cat 2 or 3, as forecast, the marina would have been a scene of total devastation as the floating docks left their pilings. Two crew who rode out the storm admitted it was scary as hell despite the absence of damage.

Our British friends, Tony and Jenny, had anchored up South River in a side creek. Tony is an experienced sailor who had sailed the Atlantic five times solo. Still, it troubled us when the hurricane passed directly over where they had anchored. When we returned to the marina, we could not raise them on the VHF radio, but they arrived the next day. It had taken a while for them to untangle the three anchor rodes Tony deployed. Unfamiliar with hurricanes, Tony had been on the bow enjoying the calm air after a hot breakfast, thinking that the storm had passed, when the back side of the eyewall abruptly blasted him with winds so forceful he had to crawl on his knees to regain the cockpit. Of course, none of us had expected the front side of the hurricane to last as long as an entire storm usually does. They hunkered down for round two.

Back on our home dock without power or water or any modern conveniences, we were relieved to know that everyone safely came through the worst storm to hit that part of the coast in decades.

Hurricane Sandy

No longer hurricane novices, each year when hurricane season begins, we commence a routine of checking the National Hurricane Center web site daily for newly forming tropical disturbances. Most will never reach the North Carolina coast of the US, but from the opposite side of the Atlantic Ocean, no one can know which will or which will bring devastation. Hurricanes confront various obstacles as they cross the tropics. Dry air, high altitude wind shear, land mass (islands such as Puerto Rico, Haiti, or Cuba), and high pressure systems can interfere with the growth and strength of a nascent storm. Nevertheless, hurricanes leave damage in their wake until they expire.

After our experience with Irene, namely the uncertainty and inaccuracy of the NHC forecasts, I relaxed and spent more time following the forecast trends as well as using multiple sources to evaluate what track might be most accurate, most threatening. Based on Irene, we learned that damage from a Cat 1 could be limited if the storm passes to our east. On that track, the main winds blow from the northwestern quadrant which is more kindly than the northeastern quadrant, the zone of destruction. We tested the theory during the next two hurricanes that approached our area.

For both Sandy and Arthur, we stayed aboard *Wild Haggis*. Winds howled and whistled and halyards banged endlessly on the masts of unoccupied boats. The northerly winds raised the water level and pushed a small swell down Whittaker Creek throughout the storm. We tied the boat bow to the wind, so the running swells were not uncomfortable even though they kept us in motion as if at sea for the duration. Cooking dinner was a challenge; in fact, other boaters chose to sleep in the marina clubhouse and bought pizza rather than try to cook aboard their boats. Also, the rising water raised the deck of the boat so high that neither Beth nor Scout could climb down onto the dock to go ashore.

"Too late" in the season (we wished), just a month before the official end of hurricane season, Hurricane Sandy ripped across Jamaica and Cuba heading north for The Bahamas. Sandy was already stronger than forecast eighteen hours earlier, and her track, once predicted to pass far enough offshore to be comfortable for us, kept slipping westward, closer to the North Carolina coastline.

During this stage of an approaching hurricane, I continue to be surprised by the margin of error for weather forecasting by the National Weather Service.

Despite all the data and historical computer modeling, Nature still charts her own course and amazes the experts with her independence (Nature is not limited to the known science of Man) and her intensity, her ability to fuel storms beyond what Man can anticipate.

By the next afternoon, whatever preparations we thought necessary would be complete, and three days of waiting and watching would commence while the storm passed offshore. The north winds would blow, and the water would rise. A storm surge of as little as two-three feet might bring the river over our dock. Winds and rain Friday night, Saturday, Saturday night, Sunday, Sunday night, Monday and possibly into Monday night. A looooongg time to sit storm-bound in the cabin of a boat listening to the whistling and howling winds and heavy drumming of the rain, but nothing that a good book and some music and movies could not alleviate.

The good news? None of the models showed Sandy coming ashore in North Carolina. The bad news? Notwithstanding the model tracks, the hurricane force winds already extended fifty miles from the eye and the tropical storm force winds 140 miles. If Sandy grew and/or her track shifted west, those winds would grow with her so that we could ultimately see even more significant winds.

All of the above are part of what we consider when staring at an oncoming storm. We do NOT assume the worst, but we do prepare for it.

1218 Update. Reports showed Sandy heading due north near our longitude (her course is less than 50 miles east of our longitude) with a predicted turn to the west (toward the US coast), which meant that there would need to be a long push to the east to move her offshore of North Carolina as Cape Hatteras protrudes far into the Atlantic. While the turn to the northeast was expected by the forecasters, they had been off so far. Were Sandy to come ashore west of us, we would be in the worst possible quadrant.

Hurricane Sandy: Day Three Morning

0425. Checked and tightened spring lines. Water to bottom of dock joists. Another eight inches and our dockmaster, Butch, would kill the dock power to protect us and the electrical system. Fortunately, all of us have batteries, and some have their own generators aboard.

0500. NHC Advisory update. Sandy downgraded to Tropical Storm as she turned north-northeast moving at 10 mph. Revised track projected Sandy farther off North Carolina coast and reduced peak winds and gusts for our area. Wind field expanded to 450 miles from the center of the storm. Our water level held steady.

0800. NHC Advisory update. Sandy was again a hurricane and continued to move off to the north-northeast.

The day before had been sunny and breezy with several sails on the river. Of course, the talk on the dock was all weather and winds and surge levels. Everyone was removing canvas, securing anything that could not be removed and tying then re-tying dock lines. (Dock lines tend to stretch, and I frequently can shorten mine by a foot at a time with no effort.) Periodically, we re-checked the NHC updates as well as other weather sources to keep abreast of any changes in the forecast.

A note here about the various weather sources. All do their best with the most current technology. But this is Nature, Mother Nature, a force with no intellect to engage in rational discussion or debate. She moves as she moves with no influence from Man. Having said that, I have a couple of pet peeves about the forecasting world.

One, all data comes from the same official sources, but is not reported with the same conclusions. In some ways this is helpful as it highlights the potential fallibility of the various reports. Two, for our specific area, the National Weather Service predicts coastal flooding based on feet "above ground." This is a meaningless reference. NWS, apparently in response to this same kind of criticism, doubled down with two paragraphs in their briefing statement, clarifying that "Ground level is essentially referencing ground that would typically remain dry." The piedmont, the mountains? Seems to me that "ground that would typically remain dry" varies with the elevation of the affected land in which case it would be useful for NWS to use "sea level" as the point of reference. After all, most of the people I know and have known along the coast know the elevation of their own property within a foot just because of storm surge.

Regardless my complaints, the NWS briefing package is very useful with good graphics. For me, there is no such thing as "too much information" even though a lot of info can be confusing and disorienting if not conflicting. At the same time, we have had calls from people who say they were unaware that a storm, which has already devastated Jamaica, Cuba and The Bahamas and killed almost two dozen people, was moving in our direction. I can imagine someone from the infamous Jersey Shore TV show (that I have never watched, but I read the news sometimes) declaring in the midst of the storm two days hence, "A hurricane landfall in New Jersey? Who knew?" We did, and they should too.

It remained quite breezy, and our lines groaned occasionally, but it was dry overnight last night, the storm rain spinning at sea. The wind rocked us in deep slumber. That would change today.

With preparations complete, most settled into the waiting chapter of the event. It will either be better or worse than expected. Nothing we can do about that.

Hurricane Sandy: Day Three Evening

Soon after my morning post, the drizzling rain began. It rained continuously all day. Gray skies, gray water, gray air.

The wind moaned as if tired of the effort, accented by the pulsing lyrical static of persistent rain. With the milder, pre-storm winds, the water rose slowly, not yet inundating the dock joists. *Wild Haggis* and all her sister boats floated nearly level with the docks, an odd view from our cockpit.

Sandy accelerated to the northeast at 13 mph, heading farther away from our coast. While her track was favorable, her tropical storm force winds reached out 520 miles. The velocity and duration of our storm winds would likely increase as we plunged into night and the arrival of the worst of Sandy during the next 36 hours.

I chose to see the presence of sea gulls, pelicans, and cormorants as reassuring. It was a quiet time for reading and watching a movie. In another 12 hours, we would wake to deteriorated conditions and peer into a new chapter of a long storm.

Hurricane Sandy: Day Four Morning

It was a dark and stormy night. Really.

The droning, whistling winds, halyards clanging on the mast. Rain and waves slapping the deck and hull. The docks remained above water, but often awash. Even Whittaker Creek had whitecaps and streaking foam. *Wild Haggis's* water line was even with the dock planks.

Scout pushed his muzzle between my hip and the arm of my chair. I knew he did not understand why we could not get him off the boat, but he flicked his tail happily anyway. I scratched his head.

Sandy continued her sprint northeast, but her wind field extended 700 miles from the eye. Big and growing larger. And we had not yet felt her strongest winds.

All boats at the marina seemed to be riding well and secure. Several crews gathered in the clubhouse last night and this morning for internet, conversation, and coffee. We stayed aboard and watched a suspenseful movie. Given the natural suspense surrounding us, I am not sure the movie was the best choice. The storm rocked our fitful sleep as we remained attuned to any changes in motion or alarming thuds.

It was another long day of listening to the storm winds and rain and watching the water rise. Cameron asked if we would have "bragging rights" about riding out a hurricane aboard our boat. We replied, "Absolutely." Then again, it was a long way from being over, words I typed in my blog as a huge gust howled overhead.

The End of the Storm

Blue skies and sunshine! Notwithstanding our Tropical Storm Warning that would continue through noon, and although it may not have been over 'til the, you know, that lady sings, we declared an end to our experience with Sandy.

The previous night, winds clocked around to the northwest, diminished a bit and blew out much of the surge. As we floated once again at a near normal level, Scout hopped off the boat, happy to have business ashore. Still, the approaching cold front would continue the high winds for a few days, common enough that time of year.

While relief swept through the marina, a tragedy was occurring offshore 150 miles east of Cape Lookout. A replica of the *HMS Bounty* (built for the 1962 movie, *Mutiny on the Bounty*) sank with the loss of two crew. A wooden tall ship, we wondered why the ship had been in the path of the hurricane. It is not uncommon for large ships to seek open ocean rather than risk damage in port where their options are limited. In open ocean, far from land, there is room for the ship to run before the storm or heave to, at least that is the theory. Apparently *Bounty*'s captain felt safer at sea, but his decision to cross paths with Sandy cost him his life and his ship.

Hurricanes extend our sense of time. Early concern stretches into preparations, analysis, and decisions. Anticipation builds as the storm approaches. Forecasts change as data changes and trends become clearer. Most often, the actual hurricane only lasts part of a day. Sandy battered us for almost 48 hours, though neither winds nor rain nor storm surge were as severe as predicted. On the other hand, as with most hurricanes, it would be several days before we knew the full impact, especially as Sandy merged with arctic air and a cold front when it reached the northeast.

In the case of both Sandy and Arthur, the forecast consistently and reliably kept the track just off the coast of North Carolina, so we felt relatively safe with the boat secured in its slip. On the other hand, Sandy wreaked havoc in New York and New Jersey where it flooded the subway and washed thousands of boats inland. From a southerner's perspective, the Yankees seemed unprepared for a big storm. Maybe that is unfair, but I know that the damage the northerners suffered created a big hike in *my* insurance premium. We had only gotten wet.

Hurricane Arthur

In late June 2014, a tropical disturbance sprouted along the east coast of Florida – scattered thunderstorms without any real structure or organization. Soon it evolved into a tropical depression and the first named storm of the Atlantic Hurricane Season, a term that always reminds me of sports seasons for some reason. Pre-name, Arthur had drifted south for days, but then it slowly turned and began to tramp northward. A friendly high pressure system to the west was poised to intervene and turn Arthur in its track as it approached the North Carolina coast. As always, timing was the issue. When would the two systems meet, and when would conditions push Arthur to the east away from the coast?

Hurricane Arthur eventually did turn, just later than we hoped. Hurricane Arthur also intensified to a Cat 2 hurricane as it crossed Onslow Bay (the body of ocean between Cape Fear and Cape Lookout) for landfall midway the east-west reach of Shackleford Banks, home to wild ponies, lost treasure, and dreams buried by earlier hurricanes. But I have gotten ahead of myself.

Two days before the Fourth of July, the dock was busy with boaters preparing their boats. Remove loose items from topsides, secure anything that cannot be removed, check and double dock lines. Consider all necessary preparations. Make lists, check lists, think of what needs to be added to lists. Chafe, windage, storm surge, loss of power.

As the official forecasts are released every three hours and factors and conditions change and develop, the ultimate risks are uncertain as they must be with natural forces, so a low buzz of anxiety roots and breathes along the docks. Speed of approach? Direction? Time and locale of landfall? Wind speed? Forecast strengthening? In the end, we ask many questions and speculate on many possible outcomes but know that the storm will be the storm that it is after we have committed to any decisions we made. Logic and reason will change nothing. The unknown and unknowable determines our fate.

Ever present, the ultimate second guessing: should we leave for a more protected anchorage? Should we haul the boat onto land? Each option has benefits and weaknesses. No answer is right, but any choice could be wrong. We could sink. Several of us live on our boats so a wrong choice could destroy our homes. We all work hurriedly and help wherever more hands or muscles are needed. Tighten lines. Hoist inflatable dinghies onto the dinghy/kayak rack and cross-tie.

The days are long as we prepare, the sweltering humidity draining us of salty, sticky sweat. Late afternoon, the pool calls. Pausing, we can enjoy the sunshine, blue skies, blue river accented with white caps whipped by a fresh breeze. Consensus calls for beers and grilled veggies as the sun sets. There is more to be done the next day – before the rains, if possible.

We continue to check the updates and discuss the variables, improvements in factors and diminishments. Overnight, Arthur spread its hurricane force winds and tropical storm force winds farther. A 25 mile diameter hurricane force wind field became 35, and the track shifted west. Instead of striking land first at Cape Hatteras, Arthur was forecast to first strike Cape Lookout, only 30 miles to the east of us. The eyewall would be close enough to hit Oriental if the track did not change. Nevertheless, the National Hurricane Center continued to predict Arthur would turn to the northeast and accelerate.

The days of the week lost meaning. Day followed night as weather update followed weather update. We picked apart each bit of new information for a glimpse into a future we could not see. Time itself lost meaning. There was only the countdown to projected landfall of what became a Cat 2 hurricane with maximum sustained winds of 100 mph and a hurricane force wind field that extended 40 miles from the center of the eye, well within striking distance if the hurricane made landfall at Cape Lookout. Our decision to stay began to look riskier.

A partial list of worries, concerns, and anxieties in no particular order:

- Major rigging failure on the boat
- We could be severely injured, maimed or dismembered
- Storm surge could overwhelm us, preventing us from escaping the dock
- Storm surge could lift the boat so high that a dock line or more snap
- Lightning could strike the mast (an aluminum lightning rod 62 feet tall)
- A tornado could hit
- Some other boat in the marina could break loose and collide with ours
- Another crew gets into trouble at a point during the storm when we cannot safely reach them to assist

- A "last minute" change in direction that places us in the dangerous sector of the storm
- The hurricane intensifies at the "last minute"
- Both of the last two above occur simultaneously
- The boat could sink
- We could die

All manner of possibility and impossibility strangle the brain as we attempt to imagine and rationalize risks we can, at best, mitigate, not eliminate. Once in the storm, there is little chance to flee, to change your mind, and safely exit.

As the outer rain bands of Arthur reached the southern coast of North Carolina, we gazed at scattered clouds in blue sky. Nothing threatening. The water down a bit due to southern winds. We gathered for 5 o'clock-on-the-dock beer and cocktails, as many of us usually did. The skies were shades of gray; the blue vanished. A rain squall formed across the river. We all had prepared as best we could. Only the actual storm would tell whether our preparations were adequate. Nervous joking all around, we scurried for our boats as the squall struck. It was short-lived, but followed by another and another until a half inch of rain had soaked the docks. The skies darkened completely well before sunset.

But then the sky brightened, the rain decreased to a drizzle, and the wind softened. We stepped into the cockpit, eager to enjoy any remaining outside time possible. Once we closed the boat for the storm, all hatches and portholes would be secured, and only the dorades and small solar fans would let fresh air into the cabins. An east-southeast breeze built to 30-35 knots and heeled the boat to port, an angle from which it never righted for the next several hours. Our crew sat down for a dinner of salmon salad and fresh vegetables from Paul's Produce. A squall surrounded us with crackling rain and pulsing wind. With a Hurricane Warning and concomitant Tornado Watch, the details of the weather forecasts, wind speeds and rainfall counts, meant less and less. If Arthur turned northeast as predicted, it would offer us a decent, not generous, buffer from the worst of the hurricane. If it accelerated as predicted, it would toss us about less rather than more. But, whatever the prediction, the opposite or something worse could happen. We would know when we it did... or did not.

List of boats with crew riding out the storm (14 souls plus one dog and one cat):

- *Hale Kai*
- *Kindred Spirit*
- *LZ Sea Dogs*
- *Katkandu*
- *My Dream*
- *Wild Haggis*

The storm began fitfully with warm and moist humidity replaced by the cooling winds from thunderstorms. Rain was alternately slammed by heavy gusts and fell rhythmically. Inside the storm, the rain pounds a heavy staccato with a background of droning winds. For hours, the sounds were rain in varying volumes, wind strong and stronger, the noise of both wind and rain, of waves slapping the hull and surging through the pilings. Sitting in our saloon, the motion was continuous as was the roar of the storm. With several layers and dimensions of wind, rain, waves, rigging, the popping of canvas and banging of halyards, a complex symphony of nature at battle never slowed. Each change of sound, each blast of wind, each noise that broke free from the storm sent caution signals to my brain. Problem? Or just another new and different sound in the lexicon of an overwhelming force?

At 2100 Thursday, July 3, Arthur was declared a Cat 2. It was tracking toward Cape Lookout, but wobbling like a drunken sailor ashore after a long voyage at sea. Aboard our boat, the storm heaved and breathed, long, deep and regular like a magnificent monster. We rolled, ever heeled, and lurched as winds and waves collided. At 2315, the eye had jumped westward, still wobbling, and Arthur made landfall on Shackleford Banks, a few miles from Cape Lookout lighthouse. The northwest wall of the eye was less than eight miles from us. Had we anchored up South River, we would have been *inside* the eye. Fortunately, the worst of the hurricane remained the southeastern quadrant, closer to Core Banks than us, but dead center for Cedar Island to our east. The danger zone also crossed Ocracoke Island, unfairly a target for many hurricanes through the centuries.

Hearing the sound of a hard BANG, I went topside onto a pitched deck to see if we were hitting the dock. Raindrops shattered by the winds stung like pebbles on my face. Water swept over the docks, but there was no damage. Back down below, I noted the wind shifted, in an instant, to the north. The boat righted for the first time since sunset. Arthur was moving on and moving fast.

Relieved as I was that the storm had "passed" in theory, I stayed up to keep an eye on the storm surge that would not recede until the winds clocked to the west. When the wind change occurred, about 0300 July 4, I crawled into my berth, content that the danger continued only for those in Arthur's path. Still, the boat rolled and shook and shuddered in the bigger gusts of storm winds. I slowly fell to sleep.

Arthur had a new surprise for us. The adage, "what goes up must come down", applies to storm surge as well as gravity. What surge Arthur had pushed into the river had drained and more. Pine cones and needles, leaves and branches, marsh grass and bark littered the dock, very minor debris all things considered. I looked toward the peninsula to see if the dead pine tree holding the osprey nest had survived. It had. One of our friends, Wayne, who spent less time on his boat than most of us, knew that he needed to tighten his docklines as the water level rose so that his boat would not float too loosely in the slip and bang into the pilings. He diligently checked his lines as the water level lifted the boats 4-5 feet above normal. A couple of us cautioned him to check his lines but not to keep the lines too tight since he would need to loosen them when the wind switched around. He was so meticulous that he stepped onto the dock as late as 0300 to tighten the lines one last time, when the eye of the hurricane had passed and the wind direction shifted 180 degrees. Instead of northerly winds pushing the water level higher, the winds began to push the water out of the river. The level began to fall. When I woke at sunrise to a peaceful morning of scattered clouds and a calm river, I boiled some tea and then climbed onto the dock far above my deck. The water was so shallow that our hull rested on the soft mud bottom. I walked along the dock and noted that Wayne's docklines seemed a bit taut. Testing it with my hand, I confirmed that I could play music on the tensioned line, so I popped loose the knot, and his boat dropped a couple of feet into the water. The boat had been hanging by the proverbial thread. Thank goodness the 30,000 pound boat did not tear out a cleat or break the piling (which can rot in the mud at the base, the damage invisible until the piling begins to wobble). With the winds diminished, water soon flowed back into the river and floated all of us back to normal.

Five years before Arthur, I would have said that anyone who rides a Cat 2 hurricane on their boat is foolish. I was wrong, but I still do not recommend it. There are too many factors over which you have neither control nor, possibly, knowledge. The proverbial devil is always in the details. Arthur was relatively small despite Cat 2 winds in part of the eyewall. It moved fast, sparing us from both wind and surge damage created by larger, slower storms. Our maximum gust as measured on *Hale Kai*'s anemometer was 59 knots, a huge difference from 90 knots when you consider than wind force increases exponentially.

Everyone survived the hurricane safely, and there was no boat damage in the marina.

Did we make a good decision, or was it good luck?

Hurricane Florence

Florence formed August 31, 2018. The early track revealed little about the storm's ultimate destination as it meandered drunkenly across the tropics, but that did not prevent the weather forecasters from making all manner of guesses about what might influence the direction, intensity and speed. Although it affects us little, we watch any strike in the Leeward Islands and feel empathetic pain for damage shown on the news. As you can imagine, if there is any hint that the southeast coast might lie in the storm's path, we pay more attention. Then again, it is common, as happened with Florence, that the forecasters get the track wrong and predict an innocuous swing into open ocean. Our relief was short-lived.

NHC updates its forecast every three hours. When the storm is closer to the equator than the Caribbean, checking every update is like watching grass grow. Checking twice a day is more than enough.

Preparing for a hurricane begins almost a week ahead of landfall locally, about the same time the storm is tearing apart islands like Puerto Rico, Haiti or The Bahamas, much earlier than NHC can predict either time or location of landfall on the US coast. Boats must be hauled sooner rather than later or you risk the boatyard running out of space or jackstands or both. Whether land or sea, there are always dozens of loose items lying on decks and patios that can become airborne in hundred mile per hour winds and tornadoes. Everything needs to be stored and secured. Chairs look funny perched high in the limbs of a pine tree.

In the house, we make sure we have plenty of food (it can be days after the storm, longer if flooding is bad and closes down highways, before the stores restock from the pre-storm rush), especially food that is easily prepared (in case we can only boil water). We fill a tub with non-drinking water (do not forget the toilet), fill the cars with fuel and the fuel cans as well. Extra drinking water is stored in the garage. Kayaks and the dinghy are secured to the back deck as are the grill and adirondack chairs. In short, anything outside comes inside, or we tie it down.

While preparing for the storm, we also debate whether we will stay or evacuate. Any storm Cat 2 or stronger should be avoided. We have become accustomed to Cat 1 storms despite the debris, fallen trees, and flooding. Florence was predicted to landfall as a Cat 3 or 4. Accordingly, a mandatory evacuation order was issued for our county. These storms are strong enough to tear houses apart with or without the tornadoes that usually accompany them. At that strength, Beth and I knew we needed to head inland and stay with Beth's family in Greensboro. Plot twist: Florence was supposed to track through Greensboro, slowing enough to flood everything in its path. We would have no idea when we might be able to return home as the rivers between Greensboro and here flood major highways (as they have historically when hurricanes drop thirty inches of rain). At four days from projected landfall, we were packing. Roads were clogging with some of the 1.7 million people heading inland (though still in the path of the storm). The nearest safe zone was far west in the mountains. At two days before projected landfall, we were evaluating the risk of staying at the coast and when we would run out of time to change our minds.

The models for the forecast track began to change. Florence looked like she would turn west and south before hitting land. Our area ceased being center of the bullseye with 40 inches of rain and the worst of the northeast quadrant winds (130-140 miles per hour) to hanging onto the far edge of the worst of the storm. With each major forecast update, Florence was predicted to be a little farther away from us. Even the rain forecast reduced to 15-20 inches. Unfortunately, the storm surge remained 9-13 feet, well above Isabelle and Irene, the two worst previous hurricanes that flooded Oriental. Selfishly, we did not worry about the surge because our rental house is more than thirty feet above sea level. It would have taken 17 feet or more to float *Wild Haggis* off its jack stands.

Still, we know that these storms are fickle and capricious under the best of circumstances, and Florence had already proven to be among the most erratic. Less than 24 hours before landfall, NHC knew neither the time nor location of where she would come ashore. A sudden reverse of track, while unlikely, was not impossible. Whatever the case, it was too late to change our evacuation plans.

By Wednesday morning, we were weary of preparing and needed to get outside before the storm struck. Late morning, we drove into town for ice (they were out) and to top off our gas. As we drove, the breeze began to build, then a rain squall caught us at the fuel pumps. The outer bands of the storm had arrived while the hurricane was still a few hundred miles off the coast. Cars were parked on high ground at the bank, the Methodist church, and the bridge. Raccoon Creek had already covered Hodges Street at the harbor, so The Bean (coffee shop) had closed early. Half the boats in Oriental Harbor Marina had left. All should have left, but lots of people were chancing fate.

We spent Wednesday reading and watching rain fall and wind blow. As seems to be the timing for all of these hurricanes, the serious rain and wind arrived after dark. Without any light, you cannot tell whether you are hearing gusts of wind or torrential rains. Both roared through the trees while branches and green pine cones thudded against the side of the house and the deck as if hooligans were pelting our walls with dirt clods.

By early afternoon Thursday, our power had flickered on and off a few times before dying completely. The power company (an EMC that generally performs above expectations) was kind enough to text us that they would make no efforts to restore power until "after" the storm (Friday? Saturday? Sunday?). We still did not know when the storm would make landfall. It rained the rest of the day, and we cooked a casserole in the propane grill on the back deck. No power for the refrigerator or air-conditioning. Humidity rising steadily inside the house as well as outside where the warm, damp, tropical air was almost too thick to breathe. The birds and squirrels had fled wherever, but one little green tree frog gripped the top of a window. I hoped he was not marking the height of our flooding.

With a Goal Zero (fancy solar charged battery), we watched an old episode of "The Curse of Oak Island" (they still have not found the treasure) and downloaded a couple of movies. We should have downloaded a dozen before we lost internet the following day.

For the next few days, there were two shades of light, the pitch black of night and the thick gray veil of day. Clouds of rain rolled across the roof. Gutters streamed walls of rain. Texts issued tornado warnings, but we could not access the locations. I tried both of my NOAA radios, and neither worked (we did not then know that NOAA's radio had failed, and there was no backup.) Cell service became fragmented. With no internet or effective communications (no data from cell phones), we lost track of the storm's progress. But the tornado warnings continued. Because a Tornado Warning means that a funnel cloud has been sighted, we take them seriously. Without knowing the location of the warning, we could only peer into the haze, try to gauge any change in the wild sway of the tree tops, and listen for the roar of a train. Minutes crept into hours, then we scrounged lunch (how inconvenient to have no microwave to heat leftovers). More minutes and more hours, more reading and a nap, and we decided to make dinner.

We also started the generator, a process requiring heaving a 100 pound motor from one place on the garage floor to the doorway where we could exhaust the carbon monoxide. The instructions tell you NOT to do this, to vent the generator only in the open thirty feet or more away from the house. But then the instructions also caution against leaving the generator in the rain. Conundrum. Crouching with a back straining lean, we poured gasoline into the generator. Sweat ran freely from every pore. But the motor started first pull of the cord, so I choked on my complaint of discomfort and plugged in the refrigerator cord.

Thursday ended, and Friday dawned with subdued light. It was still so dark that, after being awake between 2:30 and 5:30, seeing nothing and hearing the blur of storm noise, I returned to sleep in my bed. Beth woke me about 8:30. Our landlord had texted from Pennsylvania to see if we were still alive (and his house still standing). He was watching the storm on television, the images from eastern North Carolina in general and New Bern in particular, a nearby town, horrific with flooding and damage. Of course, we had no idea what damage existed aside from what we could see through our windows. I assured him we were in one piece, but he seemed only partially convinced.

Because we had not run the generator overnight, I repeated the process of back-breaking squat ("I'm getting too old for this shit") with a six gallon fuel can and poured as much gasoline into the generator as my back muscles could stand. Once again, sweat rolled freely from every pore, chilling (so to speak) my appetite for cooking breakfast over a hot propane camp stove in a stuffy garage that should have been ventilated better than we were venting it.

Beth cooked breakfast on our Coleman stove in the garage while the generator roared to run the fridge. The noise was obnoxious even though mostly muffled by the doors to the garage, but we had meat and seafood in the freezer that we did not want to lose as we had in previous storms. In dull light, the generator, the wind, and the rain droned on and on through a long and mostly boring day. No news, no information. Beth and I donned headlamps and read books and drank tea and read books and hoped the router would come alive with an internet connection. It did not of course.

Periodically, the rain would tease us by easing. During one respite, we put a window air conditioner in the den and connected it to the generator along with a fan. The room began to cool and dry. We dropped from the low 80s to the mid-70s. Ah, the relief. (Do not ask why we had not done this sooner.) Maybe the storm was reaching its end. We planned to cook dinner on the propane grill on the deck out back, and the idea was appealing until I lit the grill in a torrent that did not ease the rest of the night.

We did not run the generator at night due to the amount of fuel it consumes and the risk of leaving it unattended. But we slept better with less humidity.

Saturday morning, some information began to find its way through my cell phone. Our children, Taylor and Cameron, had been watching weather sources as had Beth's sister, Sharon. The storm was heading for the mountains where Cameron is now in college. In the mountains, it does not take much rain to create flash floods and landslides that wash roads and homes off the mountainsides.

But receiving the info was intermittent. Florence had made landfall near Topsail Beach on Friday, September 14, two weeks after initially forming off Cape Verde Islands, which meant that it had fully turned south away from us. But she also slowed to less than five miles per hour on her track. Storm winds remained near 90 miles per hour. We had counted hours as she crept south and began to bend to the west. We continued to have rain and gusts and soupy humidity, but we turned on the air conditioner in the morning. In the woods out back, happy frogs sang symphonically which we took as a sign the worst was past.

By early afternoon, we were antsy with cabin fever, so we went for a short drive in the rain. Janeiro is a nearby community with a causeway enclosing Dawson Creek. The boulders from its seawall had washed across the road. River waves had broken through the concrete block walls of an old cottage. Marsh grass matted along the road shoulder and in the yards. Large pines and oaks had broken or fallen. A couple of mobile homes had slipped off their foundations, and refrigerators lined the road where they had floated free from their garages. In a soybean field a quarter mile from the river rested a sailboat.

We returned home with a better appreciation for how much devastation we had dodged. Despite continuing rain and breezy winds, it was clear the storm had moved on to flood Wilmington, a city that soon became a literal island with all roads blocked by water. People here started cleaning up despite the continuing rain.

In a light rain shower, I cooked pork chops on the grill. We sat down for supper with our small solar light and had barely cut into our chops when the electricity snapped back on. In that moment, we suddenly leapt into the 21st century after three long days of waiting. The rain and wind continued into Sunday and Monday when the sun finally found some patches of blue sky.

Hurricane is a single word for a storm coupled with a name. But the experience extends through three phases: preparation/anticipation, the experience of the storm itself, and the aftermath. We did not lose any trees, so we had only debris in the form of pine branches, easy enough to rake. On the other hand, Beth's schools closed for another week. The scope of damage to the schools was unknown. More than 4000 homes in New Bern flooded as well as the downtown businesses closest to the confluence of the Trent and Neuse Rivers. The Neuse was not expected to crest upriver in Kinston until the subsequent week. A storm that lingered for a few days left misery that residents toiled with for weeks (months if their house flooded).

Yes, we were lucky.

TARBERT, Isle of LEWIS
and HARRIS to UIG, Isle of SKYE
Scary Ferry #2

On another trip to Scotland, we spent the night in Portree on the Isle of Skye, a brief ferry ride from Kyle of Lochalsh, then toured the northeast coast of the island, driving up into the Quiraing with its legends of reivers hiding stolen cattle in the rough hills. We viewed the water falling over the sea cliff named Kilt Rock and walked through the small ruins of Duntulm Castle overlooking the clear dark blue and green water of The Minch (known as *Skotlandsfjörð* in Old Norse), a strait dividing the Highlands and Inner Hebrides from the Outer Hebrides and extending from the North Sea in the north to The Sea of the Hebrides in the south. The Minch can funnel both currents and winds at a savage pace.

Our ferry departed from the village of Uig on the west coast of Skye, and we arrived early enough to visit a pottery shop in the village before boarding. I found a design I liked very much, a blue and yellow tartan pattern handpainted on a mug. But the potter was out of inventory and suggested he would have what I wanted if I could stop by again in a few days. I told him we were crossing to the Isle of Lewis and Harris and would return in just less than a week.

The ferry voyage across The Minch was calm and relaxing in contrast to our journeys to and from Orkney. We could walk around the ferry, visit the cafeteria, and watch the sea flow past the hull. For two and a half hours, we had no responsibility for driving a car, navigating our route, or keeping an eye out for wandering sheep that seem to get more use from the back roads than the humans do. Also, we were not pinned, crammed, and jammed into a seat with too little leg room inside a roaring tube with irritating bells telling us when we could stand and when we had to buckle our seatbelts for bumpy air. In short, we could rest without being in our B&B or an intimate pub with a comforting peat fire.

In Tarbert, we lodged with Mrs Flora Morrison at her B&B, Tigh na Mara. From her home, we toured the islands north and south for several days. We visited a remote wool shop near the beach at Seilebost with its brightly tropical sands, crofts where islanders still weave Harris tweed by hand, and St. Clements Church, a beautiful late 15th century stone chapel. Driving north through the barren landscape of Lewis, we stopped to see the Standing Stones of Callanish as a sudden snow squall obscured the site, Dun Carloway overlooking the Atlantic, a fine Iron Age (1st c. AD) broch (or fort) with a double wall offering protected passage within the stone structure, and the lighthouse at the Butt of Lewis, one of many designed and constructed by the family of Robert Louis Stevenson. Lewis and Harris have different topography, but both are rugged and desolate, raked by storms off the ocean.

On the day of our departure, Mrs Morrison insisted we eat a full breakfast as we had other mornings. She seemed to have a purpose, as if she knew something she was not sharing. When we departed, she told us to look for her husband, John, who worked for the ferry company taking tickets and handling dock lines. When we boarded the ferry, John said we could probably see Flora waving as the ferry turned around in the bay. Tigh na Mara had an open view of the bay and headlands. Sure enough, Flora was standing in the doorway of their home as the ferry pivoted with its bow and stern thrusters, the stern coming quite close to the rocky shore. We waved and imagined that there was something final and fatalistic in her farewell to us. On our way to our seats, the aroma of hot Scottish breakfast foods permeated the salon. Bangers, black (blood) pudding, sauteed mushrooms, porridge, eggs, toast, tatties, baked beans, tea and coffee. As much as we loved a hot breakfast and had enjoyed our last with Mrs Morrison, the warm, humid aroma wafting from the galley smelled of too much grease, and even the mild motion of the boat at dock threatened to nauseate us just as the ferry to Orkney had. We would hate to waste such delicious fare.

There were small swells entering the bay from The Minch. When we cleared the headlands, the gale that was blowing south slammed the ferry hard, pushing it unnaturally to starboard. The swells in The Minch mounted steadily until the ferry was plunging more than ten feet after every rise, rocking in queasy rhythm until a periodic pause as the ferry hung atop a large swell, poised for the steep drop into the following trough of the wave and crash into the face of the next swell. I was sitting in a large comfortable chair on the edge of vomiting. I dared not move, so I never ventured outside to witness the full reality of the gale.

Sitting still as if stalking a nervous rabbit, I closed my eyes and emptied my mind and tried not to think about anything, especially what I might sense about how rough were the seas and whether the conditions might cause me to regurgitate my delicious Scottish breakfast that had rested calmly in my stomach for the previous hour. I pretended to doze, nap, or sleep, and ignored all sounds and smells. We were barely fifteen minutes into the crossing when Beth told me she had to go to the restroom, undoubtedly code for "I am going to throw up". The crossing seemed as unending as was the torment of the ship's motion. All the way across The Minch, there was nothing to see through the fog, rain, and spray from the storm-torn sea.

When we landed in Uig and drove off the ferry, Beth described how she had spent the entire return voyage on the floor of the last available stall in the women's restroom. While lying in her own misery, someone opened the door to the restroom and called "Katy, are ya in here?"

"Aye."

"Are you okay?"

"No, I'm dyin', I'm dyin'." Katy's lilting Scottish accent was so sweet that Beth could only chuckle to herself between her own gagging heaves that anyone feeling as miserable as she could sound so lively.

We did not then know how lucky we were when the ferry landed at Uig. With solid land beneath our feet, Beth quickly recovered just as she had in Stromness. I ran into Uig Pottery to see whether the potter had been able to fill a kiln. He had, so I picked up a freshly thrown, fired and glazed mug with the pattern I had admired. While wrapping my purchase, the potter suggested, "Awful crossing, heh?" Then he proceeded with the tale of a ferry passage much worse than what we had just completed.

A ferry departed Uig for Lochmaddy, the harbor on North Uist in the Outer Hebrides. Plowing through a gale the entire crossing, the ferry found the entry to Lochmaddy closed out by the storm, so the captain turned south to seek shelter in a sea loch and wait for the tide to rise, hoping that would allow them passage into Lochmaddy. When morning came, the captain tried Lochmaddy again to no avail. He abandoned the island and returned back across The Minch toward Uig. As he approached Uig, he discovered that Uig too was impassable due to the gale, so he headed south to another sea loch for refuge. When he finally landed the ferry in Uig, the passengers had been aboard for two days of misery and ended their journey where they began. The potter assured me he had many more similar stories of boats and storms if I had time to listen. I shook my head, thanked him for the mug and walked back to the car. When I told Beth the tale, we concluded that we would only fly to Lewis on our next trip. Travel by ferry was just too risky.

ACKNOWLEDGEMENTS

As noted, with the exception of family, names within the stories have been changed to protect others' privacy. There are more people and friends who supported my family's experiences than I can ever remember, but in an attempt to acknowledge those I can, I thank the following:

Claire and Harry Brown, Mike Brown, Sharon and Charles Norman.

Michael McOwen for his friendship, our surf sessions, the greening of the Wright Memorial as well as designing, typesetting, illustrating, and publishing my long poem, *Wake*.

J. R. Bunn. Ed Brangman, Oliver Hassell, Larry Mott, and the staff of the Silver Spray Club. Ron Bayes.

Herbert Taylor. Bryan Mayo and the Mayo clan. Sterling and Douglas Remer. Joe and Bernice Pitt.

David Strange for editing, designing and producing *Slickrock: Notes from the Blizzard of 1993*.

Larry Gentner, who gave me a copy of the US Army Survival Manual when I returned from the blizzard.

J. Todd Bailey, Michael C. Smith, the crew of the Air National Guard helicopter based in Knoxville, and Richard and George. Guides in the Everglades and on the Brule, Nantahala, French Broad, New, Chattooga, and Gauley. Harold Dawson Jr., W. Patton Brugh, Charles Abbitt, Robin Green, Bettie Loving, Treva and Mickey Thigpen, Richard Burgoyne. Butch Didion, William and Susan Stronach,

Ronald Dean, Mark Scheiner, Carol and Ashley Erwin, Henry Frazer, and Bobby Prescott.

Dan and Luann Reineke, Lynn and Larry Dechesser, Kim and Steve Snyder, Bill Tice, Barry Antel, Sue and Bill Schadt, Mark Crowder, Keith Bruno, Ben Casey, Greg Gallagher, Rick Miller, Elaine Creel, Glenda Vestal, Martha Myers, Maria Fraser-Molina. Anne and Chris Jackson, Darcy and Kyle, Lynn and Steve Kaufman. Tony Clark and Jenny, Judy and Pat O'Brien. Ross Pease. Allen Helmick. Ceevah and David Stevenson, Barbara and Ron Jones.

To those I have omitted, please excuse the oversight.

ABOUT the AUTHOR

J. Privette grew up in eastern North Carolina and lived in Atlanta for a decade before returning to the mountains of his home state. He wrote about his family's life in a 19th century log cabin south of Asheville in his book titled, *Mole Ranch*. When they left the mountains, they moved onto their sailboat, *Wild Haggis*, on the Neuse River. With *Wild Haggis* currently on the hard, they continue to live near the river. His passions, after his wife and children, are paddling, sailing, and flyfishing. He continues to drive his rusty 1978 FJ40 with an exploded muffler.

Photography: www.jprivette.com

Books: With the exception of *Wake* and *Slickrock: Notes from the Blizzard of 1993*, his books can be purchased by ordering through most booksellers. Please support your independent book shops.

www.ingramcontent.com/pod-product-compliance
Lightning Source LLC
Chambersburg PA
CBHW030913090426
42737CB00007B/180